BACKPACKER'S BRITAIN

VOLUME THREE: NORTHERN SCOTLAND –
THE HIGHLANDS AND ISLANDS

CICERONE

2 POLICE SQUARE, MILNTHORPE, CUMBRIA LA7 7PY
www.cicerone.co.uk

ABOUT THE AUTHOR

Graham Uney runs Wild Ridge Adventure, a company specialising in walking and scrambling holidays, and rock climbing and navigation courses. He also writes for a large number of outdoor and wildlife magazines, as well as working as a professional wildlife and landscape photographer. Apart from indulging in backpacking, hillwalking, rock climbing, winter mountaineering and wildlife watching, he enjoys sampling real ale (particularly from the Hesket Newmarket Brewery) and single malt whisky (especially that from Islay, and the Welsh Penderyn). He lives in the north Pennines with his partner Olivia.

BACKPACKER'S BRITAIN
VOLUME THREE: NORTHERN SCOTLAND –
THE HIGHLANDS AND ISLANDS
by
Graham Uney

CICERONE

2 POLICE SQUARE, MILNTHORPE, CUMBRIA LA7 7PY
www.cicerone.co.uk

First edition 2006
ISBN-10 1 85284 458 2
ISBN-13 978 185284 458 5

A catalogue record for this book is available from the British Library
All photographs by the author unless otherwise stated

ACKNOWLEDGEMENTS

As always with a book like this, there are countless people who have offered help and advice, and to each one I am very grateful.

In particular, I must yet again thank Olivia, for making the whole thing a lot of fun. Special thanks must also be given to Beryl and Dick Tudhope, who have shared many great days in the hills with me, and supplied photographs of areas where it always rains when I go there! I would also like to thank Neil and Paul at Wilderness Scotland for giving me the opportunity to explore some of Scotland's greatest wilderness areas.

My thanks are also due to the staff at Visit Shetland and Visit Scotland, who helped out by organising various press trips to obscure destinations.

Backpacking in Scotland throughout the year is a lot more comfortable if you have the very best equipment. Many thanks to Hilleberg for giving me the use of one of their Akto tents – I wouldn't be without it now!

There are many other people who, in one way or another, have contributed to the making of this book, and I would like to thank you all for encouraging me to get out into those hills!

ADVICE TO READERS

Readers are advised that, while every effort has been made by the author to ensure the accuracy of this book, changes can occur that may affect the contents. It is advisable to check locally on any aspect that may affect your enjoyment of the services, facilities or routes mentioned. The publisher would welcome notification of any such changes.

Cover photograph: Backpackers on Beinn Bhuidhe in Knoydart

CONTENTS

WARNING

Mountain walking can be a dangerous activity, carrying a risk of personal injury or death. It should be undertaken only by those with a full understanding of the risks, and with the training and/or experience to evaluate them. While every care and effort has been taken in the preparation of this guide, the user should be aware that conditions can be highly variable and can change quickly, thus materially affecting the seriousness of a mountain walk.

Therefore, except for any liability that cannot be excluded by law, neither Cicerone nor the author accepts liability for damage of any nature (including damage to property, personal injury or death) arising directly or indirectly from the information in this book.

To call out the mountain rescue, phone 999 from a landline. From a mobile, phone the international emergency number 122 – this will connect you via any available network. Once connected to the emergency operator, ask for the police.

Map Key

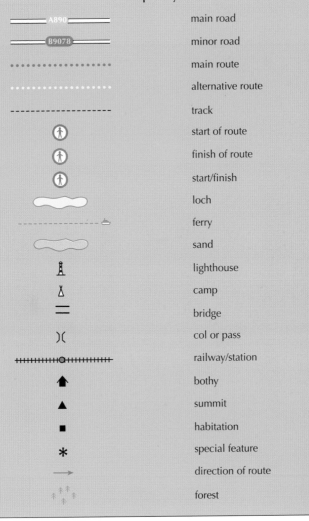 A890	main road
B9078	minor road
	main route
	alternative route
	track
	start of route
	finish of route
	start/finish
	loch
	ferry
	sand
	lighthouse
	camp
	bridge
	col or pass
	railway/station
	bothy
	summit
	habitation
	special feature
	direction of route
	forest

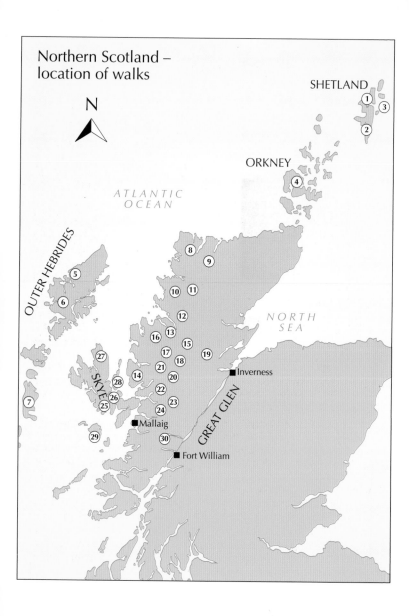

Northern Scotland –
location of walks

N

SHETLAND

ORKNEY

ATLANTIC
OCEAN

OUTER HEBRIDES

NORTH
SEA

SKYE

Inverness

GREAT GLEN

Mallaig

Fort William

INTRODUCTION

Hillwalkers crossing the moor beneath Suilven (Route 10)

BACKGROUND

The mountains of Britain encompass one of the richest, most diverse landscapes to be found anywhere in the world, although for many hillwalkers the Highlands of Scotland are, more than any other region in Britain, true backpacker's country.

Vast, open tracts of wild moorlands, high mountains, rocky coasts and long, winding glens make many Highland areas inhospitable to all except those willing to carry their own shelter and supplies, but in this wilderness there are many hidden corners where only the backpacker can explore. There are places that take days to reach on foot, where only the dedicated backpacker will venture – this is the preserve of the seasoned hillwalker, and wilderness exploration at its best.

Although many of our mountain and moorland regions are within easy reach of town and city, the northwest Highlands are more demanding of time and effort to get to for most of us, yet the rewards are all the greater for it. Some go to the northwest Highlands just or the superb walking, others go in search of rock to climb, wildlife to watch, rivers to canoe, or even whisky to drink, and many are happy to pursue all of these activities, and more, to an equal degree.

Many areas are best explored over a period of time, so for the weekend walker it makes sense to take a tent and sleeping bag on forays into the wilderness, and this is surely the best way of getting to know a particular part of the country. Crossing a range from end to end, or climbing a set of peaks around a desolate Highland glen, will introduce the walker to hitherto unknown regions, and if the trip involves the commitment of an overnight stopover or two, so much the better. To spend a night in a simple but comfortable shelter among lovely mountains, waking to a sunlit dawn of cackling grouse on vast, open expanses of purple moorland, or the guttural roar of rutting stags crashing around rocky slopes, is one of life's great pleasures, and one that is only available to those with a will to discover these quiet places, and to make a temporary home among the mountains and wild shores.

But although there is much to be discovered within the mountain ranges of northern Scotland, some of the coastline and lesser hill ranges deserve mention too, for they are just as vital a component of our natural heritage as any of the higher regions. There is an almost limitless variety of backpacking routes throughout northern Scotland and its islands, all as good as each other in terms of the sense of achievement to be had from a successful trip.

Thirty of the greatest backpacking routes within the boundaries of northern Scotland and the northern islands are described here (for the purposes of this book I have taken the boundary between

northern Scotland and southern Scotland as the Great Glen – that huge trench, with its string of lochs, stretching between Inverness on the Moray Firth in the northeast of the country, and Fort William on Loch Linnhe in the west). With the exception of Route 23, which takes five days to complete, all the routes take either two or three days, with an overnight stop at a bothy or a youth hostel, or in a tent, either wild camping or at a recognised campsite.

All the routes should be suitable for a long weekend away among the hills, but I should add that although this book contains what are in my opinion the very best backpacking walks in the region covered, there is endless scope for further exploration. The routes described should be seen as an introduction – an aperitif perhaps – to the possibilities of other, longer routes that can be planned and tackled by those who have gained experience by following the ones included here.

The first book in this Backpacker's Britain series covered northern England, and the second Wales. This is the third volume, on northern Scotland, and it is hoped that three more will follow, giving detailed backpacking routes in southern Scotland, southern England, and Ireland respectively.

HOW TO USE THIS GUIDE

This book is aimed at anyone with a love of wild, mountain and coastal walking, but as many of the routes take the walker into remote and potentially dangerous terrain, you should ensure that you have

Walking through Glen Carnach (Route 23)

Walkers in Knoydart (Route 24)

previous experience of mountain walking and wild camping before tackling any of them. Good hill fitness is essential, as is the ability to accurately navigate using a map and compass (GPS, though a useful aid, is no substitute for the real thing!).

The routes are ordered so as to move generally southwards, starting in Shetland and finishing in Lochaber. Most are circular, but a few are linear, and they range from those requiring two days to complete, through to a five-day traverse (see Appendix 3, Route Summary Table, for more details).

It is difficult to suggest a best time of year for walking in Scotland – it can be great during any season. Generally speaking, mid-winter (January to March) will give very hard conditions with most routes snow-bound – but snow-holing instead of camping can be fun. April to June is a

really good time to be in the Highlands, as the weather is often at its best then, and there are few midges, whereas July and August can be very hot and wet, and the midges are at their peak. September to December is also a very good time for a backpacking trip, and most of the midges will have gone to ground by then, but remember that you will have fewer hours of daylight in which to walk, and more time will be spent brewing up tea in tents or bothies!

Each route in the guide begins with an **information box.** This give details of the **number of days** needed, **distances**, **height gain**, and where to **start** and **finish** the walk. The **Ordnance Survey Landranger maps** you will need along the way are also included in this box. (Explorer maps are not necessary for backpacking in Scotland, as the extra detail given on them often doesn't apply up here.)

For each route there is also an **Area Summary** and a **Route Summary**, followed by a box giving details of **Tourist Information, Transport, Getting Around, Accommodation and Supplies** and **Escape Routes.**

Note The sketch maps that illustrate each route are intended only as a rough guide – **it is essential to take with you the relevant map**.

Throughout the book incidental descriptive text is distinguished from the route directions, and place names from the sketch maps are highlighted in bold type to aid orientation.

GETTING AROUND AND ACCOMMODATION

The Scottish Tourist Board is a mine of information when it comes to planning trips into the hills – I really couldn't have done without their help! Their website is useful for booking accommodation, as well as giving transport information – www.visitscotland.com (see Appendix 1, Useful Addresses).

Accommodation needs to be planned, and often booked, ahead. You will find anything from a simple campsite, to hostels, bed and breakfasts, guest houses, hotels, self-catering cottages and even castles, by contacting the Scottish Tourist Board. Accommodation is plentiful for most of the year, but be aware that many providers close for the winter season – from October to March – and checking ahead is essential during this time.

For most of the routes in this book it is definitely easier if you have your own car, but public transport is possible for many of them – details are given in the Route Information box at the start of each walk, and the Scottish Tourist Board can also give details of individual bus, ferry and flight companies.

SAFETY IN THE HILLS

Great tomes have been written on this subject, and readers are referred to the specialist books suggested in the bibliography in Appendix 2, but for the most part, common sense is the main requirement. By this I simply mean going into the hills well equipped for the task in hand, both in terms of taking the right gear with you, and having the necessary navigation skills to accurately find your way in all weathers.

Many people stress the importance of leaving written word with a responsible party before heading off into the hills, and this is very good advice for those new to hillwalking, but for me, one of the real joys of hillwalking, and backpacking in particular, is the freedom it gives, including the liberty to change plans if, for instance, you have found the going easier than expected, or the weather has improved and you find yourself wanting to extend your stay in the mountains. This is not possible, and should certainly never be considered, if written word of your intentions has been left. The choice is up to the individual, and generally the best advice is to leave a route card, but if you do this you must stick to it rigidly. Obviously, if you choose not to leave a

A backpacker crosses a river on the way to Suilven (Route 10)

route card, you will be very much on your own should an accident occur.

Some of the hazards that you need to be aware of in the Scottish mountains are:

- river crossings
- cliffs
- snow fields at certain times of year.

Rivers can rise and fall quickly in the Highlands, and people do die trying to cross them when in spate. Not all river crossings are by bridge – shallow water can be crossed quite easily by keeping your boots on (to avoid your feet being crushed by moving boulders or cut on sharp rocks) and facing upstream. However, **if in any doubt at all**, either find a way around, or camp and wait for the water level to go down.

Many of the routes in this book take you along narrow ridges and the tops of cliffs. The dangers here are obvious, but be aware that carrying a large backpack means that you will not be as agile as normal.

Any scrambles on rock included in the routes can be avoided by using the alternative route that is always given.

In spring there are often large areas of snow to cross, and carrying an ice axe and crampons is the sensible way to travel safely at this time (and it is of course essential that you know how to use them properly).

In an emergency, mark the position of the injured person on your map, then get to the nearest **landline** phone and call 999. Ask for the police and tell them you need a mountain rescue. The rescue team will come to the phone you are at and use your map to locate the injured person.

Hillwalkers on Mealaisbhal (Route 5)

There's some superb ridge walking above Glen Affric (Route 20)

Be aware that mobile phone coverage is poor in northern Scotland, and that by phoning 999 from a mobile you will be connected to a central call centre, which often delays rescue, sometimes by hours. I always put the number of the local police station into my phone before heading off into the hills.

This is a subject that gets many people very flummoxed, and even some hillgoers who claim to have mastered it would struggle, should push come to shove. It is beyond the scope of this book to go into detail on this fascinating art, and it is hoped that anyone without navigation skills who is planning to head off into the hills would first book themselves onto a navigation course organised by professionals, or at least read a good book on the subject (see Appendix 2). Having said that, a few very general pointers are as follows.

The main skill to master is that of setting the map. To oversimplify things, it is perhaps best to point out that the top of all OS maps is grid north, and the red directional needle (the one that turns in the compass housing) points to magnetic north. It is an easy matter to place the compass on the map and turn the map around until this needle is pointing to the top of the map. This will then set the map in line with all the features on the ground – walls, fences, streams, hills – so that everything on the map is then in line with its corresponding ground feature. This is actually slightly flawed, as grid north and

magnetic north are not exactly the same. Basically, the compass points slightly left of grid north at the moment, and the key at the edge of the map will tell you how many degrees the difference is for any year. You then simply subtract that difference from the dial on your compass and you are in business.

To measure distances on the map you need to know the scale – usually either 1:50,000 (OS Landranger maps) or 1:25,000 (OS Explorer, Outdoor Leisure and Pathfinder maps, and Harvey's Superwalker maps). You can use the scale on the bottom of the map to find out how many millimetres on your compass represent 100 metres on the ground, and using this information you should be able to measure any distance on the map with some degree of accuracy.

So far so good, but then you need to know how many double steps you take to walk 100 metres. This obviously varies according to the size of your legs, so it is something you will have to work out for yourself. Most people take between 55 and 80 double steps to walk 100 metres, but bear in mind that this is on the flat, on a good surface. Your pacing will differ if you head uphill or downhill, and will also be different over rough terrain such as deep heather or soft snow. You can practise all of this by either going out with someone who already knows how many paces they take to walk 100 metres, or by going on a navigation course.

Another way of measuring distances, and the preferred method over longer distances (you don't want to spend all day counting paces!), is timing. The average

Wild camping at the head of Strathconon (Route 19)

walking speed is 5 kilometres an hour (km/h), so at this speed it will take 12 minutes to walk 1000 metres (1km) on flat ground. Most people add 1 minute to the overall time of a set leg of the journey for every 10 metre contour climbed during that leg. However, for timing to be really useful you do need to know your own walking speed. I personally prefer to walk at 6km/h, but others may walk at 4km/h or even slower. The other problem with timing is that it will differ according to how heavy your rucksack is, or how tired you are, or the type of terrain you are walking over. It is best to experiment with timing over known distances to get the hang of it.

The only really effective way to learn navigation is out on the hills, initially by going on a course or reading a book, then by regularly practising the techniques on your own. Several useful books are included in the bibliography (Appendix 2) for those

who want to learn, or brush up on, navigation skills.

EQUIPMENT

This is a very subjective matter. A browse through any outdoor retailer's shop will reveal a bewildering array of boots, jackets, tents, sleeping bags, stoves, maps, compasses, and those little pouches for keeping your mobile phone safe and sound. In short, there is no shortage of gear and gizmos you can buy for the hills. Some of it is essential, other bits and pieces less so.

You will probably find that you already possess some of the essential items to get started in backpacking – most aspiring backpackers have been active in the outdoors previously, and will usually own a pair of **boots**, a **waterproof jacket and overtrousers** set, and probably a **compass, map case, torch** and **first aid kit**.

To head out for a night in the hills you will need to add a good **sleeping bag** to this list. There are basically two types of bag – down filled and synthetic. Down is lighter in weight but useless if it gets wet, whereas synthetic is heavier but retains some of its warming properties when wet. Synthetic is also usually a good deal cheaper than a better-quality down-filled bag.

A good **mat** under your sleeping bag is essential to keep you insulated from the cold ground beneath. Foam mats are cheap, but better is a Thermarest, which is air filled, far more comfortable, but much more expensive.

Then you'll need a **tent** to put over yourself. I have used a number of different makes and models over the years, but for most people the best advice is to get the lightest tent you can for the seasons you intend to use it, and to pay the most you can afford – this latter point will automatically scrub all the next-to-useless models of tent from your shopping list. Recently I have been using a Hilleberg Akto, which really is superb for all-season camping, even in the wildest of areas. It is the lightest tent I have ever backpacked with, easy to pitch, and it gives me the confidence to go anywhere at any time of year.

Next you'll need a **stove** of some sort. Gas is a popular fuel, while meths-burning Trangias are very often used by youth groups. The Trangia is a very safe stove, with the additional benefit of having no working parts to break. It is easy to light and easy to use, but does take a lot longer to boil water than almost any other camping stove I have used. Personally, I would always go for a Coleman Duel Fuel model. They are very efficient, and with one of these beauties you will be drinking your soup before your mates have even raised a bubble in their pots with other stove models.

As well as your camping equipment it is also a good idea to have spare **warm, dry clothing** in your rucksack for anything more than a single day in the hills.

Obviously you will need a **rucksack** larger than a daysack to carry all this extra kit, and again there are countless makes and models on the market. Go to an outdoor shop and try them all on, aiming for something around 60–70 litres in size. Get the assistant to fill the rucksacks with tents and other heavy gear, then walk around the shop to see which feels best. Once you set off on your backpack, aim to get everything into your rucksack, rather than hanging things on the outside. Apart from looking better, this also helps to distribute the weight more evenly, and will make for a more enjoyable backpacking trip.

FOOD

Food must be nutritious and palatable, and you should plan to carry enough to satisfy your energy needs for the duration of the trip, plus some spare high-energy food in case of emergency.

Generally speaking most people burn between 3000–4000 calories a day when they are backpacking, and it is recommended that you replace this throughout the day – a backpacking trip

Backpackers in Knoydart (Route 24)

Having a rest en route for Dun Caan on Raasay (Route 28) (photo: Beryl Tudhope)

is not the time to go on a diet! Try to balance your daily intake so that you have around 60–65% carbohydrates, 25–30% fats and 10–15% protein, and aim to spread your food intake out over the day, eating little and often throughout the walk, rather than stopping for a huge food-fest at lunchtime, and spending the rest of the day feeling like snoozing it off!

On a backpacking trip it is difficult to eat similar foods to those you would normally eat at home, and the best advice is to experiment over different trips – indeed, this can become a great part of the whole backpacking experience.

As for **spare emergency food**, most people throw a few chocolate bars, flapjacks or high-energy bars into the bottom of their rucksacks. I know there are people who always eat their 'emergency rations' long before the trip is over, which of course is not ideal, and others deliberately take things that they don't actually like eating very much, which is rather

a good way of avoiding temptation. I have also heard it recommended that emergency rations should be wrapped in sticky tape, making it difficult to get into them, which is fine until an emergency occurs, and you still can't get into them!

It is also essential to take in plenty of **fluid**, partly to replace that lost through sweating, and partly to help you digest food more efficiently.

ACCESS AND THE BACKPACKER

The Land Reform (Scotland) Act of 2003 establishes access rights for everyone to most land and inland waters, provided they exercise them responsibly. These rights and responsibilities are set out in the Scottish Outdoor Access Code. For a copy of the code, call Scottish Natural Heritage on 01738 444177 or go to www.outdooraccess-scotland.com

Everyone has the right to be on most types of land to undertake outdoor

21

Red deer stags in the Fisherfield Forest (Route 13)

activities such as walking, cycling and wild camping as long as they act responsibly. This means taking responsibility for your own actions in the outdoors, respecting the interests of other people using or working in the outdoors, and caring for the environment.

Access rights don't apply to any kind of motorised activity or to hunting, shooting or fishing. They also don't apply everywhere, and exclude buildings and their immediate surroundings, houses and their gardens, and most land in which crops are growing.

Wild camping

Access rights extend to wild camping, which must be lightweight, done in small numbers, and only for two or three nights in any one place. Act responsibly by not camping in enclosed fields of crops or farm animals, and by keeping away from

buildings, roads or historic structures. Take care to avoid disturbing deer stalking or grouse shooting activities. If you wish to camp close to a house or building, seek the owner's permission. Leave no trace of your stay by removing all litter and any traces of your tent pitch or fire, and by not causing any pollution.

Stag-stalking season

This is usually from 1 July to 20 October, although most stalking takes place from August onwards (usually excluding Sundays). (The hind-stalking season is 21 October to 15 February.) During this period, you can help to minimise disturbance to stalking activities by finding out where stalking is talking place. Use the Hillphones service if available, www.snh.org.uk/hillphones, which gives recorded advice on where stalking is taking place, or pick up a Hillphones booklet in outdoor shops, hostels, tourist information centres or hotels. Although the code advises land managers to consider popular walking routes, paths and ridges when planning stalking you can also minimise disturbance to stalking by taking account of advice on alternative routes that may be posted on signs in the area. Deer control in forests and woods can take place all year round, often at dawn and dusk. Take extra care at these times and follow advice on signs and notices.

FLORA AND FAUNA

The flora and fauna of the Highlands are fascinating aspects of this beautiful landscape, and worthy of whole volumes in their own right. However, I will summarise some of the more exciting species that the backpacker might, with a watchful eye and enough patience, come across during his or her wanderings in this area.

Fauna

Chief amongst mammals in the Highlands is the **red deer**, and put simply, there are far too many red deer wandering around in the hills. The lack of a natural predator is the problem – their numbers used to be kept down by wolves, but out ancestors managed to get rid of those. Too few deer are being culled, and although some estates are very good at culling, numbers of deer are still increasing. This might sound like wonderful news in one sense, but it also means that there simply isn't enough land to support the huge numbers of deer on it – a recent estimate is around 700,000 in the Highlands. Many

deer starve to death in winter, but as breeding numbers are high, the population still continues to grow. So taking all this into account, you'd be very unlucky not to see at least some red deer while out backpacking in the wilds (although you won't find deer in the Northern Isles).

Of the larger birds, **ravens**, **buzzards** and **golden eagles** are the species most likely to be seen. Raven numbers are decreasing, but buzzards and golden eagles are doing very well. On all the mainland walks in this book you could enjoy good views of these birds, but again they are pretty much absent from the Northern Isles.

Other predators to look out for include **otters**, the **pine marten** and **Scottish wildcat**. Of these, you are most likely to come across otters, particularly on any of the walks on the west coast, although there are also very high numbers in Shetland, and a fair few in Orkney, so if you're quiet you might just be lucky.

On ferry crossings you should look out for **seals**, both common and grey, while cetaceans (dolphins and whales) are often seen. In particular, you should keep your eyes peeled for **bottle-nosed**, **common** and even **Risso's dolphins**, the **minke whale** and the **harbour porpoise**. **Humpbacked whales** have been seen around the Small Isles, and this also seems to be a fairly regular area for **basking sharks**.

Back on dry land there are always **red grouse** on the moors, and here you should also see **curlew**, **dunlin**, **snipe** and

Sunset over the Black Cuillin from Knoydart (Route 25)

golden plover in the breeding season. Mountain tops are not without wildlife either – you'll find the **snow bunting**, **ptarmigan** and **mountain hare**.

In woodland you might see the secretive **roe deer**, while the trees attract **red squirrels** and many small birds. In ancient pine forests, such as in Glen Affric, there's also a chance of seeing the **crested tit** and **Scottish crossbill**, which is unique to Scots pines in the Highlands.

All these species are best viewed from a distance – indeed, you will no success at all if you try getting too close to birds and mammals, and it is actually illegal to deliberately approach many nesting birds. It is obviously sensible not to try to get anywhere near deer, either, particularly during the rut, when the males will see you as competition – and they do have very big antlers!

Flora

It is also illegal to pick wild flowers, and there are plenty of these to be seen in the Highlands. Specialities include **bog asphodel**, **bog myrtle**, **ling**, **bell** and **crossed-leaved heathers**, **lousewort**, **milkwort**, **cow wheat** and a whole range of **orchids.** **Bilberry** and **crowberry** can be seen on high mountainsides, and occasionally you might come across **bearberry** and **cowberry**.

Each region and island has its own specialities, which can make the study of the flora of Scotland particularly fascinating, and while you are not likely to want to suffer the extra weight of a field guide to flora when backpacking, doing a bit of research before a trip can greatly heighten the enjoyment when you stumble across your first **grass of Parnassus, spring squill** or **dwarf cornel!**

ROUTE 1

Shetland – Esha Ness

Number of Days	2
Total Distance	52km (32.5 miles)
Daily Distances	Day 1 – 31km (19.25 miles), Day 2 – 21km (13.25 miles)
Height Gain	Total: 850m; Day 1 – 420m, Day 2 – 430m
Maps	OS Landranger sheet 3 Shetland, North Mainland
Starting Point	Urafirth (grid ref HU303788). Park in the lay-by overlooking the inner pool of Ura Firth, just off the A970 leading toward Hillswick.

Area Summary

The Shetland Islands offer backpacking as you won't find it elsewhere. The best of the wild country lies on the coast, and there is certainly plenty of that – rough seas pour in from all sides, bringing westerly gales, northerly sleet and southerly showers, often all at once, and on these ocean-borne winds come millions of birds. A coastal backpack here in summer – for to be honest, you wouldn't want to go backpacking in these remote islands at any other time of year – will bring you up close and personal with all of our birds of sea and cliff. Puffins peer out of burrows on the cliff tops as you walk by, while below, just over the edge, a teeming mass of guillemots, razorbills, gannets, shags, rock doves, kittiwakes and fulmars jostle for space on tiny ledges.

This route takes in part of North Mavine, the northern tip of the main island of the Shetland group (confusingly known as 'Mainland'). North Mavine is almost completely separated from the rest of Mainland by a very narrow strip of land known as Mavis Grind – a strip just wide enough to take the main A970 north.

On the west side you gaze around points and islands into the North Atlantic, while to the east you are looking at the

Sullom Voe inlet of the North Sea. Heading into North Mavine the main road crosses rough moorland then splits on Hill of Orbister. The road to the west leads onto the fine Esha Ness peninsula, with its superb coastal scenery – huge, plunging cliffs falling into spectacular tidal voes (small bays or narrow creeks). This walk takes you around this exciting, windswept headland.

Route Summary

A walk that is suitable for all who enjoy wild coastal scenery. Route-finding is very easy, and there is not too much climbing, although picking your way around the thousands of inlets and headlands can be tiring. There is a path along parts of the route, particularly the main headland of Esha Ness, but the going throughout is easy, on short-cropped, flower-filled grass.

The route begins at Urafirth, preferably after a good night's sleep and hearty breakfast at Almara Guest House in Upper Urafirth. Heading south along the main road you soon find yourself in Hillswick, where you leave the road and take to the rocky shore leading around the Ness. From here on it's simply a case of keeping the sea to your left and the land to your right as you head off around the countless bays and jutting peninsulas to reach your overnight stay at Hamnavoe. On Day 2 the route continues in a similar vein, leading onwards around the coast into Ronas Voe and its fjord-like waters. A short walk along a little lane takes you back to Urafirth and the end of a fine expedition.

Tourist Information

There is an excellent tourist information centre at the Market Cross in Lerwick, tel 01595 693434, website www.visitshetland.com.

Transport

You can get to Lerwick, the capital of the Shetland Islands, by either air or ferry. Air Contact British Airways and their franchise partners Logan Air on 0845 7733377. Their flights make use of the main airport on Shetland at Sumburgh, 40km (25 miles) south of Lerwick, website www.loganair.co.uk.

Ferry North Link Ferries operate ferries to Lerwick from Aberdeen or Stromness (Orkney), tel 0845 6000 449, website www.northlinkferries.co.uk.

Getting Around
Buses A daily (Mon–Sat) bus service to Hillswick from Lerwick stops at Urafirth. It leaves at 17.10 and arrives at 18.25 – contact White Coaches on 01595 809443.

Car Hire Try either Bolts Car Hire on 01595 693636, or Star Rent-a-Car on 01595 692075. Both have offices in Lerwick and at Sumburgh Airport.

Accommodation and Supplies
Lerwick For accommodation in Lerwick try the Glen Orchy Guest House on 01595 692031, website www.guesthouselerwick.com, or the Alder Lodge Guest House on 01595 695705. The youth hostel is a cheaper option, and you can contact them direct on 01595 692114 (open April to September). There are plenty of shops, bars and restaurants in Lerwick.

Heading North A very comfortable hotel on the road to North Mavine is the Busta House Hotel – Joe and Veronica Rocks are very welcoming, the food is excellent, and it is also a good option for some local Valhalla Brewery beer! Busta House is at Busta, near Brae, and you can make a reservation on 01806 522506, or e-mail reservations@bustahouse.com (website www.bustahouse.com).

North Mavine In North Mavine I would always opt for a night at Almara Guest House in Upper Urafirth – very comfortable rooms and huge breakfasts. Contact Marcia Williamson at Almara on 01595 503261, or e-mail almara@zetnet.co.uk (website www.users.zetnet.co.uk/almara). There is also a bar selling food in Hillswick, and a small shop.

Overnight Options
Either camp discreetly, or try Johnnie Notions' Camping Böd at Hamnavoe, open from April until September and bookable through Lerwick tourist information centre, or contact 01595 694688, www.camping-bods.com.

Escape Routes
At any point during the walk the quickest return route to Hillswick and Urafirth is to head for the B9078, which runs along the Esha Ness peninsula from near Hillswick to the tip of the headland.

DAY 1

From the lay-by beneath **Urafirth** village walk southwestwards along the road towards **Hillswick** village. Pass the B9078, which heads off to your right – this is the road leading out to the lighthouse at Esha Ness, and is worth remembering as a possible escape route. Continue into Hillswick and pass the St Magnus Hotel on your right, then take a little lane on the left that leads down to the shoreline. Follow this around to the west and along a track to Findlins House, from where you can go down onto the shore and pick a way between the rocky platforms and sandy bays.

This is a great place to see otters. They prefer to come out hunting on a rising tide, and so are not necessarily nocturnal, as many people believe. We only have one species of otter in Britain, the Eurasian otter, Lutra lutra. On the rivers of England and Wales it is pretty much completely nocturnal, but by the coast in Scotland can be seen at any time of day.

Continue around the little headland of Tur Ness, which juts into **Ura Firth**, then on into the bay known as the Bight of Niddister.

Watch for fulmars as you walk along towards Baa Taing. These graceful birds are a joy to watch as they skim close to the waves out at sea. They look not unlike seagulls, but are in fact members of the shearwater family. They fly with very stiff wings, whereas gulls are much more flappy.

Continue around the Quilse and into Queen Geos, then on to the lighthouse at Baa Taing, the headland of the **Ness of Hillswick.**

From Baa Taing turn northwestwards and go along the coast, passing the finger-like pinnacle of Gordi Stack and Windy Geo, before climbing to the 70m cliff top of Oris Field. Out to sea across Houlma Sound you can see the famous rock pinnacles of the **Isle of Westerhouse** and the **Drongs**. Continue around the cliff top to the summit of Ber Dale, then onwards and downhill to the Quey and the lovely bay of **Sand Wick**.

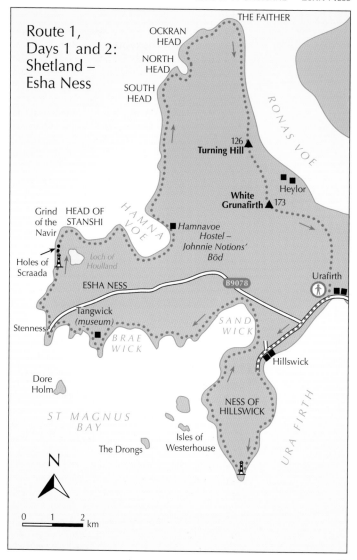

Route 1,
Days 1 and 2:
Shetland –
Esha Ness

THE FAITHER

OCKRAN HEAD

NORTH HEAD

SOUTH HEAD

RONAS VOE

126 ▲ **Turning Hill**

Heylor ■ ■

White Grunafirth ▲ 173

Grind of the Navir

HEAD OF STANSHI

HAMNA VOE

Holes of Scraada

Loch of Houlland

■ *Hamnavoe Hostel – Johnnie Notions' Böd*

Urafirth

ESHA NESS

B9078

Tangwick *(museum)*

SAND WICK

Stenness

■

BRAE WICK

Hillswick ■

Dore Holm

ST MAGNUS BAY

NESS OF HILLSWICK

URA FIRTH

The Drongs

Isles of Westerhouse

N

0   1   2
km

29

The island of Dore Holm, with its huge natural arch

Follow the coast round, climbing again until you are high above the bay, then drop down to cross Twart Burn where it enters the sea. A short hop around rough ground below the B9078 and you are soon heading southwest again, towards the Grey Face and Harry's Pund. Another short climb up to the Heads of Grocken, then a traverse around under Watch Hill to Stoura Pund and the Neap, bring you out above the big bay of **Brae Wick**. Walking out along the cliff top of the Neap you soon descend to cross a couple of small streams, then head out towards the distant headland of No Ness above the rocky flats of Scarf Skerry. Just around the bay from here lies the hamlet of **Tangwick**, with a superb museum that is well worth a visit.

Tangwick Haa Museum has a fascinating display of local artefacts and photographs, part of which is changed every year. All aspects of life in this remote part of Shetland are depicted here. The haa itself was built in the 17th century as a home for the Cheyne family, and is one of the oldest buildings in this part of Shetland. The Cheynes were lairds of the Tangwick estate and other parts of Shetland.

From the museum drop down the lane around the back that leads westwards to the beach at the Houb, then continue along the low cliffs to Gro Taing and onwards to the natural coastal arches of Fiorda Taing.

Offshore lies the spectacular island of Dore Holm, with its huge natural arch. It is quite often referred to as 'Horse and Man Rock', or 'Drinking Horse Rock' – the latter name seems much more fitting.

Go around the bay to Utstabi, then the cliffs begin to rise again as you near **Stenness**, with the Isle of Stenness and Skerry of Esha Ness lying just offshore. Continuing towards Esha Ness itself, the way leads across broken, rocky ground around the Bruddens and the Cannon before you reach the **lighthouse** at the end of the B9078.

The name Esha Ness comes from the Old Norse for 'Headland of Volcanic Rock'. Black basalts and purple andesites make up the geology, and agates and amethysts can be found within these hard volcanic rocks.

Backpacking at the Holes of Scraada

Johnny Notions' Böd

Walk around the seaward side of the lighthouse and along the top of Calder's Geo, where many seabirds will be nesting below your feet.

Calder's Geo is a huge void cutting into the cliffs at Esha Ness. Kittiwakes (known locally as 'waegs') and fulmars ('maalies') nest here, while razorbills ('sea craas') and guillemots ('looms') can also be seen. Everyone's favourite seabird, the puffin ('tammy norrie') is also present, and shags ('scarfs') nest at the bottom of the cliffs.

John Williamson of Hamnavoe is one of many great characters remembered by all in the North Mavine area. Always known locally as **Johnnie Notions** because of his inventive mind, in the 18th century he designed his own inoculation against smallpox, saving thousands of local Shetlanders from this terrible disease without losing a single patient – and all without the benefit of any kind of education! **The Böd**, which is now a small bunkhouse, stands where his house once was, and is a great place to spend the night.

Walk around Calder's Geo and continue along what must surely be some of Britain's most dramatic coastline. In two places the sea has found weaknesses in the rocks of the cliffs and forced subterranean passages through to blow-holes set well back from the cliff edge. One of the best examples of this is at the **Holes of Scraada** near the **Loch of Houlland**.

> The Loch of Houlland is a good place to see breeding arctic terns (known hereabouts as 'scooty aalins') and great skuas ('bonxies'). These birds can be very aggressive if you approach their nests or young, so be warned!

The cliffs continue, taking you past the **Grind of the Navir** as you approach the **Head of Stanshi** along the Villians of Ure, a fantastic name for a cliff top if ever there was one! Continue walking around the Geo of Ure and the Dale of Ure until you enter the delightful bay of **Hamna Voe**. Stroll into Braehoulland and walk around to the pier. If you are staying at **Johnnie Notions' Böd** you should continue around the bay past Scarff to the hamlet of **Hamnavoe** itself.

The Holes of Scraada

DAY 2

Begin the day by heading out westwards from Johnnie Notions' to the sea. Turn north and walk along the cliffs of the Villians of Hamnavoe to the Burn of Tingon. This can occasionally be difficult to cross and you may have to head inland a short way to find a safe place. North of here you'll come to the Hole of Geuda near the Geo of Ockran, another fine bay with a waterfall pouring into it from the hill above. Continue around **Ockran Head** and on past Clew Head to the superb headland of the **Faither**, which gives good views eastwards of Lang Ayre, the biggest beach in the Shetland Islands, backed by Ronas Hill, the highest hill.

Across **Ronas Voe** you can see the impressive Stonga Banks dropping to the beach at Lang Ayre. Above this rises **Ronas Hill**, at 450m the highest hill in the Shetland Islands, and enjoying almost arctic weather and terrain to match. There are many rare arctic plants growing here, and it is also a good place to see upland waders nesting in the summer.

The seas north and west of the **Faither** are often a good place for whale watching. In summer you might be lucky enough to spot minke whales, sperm whales, killer whales or even humpback whales. There are also good numbers of dolphins and porpoises. In all, 22 species of cetacean have been recorded in the waters around Shetland.

On Turning Hill you may see nesting great skuas, which will probably dive bomb you as you walk past.

This is a good place to see red-throated divers, but be careful not to disturb them during the breeding season.

The route now leads southeastwards alongside **Ronas Voe**. You can either stay along the shoreline until you hit the minor road at **Heylor**, then follow that back to Urafirth, or continue along the shore only as far as the Stack of Sumra, then begin a slow climb up over rough grass and heather to **Turning Hill.** ◀

Continue southeastwards up to Septa Field, then on to the curious lake known as Gersfield Water. ◀

Head south from the loch to the summit of **White Grunafirth**, where an OS trig pillar stands at 173m. From here head eastwards over rough ground to a track that takes you to Assater, then down to Upper Urafirth and the end of a fine walk.

ROUTE 2

Shetland – Mainland South

Number of Days	2
Total Distance	68km (42.25 miles)
Daily Distances	Day 1 – 37km (23 miles), Day 2 – 31km (19.25 miles)
Height Gain	Total: 1570m; Day 1 – 930m, Day 2 – 640m
Maps	OS Landranger sheet 4 Shetland, South Mainland
Starting Point	Scalloway Castle (grid ref HU404393). Catch a bus from Lerwick to Scalloway – there are regular buses daily.
Finishing Point	Grutness, just south of Sumburgh airport (grid ref HU404100). Regular daily buses run to Lerwick from Grutness, or simply catch a plane home from Sumburgh airport.

Area Summary

The Shetland Islands offer such superb backpacking over rugged coastlines that you could spend weeks here and never tire of it. Of the group of islands making up the Shetlands, Mainland is by far the largest and offers good scope for the explorer on foot. South Mainland is a long, narrow peninsula, never more than a few kilometres wide east to west, but extending for some distance south of the capital of Shetland, Lerwick.

Lerwick lies on the east coast of Mainland, about halfway down the length of this mainly north–south running land mass. On the opposite side of Mainland lies the only other town in these parts, Scalloway. The walk starts here and takes you southwards along the west coast of Mainland, through some wonderfully wild country with superb views out to the islands of Trondra and East and West Burra. There isn't much in the way of habitation throughout the length of South Mainland, apart from a few settlements at the halfway point and the odd farm building, and this sense of remoteness makes this a truly memorable walk.

Walk Summary

Starting in Scalloway the route initially follows the quiet road towards the bridge leading over the Clift Sound to the island of Trondra, but here leaves all sight and sound of man's presence behind. The long line of hills falling in steep slopes down into the Clift Sound are followed through to Maywick, from where more rocky coastal cliffs lead around to St Ninian's Isle.

Tourist Information

There is an excellent tourist information centre at the Market Cross in Lerwick, tel 01595 693434, website www.visitshetland.com.

Transport

You can get to the Shetland Islands' capital, Lerwick, by either air or ferry.

Air For flights contact British Airways and their franchise partners Logan Air on 0845 7733377 – they make use of the main airport on Shetland at Sumburgh, 40km south of Lerwick – website www.loganair.co.uk.

Ferry North Link Ferries operate comfortable ferries to Lerwick from Aberdeen or Stromness (Orkney), tel 0845 6000 449, website www.northlinkferries.co.uk.

Getting Around

Buses There are regular bus services to Scalloway from Lerwick, and back from Grutness. Contact the Lerwick tourist information centre for details.

Car Hire Try either Bolts Car Hire on 01595 693636, or Star Rent-a-Car on 01595 692075. Both have offices in Lerwick and at Sumburgh Airport.

Accommodation and Supplies

Lerwick For accommodation in Lerwick, try the Glen Orchy Guest House on 01595 692031, website www.guesthouselerwick.com, or the Alder Lodge Guest House on 01595 695705. The youth hostel is a cheaper option, and you can contact them direct on 01595 692114 (open April to September). There are plenty of shops, bars and restaurants in Lerwick.

Scalloway Not a lot of choice here, but the Scalloway Hotel is situated conveniently in the centre of the village (tel 01595 880444). Also worth a try is Windward bed and breakfast (tel 01595 880444) or Broch House bed and breakfast (01595 880051) www.brochhouse.shetland.co.uk.

Sumburgh Area For a comfortable night's sleep there's always the Sumburgh Hotel at Jarlshof (tel 01950 460201), www.sumburghhotel.com, whereas nearby you'll find Betty Mouat's Böd (tel 01595 694688) www.camping-bods.com.

Overnight Options
Either camp discreetly, or book a room at the superb Spiggie Hotel in Scousburgh (tel 01950 460409), www.thespiggiehotel.co.uk.

Escape Routes
There are roads running parallel to the coast to the east at most points of this walk, and although generally a couple of kilometres away at the furthest points, they do see regular traffic.

The route then takes you around the Bay of Scousburgh and on to Fora Ness before making for impressive Fitful Head. The broad sands at the Bay of Quendale provide a change in scenery before the rugged headland at the Ness of Burgi and the superb walk around Sumburgh Head to Grutness.

DAY 1
Before heading out of town it's worth having a good look around the sleepy streets of **Scalloway**.

Head out of Scalloway on the main road towards Lerwick (A970). Walk over the road bridge that goes over the East Voe of Scalloway and turn right immediately. This is the B9074, leading towards the bridge over **Clift Sound** to the island of **Trondra**.

Scalloway used to be the capital of Shetland, until Lerwick gained in importance through greater trading success. Today the place is very quiet, although it does have a busy fishing industry, and down at the harbour you could hardly fail to notice the imposing tower of **Scalloway Castle.** This was built in 1600 by the infamous Earl Patrick Stewart, using forced labour, and both the earl and his son Robert were to be executed in Edinburgh in 1615 for their aggression against fellow landowners. The castle is really little more than a fortified tower house, but it is well worth a look around (if the gate is locked you can get the key from the Scalloway Hotel).

On Main Street, at the road junction, there is the small **Scalloway Museum**, which is free and also worth a little time spent there.

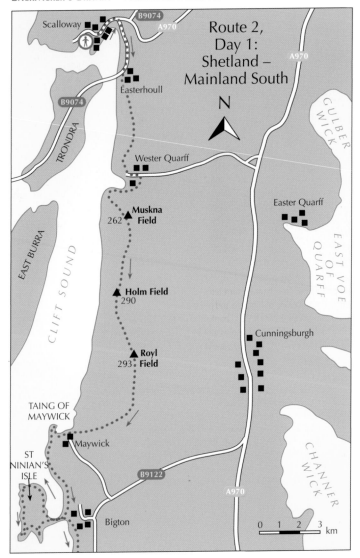

Scalloway

B9074

A970

A970

Route 2,
Day 1:
Shetland –
Mainland South

N

Easterhoull

B9074

GULBER
WICK

TRONDRA

Wester Quarff

Easter Quarff

Muskna
262 ▲ **Field**

EAST BURRA

CLIFT SOUND

EAST
VOE
OF
QUARFF

▲ **Holm Field**
290

Cunningsburgh

▲ **Royl**
293 **Field**

TAING OF
MAYWICK

Maywick

CHANNER
WICK

ST
NINIAN'S
ISLE

B9122

A970

Bigton

0   1   2   3 km

A few hundred metres before this bridge, which is visible cutting across the channel, turn left to **Easterhoull**. Go right at the next junction at Uradale and pick up the path along the east bank of the Burn of Sundibanks. This path soon crosses over to the west bank and begins a gentle climb up the ridge of the Kame of Whalwick. The views from here out westwards over **Trondra** are superb.

Scalloway Castle at the start of this walk

Continue down into a little col, then leave the path for a short time to climb to the higher summit at a spot height of 143m. Drop down to the east to pick up the track again – this leads down into **Wester Quarff** and the end of a small tarmac lane. Turn left – eastwards – here to a road junction, then turn right and continue beyond the wonderfully named Beneath-a-Burn to the ness. Head out to the coast overlooking **East Burra**.

From the coast begin a steep climb up towards Bogabreck, then continue up the moorland ridge to the summit of **Muskna Field** at 262m.

These moorlands of South Mainland hold a few breeding pairs of great skuas and arctic skuas. These great ocean wanderers return to the wild moorlands of Shetland every year and provide a bit of excitement for any passing walker. Arctic skuas will defend their territory against any intruder, especially if they happen to have eggs or young on the nest. These large birds dive bomb the hapless walker, but rarely make actual contact. The same can't be said for the great skua, or 'bonxie', as the Shetlanders call it. Bonxies are more than happy to fly at you as you walk harmlessly across the moors, and they regularly clip people with a wing or extended foot, which can be quite painful. Fortunately they do seem to aim high if you hold your arm or even a walking pole above you head, and the whole thing can actually be good fun – being bombed by a bonxie is all part of the joy of walking on Shetland.

Head on southwards from Muskna Field along the Clift Hills and down to a col at the head of Lax Dale. Climb steeply up to the top of **Holm Field** at 290m, then down again to another col at 209m. A gentler climb up to a spot height at 247m leads onto the northwest ridge of **Royl Field**. Climb the ridge to the summit at 293m – there is a trig pillar here, and the views out to the west lead the eye to far-off Foula, one of the most remote inhabited islands of Britain.

Head southwards to the Grey Stane of Bonxa then continue over rough ground to the Hamars. A short climb leads to the Hill of Deepdale, and you should continue over this and down to a sheepfold in Deepdale itself. From here head southwestwards to the deep cleft at the Burn of Claver, then down the hill with a steep drop into the sea on your right, and you'll emerge at the road head in **Maywick** hamlet. Walk westwards out to the wonderful headland called the **Taing of Maywick**, then follow onwards down the coast to the Knowe of Burgarth.

The coastal scenery here is superb, with boiling seas throwing up white spray onto the cliffs, and fulmars and kittiwakes riding the airstreams above each wave. Also look out for puffins, guillemots and razorbills, as well as shags and rock doves.

The cliffs soon diminish in height as you make towards the Tromba of Griskerry and the superb little island of Griskerry itself. Continue onwards around Ireland Wick into the village of **Bigton**.

St Ninian's Isle is today uninhabited, but there are the remains of a 12th-century church just to the north across the tombolo. In 1958 a large hoard of Pictish treasure was discovered within the church. There were 28 silver objects, including brooches, bowls and a spoon, possibly dating from about 800AD. There are replicas in the Shetland Museum in Lerwick, although the originals are on view at the Royal Scottish Museum in Edinburgh.

Just south of Bigton lies one of the most remarkable coastal features of the walk – the tombolo leading across to **St Ninian's Isle**. A tombolo is a narrow spit joining an island to the mainland, and the one at St Ninian's Isle really is superb. A single strand of white sand and shingle leads you out through nesting arctic terns to the island itself.

The tombolo to St Ninian's Isle

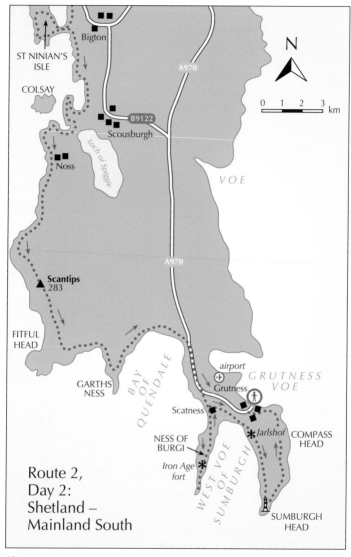

ST NINIAN'S ISLE

COLSAY

Bigton

A970

N

0 1 2 3 km

B9122
Scousburgh

Loch of Spiggie

VOE

Noss

A970

Scantips
283

FITFUL HEAD

GARTHS NESS

BAY OF QUENDALE

airport

Grutness

GRUTNESS VOE

Scatness

NESS OF BURGI

Jarlshof

COMPASS HEAD

Iron Age fort

WEST VOE OF SUMBURGH

SUMBURGH HEAD

Route 2,
Day 2:
Shetland –
Mainland South

It is possible to camp discreetly on St Ninian's Isle, or you can ask at one of the farms in Bigton if you can pitch a tent for the night. Failing that, continue along the coast to **Scousburgh** and the Spiggie Hotel.

DAY 2

From Bigton continue southwards around St Ninian's Bay to Rerwick, and round into the beautiful Bay of Scousburgh. Here the superb Scousburgh Sands are held in by Northern Ness and the lovely island of **Colsay**, lying just offshore. Walk along the sands and around Northern Ness, then continue to Fora Ness for the best views of Colsay.

Head southwards to **Noup Noss** then onwards to Wick of Shunni. Here the long climb to the summit of **Fitful Head** begins. Follow the top of the cliffs throughout for the best views, over Windy Stacks and out to the headland of Yuxness before turning south again for the top of Fitful Head, known as **Scantips** at 283m.

Walk onwards to **Garths Ness**, then pick up a track northwards to Quendale. Hop down onto the sandy beach and follow this around to Hestingott and Toab. Walk along the A970 to Betty Mouat's Böd on the left, and a little further on a lane leaves the main road and heads south for **Scatness**. Follow this to its end, then continue along a track to Tonga. A superb and narrow rocky ridge leads with the aid of a handrail out to the **Ness of Burgi**.

At the **Ness of Burgi** there is a defensive Iron Age blockhouse sited in a spectacular position on the promontory. This massive blockhouse lies behind two ditches that cut off the promontory from the mainland, and between them is a 6.4m thick stone rampart. The blockhouse was once 22m long, but its south end has been destroyed by cliff erosion. There is a single entrance leading to a stone-lined passage with door-checks and bar-holes. The blockhouse is 1.5m high and there are three cells within its 6m wide walls. The site was excavated in 1935.

Retrace your steps from the Ness of Burgi back to Scatness and out onto the A970. Turn right and down the hill to where the road is backed by sand dunes on the right. A little path

Officially described as 'one of the most remarkable archaeological sites ever excavated in the British Isles', **Jarlshof** came to light 100 years ago, when violent storms exposed massive stonework under a grassy mound above the beach at the West Voe of Sumburgh. There are six main levels, dating originally from the Stone Age (perhaps 4000 years old), through to an Iron Age broch and wheel-houses, to a sizeable Viking village and medieval farmstead. The site is owned by Historic Scotland and there is an admission fee.

through the dunes leads down onto the beach, and you can follow this round to the Sumburgh Hotel and **Jarlshof**.

From Jarlshof you can walk around the coast via a series of cairns, and uphill across close-cropped grass to **Sumburgh Head** lighthouse and nature reserve.

The cliffs around Sumburgh Head attract thousands of breeding seabirds, including puffins, guillemots, shags and fulmars. Gannets are regularly seen offshore, as well as sometimes whales and dolphins. The site is owned by the RSPB and entry is free.

Walk around the lighthouse and down the access road to a car park. Do not follow the road from here, but stick to the cliff top with the sea to your right. Walk out over **Compass Head** and down to **Grutness** where this walk ends.

Fitful Head from Jarlshof

ROUTE 3
Shetland – Yell

Number of Days	2
Total Distance	54km (33.5 miles)
Daily Distances	Day 1 – 27km (16.75 miles), Day 2 – 27km (16.75 miles)
Height Gain	Total: 690m; Day 1 – 480m, Day 2 – 210m
Maps	OS Landranger sheets 1 Shetland, Yell, Unst and Fetlar, and 3 Shetland, North Mainland
Starting Point	The pier at Ulsta, on Yell (grid ref HU463795). Unless you actually want to take your car over to Yell you can park in the car park at Toft on Mainland and catch the ro-ro ferry as a foot passenger. There are regular buses from Lerwick to Toft.
Finishing Point	The pier at Gutcher, on Yell (grid ref HU449993). Buses from Gutcher back to Ulsta, tel R Robertson and Son on 01957 722253.

Area Summary

Apart from Shetland Mainland, the smaller Shetland Islands offer some superb backpacking too. The best of the wild country here lies on the islands of Yell, Unst, Fetlar and Foula, on rugged coasts and rough moorland, and there is certainly plenty of that. Of these perhaps only Yell and Unst offer enough scope to make the long journey here worthwhile. Yell lies in the northeast corner of the Shetland Islands group, just offshore from Mainland, with the islands of Fetlar to the east and Unst to the north.

A coastal backpack on Yell in summer can be as good as you'll find anywhere in Britain. There's a lot of wildlife all around, with perhaps a better chance of seeing wild otters than you'll find anywhere else.

This walk takes you around the south and eastern coasts of the island. It starts along a quiet lane before heading for the highest point, on Ward of Arisdale, then

goes eastwards to the coast at Otterswick. The route
then follows the coast closely around to Mid Yell and
onwards to Gutcher.

Route Summary

Quite a tough walk considering that the high point of the
route is just 210m above sea level. It starts out by taking to
the very rough moorland on Ward of Arisdale, then heads
eastwards to the coast (this is all pathless terrain, and map
and compass skills are essential across the moorland). From
Otterswick the going is a little easier, taking you around some
fantastic coastal scenery to Mid Yell. The route onwards is

Tourist Information

There is an excellent tourist information centre at the market cross in
Lerwick, tel 01595 693434, website www.visitshetland.com.

Transport

You can get to the capital of the Shetland Islands, Lerwick, by either air or
ferry.
Air For flights contact British Airways and their franchise partners Logan Air
on 0845 7733377 – they make use of the main airport on Shetland at
Sumburgh, 40km south of Lerwick, website www.loganair.co.uk.
Ferry North Link Ferries operate to Lerwick from Aberdeen or Stromness
(Orkney), tel 0845 6000 449, website www.northlinkferries.co.uk.

Getting Around

Buses There is a daily bus service to Toft from Lerwick, contact White Coaches
on 01595 809443.
Ferry The roll-on roll-off ferries from Toft to Ulsta run regularly throughout the
day, www.shetland.gov.uk/ferryinfo/.
Car Hire Try either Bolts Car Hire on 01595 693636, or Star Rent-a-Car on
01595 692075. Both have offices in Lerwick and at Sumburgh Airport.

Accommodation and Supplies

Lerwick For accommodation in Lerwick try the Glen Orchy Guest House on
01595 692031, website www.guesthouselerwick.com, or the Alder Lodge
Guest House on 01595 695705. The youth hostel is a cheaper option and you
can contact them direct on 01595 692114 (open April to September). There
are plenty of shops, bars and restaurants in Lerwick.

Heading North For a very comfortable hotel on the road northwards to Yell, try Busta House. Joe and Veronica Rocks are very welcoming, and the food is excellent – plus this is a good opportunity for some local Valhalla Brewery beer! Busta House is at Busta, near Brae, and you can make a reservation on 01806 522506. E-mail reservations@bustahouse.com, website www.busta-house.com.

Yell In the south of Yell there is a bed and breakfast at Hillhead, Hamnavoe, tel Rita Leask on 01957 722274, while at Mid Yell you should get in touch with Catherine Gibb at Altna-Craig on 01957 702162. At Gutcher I would recommend staying with the Tullochs at the post office, tel Margaret Tulloch on 01957 744201.

Escape Routes
At any point during the walk the quickest return route to civilisation is to make for the B9081, which runs between the villages on the east side of the island.

straightforward, and involves a little road walking to get around big coastal estuaries, but the views throughout are spectacular, and you are not likely to see any other walkers during the entire trek.

It may be possible to get permission to camp at Mid Yell if you ask around at the farms nearby.

On Yell there are shops at the Ulsta ferry terminal, and at Mid Yell. The Wind Dog Cafe at Gutcher is popular too.

DAY 1
As the ferry slowly pushes its way over the Yell Sound from Toft, keep an eye out for porpoises and whales from the deck. You don't get very long though – within half an hour the ferry will have deposited you on the pier at **Ulsta**, and you're ready for the walk out to the east coast. (Before setting off you could pop into Robertson's shop at Ulsta to have a word about being picked up from Gutcher at the end of the walk.)

Head out along the main road then turn right along the B9081 after just a couple of hundred metres. This road climbs gently up to the Hill of Ulsta where the Loch of Ulsta lies to the left.

Watch gannets from the Yell ferry

You'll probably see nesting arctic terns here if you visit during the summer months – the moor has a healthy population, as well as a few bonxies (skuas), and wading birds such as golden plover and dunlin.

Up the valley here you'll pass the Catalina memorial, commemorating the crew lost in an air crash during the Second World War.

Continue along the road down to a bridge over the Burn of Arisdale. Just over the bridge a track leaves the road on the left and you should follow this up the wide, rough dale to the farm at **Arisdale**. ◀

From Arisdale a steep climb up to the northeast leads onto the broad ridge of **Hill of Arisdale**. Climb up through heather and moorland grasses to the summit at 210m.

The views from the Hill of Arisdale are spectacular. To the east you can see the hills of Fetlar rising out of the sea, while the rocky lumps to the southeast are the Out Skerries. Westwards the bald plateau of Ronas Hill forms a bare knoll rising over the surrounding moorland. Ronas Hill is the highest point on Shetland.

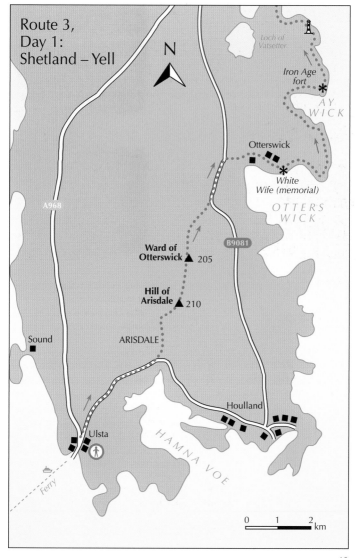

Route 3,
Day 1:
Shetland – Yell

N

Loch of
Vatsetter

Iron Age
fort

AY
WICK

Otterswick

White
Wife (memorial)

OTTERS
WICK

A968

B9081

Ward of
Otterswick ▲ 205

Hill of
Arisdale ▲ 210

ARISDALE

Sound

Houlland

Ulsta

HAMNA VOE

Ferry

0   1   2 km

The White Wife at Otters Wick

Continue northeastwards along the ridge to the Ordnance Survey trig pillar at **Ward of Otterswick**, at 205m. A little to the north lies a large cairn – walk on to this, then descend eastwards to the B9081 near a little chapel.

Turn left along the road then right at a junction, passing what is marked on the map as a pub, although it does-n't look anything like it when you get there. Turn right again to Midgarth and walk along the dead-end road to a car park and a stile on the right. Go over the stile and follow the path beneath the farm buildings at Queyon. The path passes down through fields then onto moorland, leading easily down to the coast at the **White Wife**, overlooking the bay of Otters Wick.

On the shore at Otterswick village there is a prominent figurehead known as the White Wife. This came from the Bohus, a German training ship that was wrecked on the Ness of Queyon in 1924.

Walk onwards around the coast to the Ness of Queyon, looking for signs of wildlife as you go.

> The rocky shore here is a good place to see seals, and they are often out on Black Skerry in the bay, while otters are also occasionally seen. Out in the bay you might also spot common porpoises feeding on shoals of surface-feeding fish.

From the Ness of Queyon turn northwards to Salt Wick, then around the Haa of Ay Wick and into the little bay of **Ay Wick** itself. Continue around the coast to the remains of a **fort**. ▶

The Ay Wick fort dates back to the Iron Age, though there isn't a lot to see today.

Onwards the route takes you around the White Hill of Vatsetter and the **Ness of Vatsetter** to the small cover known as the Wick of Vatsetter.

From Vatsetter you have a choice of routes to **Mid Yell**. You can either continue around the coast to the Ness of Lussetter and on to Mid Yell alongside **Mid Yell Voe**, or you can go over the Hill of Lussetter. To do this, walk along the side of **Loch of Vatsetter** and on to North Westerhouse. A path starts just to the left of the house here and climbs easily to the summit at 102m. The path continues down the other side to Mid Yell at Cashigarsh. Turn left along the shore to the centre of the village.

DAY 2

Start the day by walking westwards out of the village towards Hillend. Here you gain the B9081 again. Turn right and follow it down to the mudflats at the head of Mid Yell Voe.

Continue along the road until the junction with the A968 is reached. Turn right along this, rising gently above Mid Yell Voe, again with good views across the mudflats. At Camb, the next hamlet along where the road swings away northwards, take a little lane down to the pier at **Seafield**. Just beyond the pier the lane swings sharply to the left and climbs steeply uphill. Leave the road at this bend and take to the shore, making your way around the wonderful knap of Head of Hevdagarth – there are good views across Mid Yell Voe from here. The route soon takes you around the coast to **Kaywick**, then on to

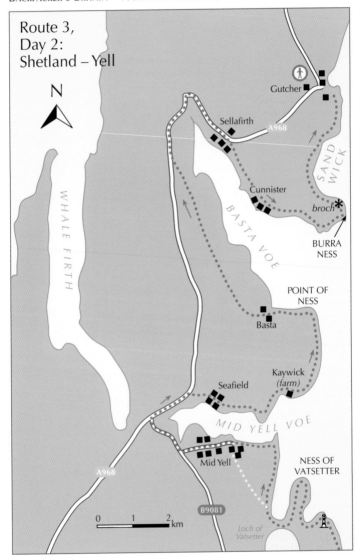

Route 3, Day 2: Shetland – Yell

N

Gutcher

Sellafirth

A968

Cunnister

BASTA VOE

broch ✳

BURRA NESS

POINT OF NESS

Basta

SAND WICK

WHALE FIRTH

Kaywick (farm)

Seafield

MID YELL VOE

Mid Yell

NESS OF VATSETTER

A968

B9081

0   1   2 km

Loch of Vatsetter

the Ness of Kaywick where the views open out across the Hascosay Sound. ▶

This muddy area is a great place to see wading birds. When the tide is out you should see oyster-catchers, ringed plover, dunlin, curlew, redshank and possibly teal.

The island of Hascosay just across the sound is one of the best places in Britain to see otters, although when a wildlife film crew went there in 1979 to make a BBC Wildtrack film they failed to find any! The soil on Hascosay is said to have magic qualities that keep mice away, prompting residents of other islands to take it from Hascosay. Its true mouse-deterring properties have never been thoroughly explored, however.

Continue on northwards to the **Point of Ness,** then round to the Haa of Udhouse with its lovely little beach at **Basta**. You are aiming for **Burra Ness**, across the water to the north, but first a long detour has to be taken around **Basta Voe**.

From the Haa of Udhouse walk out along the driveway to the houses at Basta, then look for a path on the right that takes you across the Burn of Basta. This path continues across moorland to Colvister, where it becomes a track leading out onto the A968. Turn right along the main road and walk around Basta Voe to Sellafirth. Here a little lane heads off to the right through the Knowes of Cunnister to the hamlet of Cunnister itself, then on to Kirkabister. From here you are back along-side the beautiful, windswept coastlines around to Burra Ness. On Burra Ness there is quite a good example of a broch ruin, with walls 4.5m thick and a scarcement (a ledge to support a floor) visible 4m above ground level.

From the **broch** a path leads around the coast to **North Sandwick,** then onwards via a standing stone to **Gutcher** and the end of the walk.

ROUTE 4

Orkney – Western Mainland

Number of Days	2
Total Distance	38km (23.5 miles)
Daily Distances	Day 1 – 21km (13 miles), Day 2 – 17km (10.5 miles)
Height Gain	Total: 380m; Day 1 – 250m, Day 2 – 130m
Maps	OS Landranger sheet 6 Orkney Mainland
Starting Point	The car park overlooking the Brough of Birsay in the far northwest corner of Mainland (grid ref HY243284).
Finishing Point	Stromness pier (grid ref HY253087).

Area Summary

The Orkney Islands differ greatly from the Shetland Islands. For the most part they enjoy easy access from mainland Scotland, and are a lot less rugged than the Shetlands. Much of the land is either arable, or reasonably low-lying moorland. This apart, there is a great deal for the walker to explore, with fantastic coastlines to the west of Mainland, and some great nature reserves throughout the archipelago, many of which are of international importance as breeding sites for rare birds, and also as regular migration hotspots for wayward birds that really should be elsewhere!

Some of the walking in this island group really is as spectacular as it gets. Hoy is superb for coastal scenery, and has some modest hills too, while Orkney Mainland offers the most scope for exploring with a backpack.

Route Summary

A walk suitable for all, this coastal trail is easy to follow throughout – just start at the northwestern tip of Mainland and keep the sea to your right until you hit the bright lights of Stromness – no navigation needed! That said, there is a feeling of remoteness here – you pass the odd farmstead as you walk south, but it's only around Skara Brae, the best-preserved Stone Age village in northern Europe, that there will be any real sign of other tourists. South of Skara Brae it goes a bit wild again, with dramatic scenery dominated by the island of Hoy dead ahead, with the Old Man, a famous sea-stack, standing proud off its west coast.

You'll camp on a small headland along this section of the walk, and complete the pleasant journey into Stromness the following day, perhaps with time to spare for a visit to the Ring of Brodgar stone circle. Note, though, that this is a linear walk, so transport will have to be arranged at either end. Parts of the walk are pathless, although the going underfoot is never difficult.

Tourist Information

There is an excellent tourist information centre on Broad Street in Kirkwall, tel 01856 872856, website www.visitorkney.com.

Transport

You can get to Kirkwall, the capital of the Orkney Islands, easily by either ferry or air from the Scottish Mainland.

Air Contact Logan Air on 0845 7733377 or British Airways on 0870 8509850 for flights, which arrive from Aberdeen, Edinburgh, Glasgow, Inverness or Shetland to Kirkwall airport, websites www.ba.com, or www.loganair.co.uk.

Ferry For ferries to Orkney you must get to either Aberdeen or Scrabster (Northlink Ferries, tel 0845 6000449, website www.northlinkferries.co.uk), Gills Bay (Pentland Ferries, tel 01856 831226, website www.pentlandferries.com) or John o' Groats (John O' Groats Ferries, tel 01955 611353, website www.jogferry.co.uk).

Buses There is a limited bus service around Mainland. Contact the tourist information centre in Kirkwall for information, tel 01856 872856, website www.visitorkney.com.

Car Hire Try either Scarth Car Hire on 01856 872125, or WR Tullock on 01856 876262. Both have offices in Kirkwall.

Taxis There are taxi ranks down by the pier in Kirkwall, and it is possible to arrange to be dropped off at Birsay and picked up at Stromness.

Accommodation and Supplies

It is best to stay in Kirkwall when you first arrive in Orkney and arrange your onward transport from there to Birsay. Good options for accommodation are the

Ayre Hotel overlooking the harbour (tel 01856 873001, website www.ayreho-tel.co.uk), or the Albert Hotel (tel 01856 876000).

There are also lots of cheap bed and breakfasts, and a good youth hostel on Old Scapa Road (tel 01856 872243). There are also shops for supplies in Kirkwall, and it is best to buy all you need before heading out to the coast.

At the end of the walk there is plenty of accommodation in Stromness. Try the youth hostel on Hellihole Road (tel 01856 850589), or for more comfort go for one of the many bed and breakfast options around town.

Overnight Options

There's nothing much along this west coast of Mainland, and you will invari-ably have to camp wild, well away from habitations.

Escape Routes

You can head east from the coast at any point, and within 4km you will hit either the B9056 or the A967. There are lots of settlements in the country between the coast and these roads.

DAY 1

At the northwestern tip of Mainland lies the small island of the **Brough of Birsay**. The short spit of land that connects the island to the mainland is only accessible at low tides, so be careful not to get stranded. The island was an important Pictish stronghold from around the 6th century, and many interest-ing archaeological remains have been found here from this period. There is a small charge at the kiosk for visiting the island, payable to Historic Scotland.

You can walk around the cliff-top path, where you should see puffins, guillemots, razorbills and fulmars nesting during the early summer. Another path leads from the lighthouse on the very western tip of the island, across the centre and back to the kiosk.

Once you've had a walk around the island, return to the kiosk via the scramble across wrack- and weed-covered rocks to get back onto Mainland. Follow the minor road towards a junction near the Earl's Palace, and bear right past St Magnus church to a track leading along the top of the low cliffs.

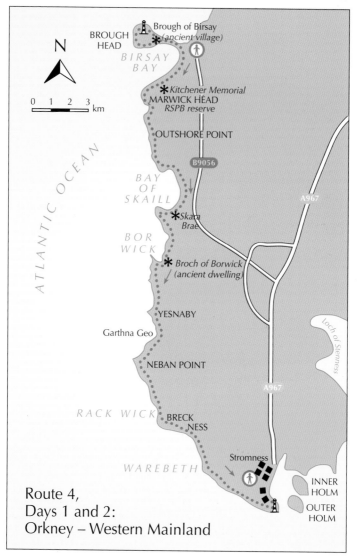

Brough of Birsay
(ancient village)

BROUGH
HEAD

*BIRSAY
BAY*

N

0 1 2 3
km

* Kitchener Memorial
MARWICK HEAD
RSPB reserve

OUTSHORE POINT

B9056

*BAY
OF
SKAILL*

A967

* Skara
Brae

*BOR
WICK*

* Broch of Borwick
(ancient dwelling)

ATLANTIC OCEAN

YESNABY

Garthna Geo

NEBAN POINT

A967

Loch of Stenness

RACK WICK BRECK
NESS

WAREBETH

Stromness

INNER
HOLM

OUTER
HOLM

Route 4,
Days 1 and 2:
Orkney – Western Mainland

Walking at the Brough of Birsay

The Earl's Palace was built in the late 16th century by Earl Robert Stewart and was once described as 'a sumptuous and stately dwelling'. There's not much to see today, but you can have a look around to get a feel of the place. Free admission.

Walk around **Birsay Bay** towards a prominent tower (the **Kitchener memorial**) on the cliff top. Keep a lookout seawards for passing minke or pilot whales, while grey seals can often be seen closer inshore, basking on the rocks beneath the cliffs. Seabirds nest on the cliffs at your feet, while the flower-filled meadows are a good place to see singing skylarks, meadow pipits, and nesting wading birds such as lapwings, oyster-catchers and redshank.

The cliffs rise in height as you near the Kitchener memorial, sitting on top of spectacular **Marwick Head**, 91m above sea level.

The Kitchener memorial was erected after the First World War to commemorate Lord Kitchener and the crew of HMS Hampshire, which was sunk off this coast in 1916 by a German mine. Only 12 of her crew survived.

Continue around the headland from the memorial to the tip of Marwick Head, above the rocks of Choldertoo.

Marwick Head and the Kitchener memorial

Marwick Head is an RSPB reserve that is an important nesting site for thousands of seabirds. Expect to see puffins, razorbills, guillemots, fulmar, shag, kittiwakes and rock doves during the main nesting season, which is from May until the end of June. Look for wild flowers on the cliffs too, including sea thrift, sea campion and rose root.

Carry on around the cliff-top path, with superb views ahead of the island of Hoy with its famous sea-stack, the Old Man, off its western coast. The path leads down to the little stony bay of the Choin of Mar Wick, where there is a small car park. Our walk continues around the coast, rising again to the headland of **Outshore Point**. Although now outside the RSPB reserve at Marwick Head, there is still plenty of wildlife to be seen.

From Outshore Point it is a further, wonderful 4km of cliff-top walking to the **Bay of Skaill**, where you come to the B9056 and a small car park with public toilets.
Just around the bay you'll find Skaill House and the entrance to **Skara Brae**.

Skaill House is an early 17th-century mansion containing a few interesting arte-facts, including the dinner service from Captain Cook's Resolution, but all this is not terribly exciting when Skara Brae lies just a few hundred metres down the road!

Skara Brae rose from the sand dunes in a violent storm during 1850. The sand was blown off the remains of this 500-year-old site, revealing to the world the best-preserved Stone Age village in northern Europe. It is known that the site was occupied for around 600 years from about 3000BC, and you can still see the stone furniture, fireplaces, drains, and even damp-proof coursing in the foundations! The entrance to Skara Brae is through a modern visitor centre, and there is a charge.

Drop down onto the beach and walk around the outside of the Skara Brae complex until you can regain the cliff top. Continue around the headland to Hole o' Row, a fine natural arch. The route continues around Yettna Geo to Row Head, then on to the **Broch of Borwick**. From here you head around the Hill of Borwick and on to a car park at the end of a minor road.

The Broch of Borwick is perched high on an eroding headland surrounded by a spectacular sea cliff. The site takes its name from adjacent Bor Wick bay, an inlet lying almost halfway between the Bay o' Skaill and Yesnaby. Thought to date from the first millennium BC, the broch was probably in use for over 1000 years, finally abandoned between 500AD and 600AD.

The next section of the route takes you along some of the wildest coastline in the Orkney Islands group. There is little south of here until you round the headland overlooking Hoy Sound and enter **Stromness**.

Walking on southwards from Yesnaby towards **Garthna Geo**, you are probably beginning to think about finding a suitable campsite for the night. I have found a few good sites around here, but in order to encourage you to wild camp responsibly it is better if I do not give exact details of the ones I have used. There really are some lovely places to pitch up for the night, with a great view of the wild North Atlantic from your tent door.

DAY 2

Begin the day by packing up slowly and enjoying the morning view of the ocean. Once you've had a relaxing brew-up, begin the pleasant walk southwards towards **Neban Point**, another superb place for close-up views of seabirds.

The route continues along the Bight of Mousland to the little headland of Neblonga, below the small hill of Black Craig. Look on Skrowa Skerry for basking seals, shags and turnstones as you descend from Black Craig, then continue around the bays of Billia Croo and **Rack Wick** to the headland of **Breck Ness**. Walk around this, passing the Breck Ness Broch and perhaps dropping down onto the shore below the low cliffs if the tide is out. The rock pools here are fun to explore as you begin the journey eastwards to Pulse Skerry.

Here regain the cliff top, which has a good path now, leading towards **Stromness**. The walking here is easy, but pleasant, and you soon find yourself on a minor road leading into the centre of Stromness.

Stromness is a good place to spend the night before heading back to Kirkwall.

Stromness, the second biggest town on Orkney after Kirkwall, sits on the natural harbour of Hamnavoe. In the 18th century the growth in the whaling industry made it an important last port of call for ships heading north to the cold waters of Greenland. Many local men were recruited into the ranks of crewmen on these whaling ships.

ROUTE 5

Lewis – Western Mountains

Number of Days	2
Total Distance	40km (24.75 miles)
Daily Distances	Day 1 – 19km (11.75 miles), Day 2 – 21km (13 miles)
Height Gain	Total: 1140m; Day 1 – 890m, Day 2 – 250m
Maps	OS Landranger sheet 13 West Lewis and North Harris
Starting Point	A small lay-by at a gate with a track leading down to the beach at Mangurstadh in West Lewis (grid ref NB013307). Reach this from Stornoway by following the A859 south from the town and turning onto the A858 towards Callanish. Just before Callanish take the B8011 and follow it beyond the superb beach at Traigh Uig. Drive on up the hill, passing a gravel pit on the left and a track just beyond. Ignore the next turn on the right to Mangurstadh and look for the lay-by after another 1.5km.

Area Summary

The Outer Hebrides, also variously called the Western Isles, or the Long Island, consist of a narrow chain of islands 209km long, lying around 64km off the northwest coast of the Scottish mainland. Much of the interior of these islands is bleak and barren, with mile after mile of peat bog bejewelled with tiny lochans and rocky hills. There are also some superb coastal cliffs, and the finest beaches in Britain, with wild mountain tops rising from the shore. Remote crofting communities are scattered around, and with 5000-year-old archaeological remains in their midst, a visit to these islands is a truly unique and magical experience.

The northern part of the Outer Hebrides is made up of Harris and Lewis. People tend to think of them as two separate islands, whereas in fact they are all one land mass. In past times it was easier for people to travel from Lewis to Harris, or visa versa, by boat, rather than trudging across the harsh landscape, so many local people simply thought of Harris and Lewis as being separate.

This walk is in the mountains of west Lewis, one of the wildest areas of this beautiful land.

Route Summary

A walk suitable for experienced backpackers. The route takes you through some very wild and remote terrain, far from help, and although the mountains traversed are never too high, they are nevertheless incredibly rocky. There is a low-level alternative for those who would like an easier walk.

The route leads into the mountains from near the Sands of Uig. Great mountains crowd around on all sides as you walk up a wonderfully wild glen, then you leave the track and make for the heights of Mealaisbhal. A series of rocky hills is then traversed before dropping down on the south side of the range into the wilderness at the head of Loch Tamnabhaigh. A wild camp is taken on the little peninsula of Rubha Garbh. The following day gives a superb coastal walk around to Mealasta, then on around the point of Aird Feinis and back to the starting point.

Tourist Information
There is a good tourist information centre on Cromwell Street in Stornoway, tel 01851 703088. The Outer Hebrides Tourist Board also has a useful website www.visithebrides.com.

Transport
There are two ways of getting to the Outer Hebrides.
Air You can fly to Stornoway from Inverness, Edinburgh or Glasgow. For details of British Airways flights, tel 0345 222 111, or visit their website at www.british-airways.com. British Midland also flies from Edinburgh to Stornoway, tel 0870 60 70 555, or visit their website at www.flybmi.com. From Inverness you can also fly with Highland Airways to Stornoway, tel 0845 450 2245, or visit their website at www.highlandairways.co.uk.
Ferry You can get to Stornoway from Ullapool, or to Tarbert on Harris from Uig on Skye with Caledonian MacBrayne, tel 08705 650000. You can also check timetables and book online at www.calmac.co.uk.

Transport on Lewis A car is essential to get to the start of this walk. You can hire one in Stornoway with Lewis Car Rentals on www.lewis-car-rental.co.uk, tel 01851 703760, or Mackinnon Self Drive on www.mackinnonselfdrive.co.uk, tel 01851 702984.

Accommodation and Supplies
There are a few guest houses in the Callanish area on Lewis. Try Leumadair, tel 01851 621706, e-mail info@leumadair.co.uk. Further north at Galson is the superb Galson Farm Guest House, tel 01851 850492, www.galsonfarm.co.uk. They also have a comfortable bunkhouse at Galson!

You can buy all the supplies you need in Stornoway, but there are no shops along the route.

Overnight Options
No option but to camp – but what a location to camp in! Pick a wild site somewhere on the Rubha Garbh peninsula at the mouth of Loch Tamnabhaigh.

Escape Routes
To the west lies the narrow, dead-end road running from Uig to Mealasta, while to the east the glen has a good Land-Rover track running north to Uig. (**Note** Following this Land-Rover track southwards just leads even further into the wilderness.)

DAY 1
From the small lay-by walk back along the road to the track near the gravel pit. Turn right onto this track and follow it down to the crossing of Abhainn Stocaill. The track takes you around a big bend to the left, then back right as the views open up before you.

Red-throated divers regularly nest here, and it is also a good location for dunlin and golden plover on the moorland, and common sandpipers by the shore.

The line of hills on the far side of the glen leads the eye right up to its head. The hills here are some of the rockiest in the Outer Hebrides. Keep a lookout for golden eagles – this is an important territory for them, and it is not unusual to see a pair hunting along the ridges.

Continue to the rise of a knoll then head west across a boggy moor to the east side of **Loch Brinneabhal**. ◀

Walk around to the south side of the loch from where a rocky slope leads onto the north ridge of **Brinneabhal**. The top of this low hill at 213m is a good place to view **Uig Sands** to the north. Leave the top by heading southwest along a vague ridge, passing just north of a little lochan. Continue southwestwards beneath the steep, craggy northern slopes of **Mealaisbhal** until you reach the gentler northwestern slopes.

Callanish stone circle on Lewis

Here turn to the southeast up bouldery slopes, then eastwards to a small knoll on the ridge known as Mula Mac Sgiathain. From the knoll a good rocky scramble leads directly southwards to the summit of Mealaisbhal at 574m. (A slightly easier alternative lies to the left, up grassy slopes to a col, then right along the ridge to the top.) A pile of huge boulders marks the highest point.

Thirty-three kilometres west of Lewis the Flannan Isles can be seen on a fine day from the top of Mealaisbhal. There are three small clusters of islands in the group, the main one having two islands, Eilean Mor (Big Island) and Eilean Tighe (Islands of the House).

Head southeast from the summit down a ridge of boulders and grass leading to a col with two lochans at 293m.

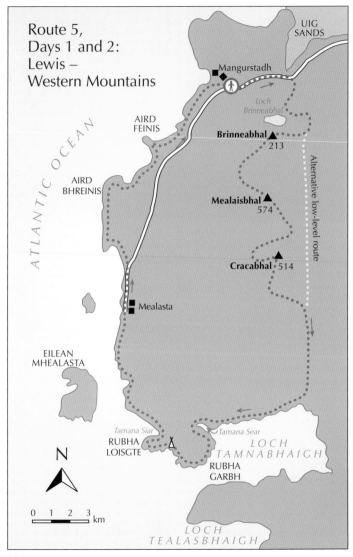

Route 5,
Days 1 and 2:
Lewis –
Western Mountains

UIG
SANDS

Mangurstadh

*Loch
Brinneabhal*

ATLANTIC OCEAN

AIRD
FEINIS

Brinneabhal ▲
213

AIRD
BHREINIS

Mealaisbhal ▲
574

Alternative low-level route

Cracabhal ▲ 514

■■ Mealasta

EILEAN
MHEALASTA

Tamana Siar

Tamana Sear

RUBHA
LOISGTE

Ⴟ

*LOCH
TAMNABHAIGH*

RUBHA
GARBH

N

0 1 2 3
▬▬▬▬ km

*LOCH
TEALASBHAIGH*

Again you must skirt under crags to gain easier slopes leading to your next summit, **Cracabhal**. Head southwestwards to Loch Clibh Cracabhal, then pick up the west ridge leading to the summit of this fine hill at 514m.

Descend to the south to a col, then head east down into the head of the glen draining Loch a' Chama. Here you pick up the Land-Rover track that you started out along earlier in the day. Turn right and follow this down the glen, heading southwards for the sea at Loch Cheann Chuisil.

As the track drops down to sea level, bear in mind that you'll need to cross over the river to the west side at some point. The water here can be difficult to cross in flood, so it might be better to go higher up if there's been a lot of rain.

Once on the other side, walk round the coast across rough slopes beneath Sgaladal to cross another burn at Gleann Sgaladail. Continue around the coast to the little cove at **Tamana Sear**, then around to your overnight campsite at **Rubha Garbh**.

DAY 2

Pack up the tent and start off by following the coast round into the bay at Tamana Siar to the west. Continue around the coast to the rocky headland at Aird Dhrolai Geodha, then turn northwards with the coast.

The view to the Sands of Uig from Mealaisbhal

Keep an eye open for red deer on these slopes. There are good populations of deer all over these hills, and for the most part the stags and hinds will be apart for much of the year. They generally only get together in one big mixed herd during the rutting season in October and November.

Continue northwards along the coast, with great views out westwards to **Eilean Mhealasta**.

A little further north you will reach the road head at **Mealasta** village. Follow this for a short while, then make your way back to the cliff top. It's easy walking round the headland of **Aird Bhreinis** and on to the bay at Camas Islibhig.

Mhealasta island lies about 750m offshore and is used as grazing land for sheep. As you continue northwards, keep an eye on the shoreline for otters. Although they are not easy to see there is a small population on these coasts. **Otters** inland on the mainland and in England and Wales are almost always nocturnal, whereas on the coasts of Scotland they tend not to be so choosy. These otters are governed more by the tides, preferring to hunt on a rising tide, whatever the time of day or night. Many people talk about these coastal otters as 'sea otters', but although they live and feed in the sea, they are the same species as the otters found inland in Britain, the Eurasian otter, Lutra lutra. There is such a thing as a sea otter, but this is a North American species. Eurasian otters, even those that live in coastal waters, need freshwater to clean their fur in daily.

During the summer months there will be lots of seabirds in this area. Fulmars, shags, rock doves and kittiwakes nest on the cliffs, while you may also see puffins, guillemots and razorbills. Out at sea occasional pods of pilot whales and sperm whales are seen, although you need a very calm sea to stand any chance of a clear view.

Walk around the bay and out to the headland of **Aird Feinis**. Continue along the cliff tops to a descent onto the small but beautiful beach at Traigh Mhangurstadh. Walk up the beach on the right and you'll pick up a track taking you the short way back up the hill to your car.

ROUTE 6

North Harris – Mountains and Moorlands

Number of Days	2
Total Distance	31km (19.25 miles)
Daily Distances	Day 1 – 15km (9.25 miles), Day 2 – 16km (10 miles)
Height Gain	Total: 2060m; Day 1 – 920m, Day 2 – 1140m
Maps	OS Landranger sheet 13 West Lewis and North Harris
Starting Point	A small lay-by on the right where a metalled access road leads up the glen by the waterfalls at Abhainn Suidhe (grid ref NB053077). Reach this point from Tarbert on Harris by heading north out of town on the Stornoway road. After a couple of kilometres take the B887 on the left leading to Bun Abhainn. This spectacular road takes you along the coast with the mountains of North Harris towering over you on the right. The road ends at Huisinis, beyond the parking space where this walk starts.

Area Summary

The Outer Hebrides, also variously known as the Western Isles or the Long Island, are a narrow chain of islands 209km long, and lying about 64km off the northwest coast of the Scottish mainland. The northern part of the Outer Hebrides is made up of Harris and Lewis. These are often thought of as two separate islands, whereas in fact they are all one land mass. In past times it was easier for people to travel from Lewis to Harris, or visa versa, by boat, rather than trudging across the harsh landscape, so many local people simply thought of Harris and Lewis as being separate.

The walking out here is superb, particularly in the hills of Harris, where long ridges stretch away into the wilderness, each cut by deep glens with dashing waterfalls and hidden lochans. This walk is in the hills of north Harris, the most mountainous part of the Western Isles.

Route Summary

The mountains of Harris are one of my favourite areas for a backpacking expedition. Good ridge walks lead you into the heart of mountains where the only other living things you are likely to see are golden eagles and red deer. While other walkers head for Clisham, the highest mountain in the Outer Hebrides at 799m, this route takes you into much finer mountain country.

From the roadside near Abhainn Suidhe you follow a metalled road for a short way then continue into the mountains along a track to Loch Chliostair. A ridge leads onto the heights of Tiorga Mor from where you head north into the wilderness to Loch Reasort. The route back takes in the ridge on the other side of the glen, over Ulabhal and Oireabhal. The walking is quite rough underfoot, but never excessively so, and once on the ridges much of the going is on short-cropped grass. This is also one of the shortest backpacking routes in this guidebook, so it is suitable for anyone with a

Tourist Information There is a good tourist information centre on Cromwell Street in Stornoway (tel 01851 703088). The Outer Hebrides Tourist Board also has a useful website www.visithebrides.com.

Transport
There are two ways of getting to the Outer Hebrides.
Air You can fly to Stornoway from Inverness, Edinburgh or Glasgow. For details of British Airways flights, tel 0345 222 111 or visit their website at www.british-airways.com. British Midlands also flies from Edinburgh to Stornoway, tel 0870 60 70 555 or visit their website at www.flybmi.com. From Inverness you can also fly with Highland Airways to Stornoway, tel 0845 450 2245 or visit their website at www.highlandairways.co.uk.
Ferry You can get to Tarbert on Harris from Uig on Skye, or Stornoway from Ullapool with Caledonian MacBrayne, tel 08705 650000. You can also check timetables and book online at www.calmac.co.uk.
Transport on Lewis A car is essential to get to the start of this walk. You can hire one in Stornoway with Lewis Car Rentals on www.lewis-car-rental.co.uk, tel 01851 703760), or Mackinnon Self Drive on www.mackinnonselfdrive.co.uk, tel 01851 702984.

Accommodation and Supplies
There are a few guest houses in Tarbert on Harris. Try Dunard (tel 01859 502340) or Leachin House (tel 01859 502157). There's also a private bunkhouse, Rockview (tel 01859 502211). Next door to Rockview is the best fish and chip shop in the Outer Hebrides! You can buy all the supplies you need in Stornoway, while there are a few shops in Tarbert too, but be aware that here everything closes on Sundays, so be prepared. There are no shops along the route of the walk.

Overnight Options
Camp in among the mountains at the head of Loch Reasort, one of the wildest and most beautiful parts of the Outer Hebrides (grid ref NB104175).

Escape Routes
The two mountain ridges followed by this walk have a deep glen between them. Running through this glen is a good track that goes over a high pass and down the other side as far as Sron Uladal. Although these are rocky hills, it is possible with care to pick a way down to this track at all points of the walk, then follow this southwards out of the mountains to your car.

little experience of mountain walking who wants to get into a remote wilderness area.

DAY 1
Begin just east of **Abhainn Suidhe**. Follow the track northwards up the glen, first beside Lochan Beag then above the river feeding this loch from the larger **Loch Leosaid**. Turn left through a gate onto the main track leading up the glen. ▶

Ahead lies the impressive-looking bulky mass of **Tiorga Mor**. Continue along the track, passing a small hydropower station. The track passes beneath the water pipeline that brings water down from **Loch Chliostair** above to feed the station. At this point leave the track and begin climbing the steep slopes on the left, gaining a flat plateau area on the southeast ridge of Tiorga Mor, just above the loch. Continue climbing up the slabby rocks of the southeast ridge towards the summit, passing lovely Loch Maolaig on the way up. ▶

This ridge of Tiorga Mor is quite rocky and rough, but grassy gullies lead up through the slabs and make for an easy and quick ascent. As you climb Tiorga Mor the views open

The Abhainn Leosaid flows into the loch at the point where this track crosses it, and here are the most amazing orange rock beaches. Look out for common sandpipers during the summer.

The hidden bowl that holds Loch Maolaig is a good place for red deer, out of sight of anybody passing along the track far below.

The view to the hills of Western Lewis from Huisinis

out all around, and soon you will reach the top, with its lofty cairn and Ordnance Survey trig pillar at 679m.

Way out to the west in the open wastes of the North Atlantic a group of huge rock stacks breaks the surface. This is the St Kilda archipelago, a national nature reserve since 1957, and now a world heritage site. St Kilda can be seen easily from Tiorga Mor on clear days, while eastwards the view is of a crowd of mountain ridges and summits leading to Clisham, the highest mountain in the Outer Hebrides.

From the summit a superb ridge leads off to the northeast, down to the col at Lag Glas then up to the summit of Tiorga Beag. Head northwards down a broadening ridge, bearing slightly to the northeast to the rock arm of **Mas a' Chnoic Chuairtich**.

This hillside is also a good place to see red deer, while across the glen to the east there is a huge nose of overhanging rock – Sron Uladal. This is a well-known site for golden eagles, and you may be lucky enough to see a pair below you as you walk.

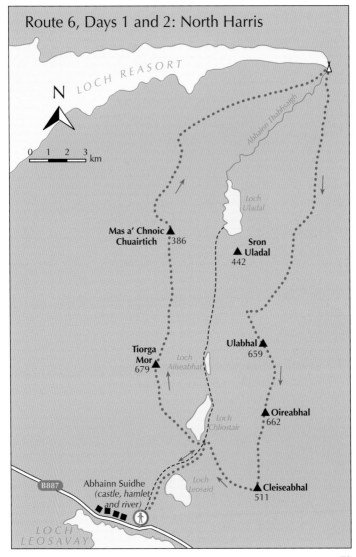

Route 6, Days 1 and 2: North Harris

LOCH REASORT

N

0 1 2 3 km

Abhainn Thabhsaigh

Loch Uladal

Mas a' Chnoic Chuairtich ▲ 386

Sron ▲ Uladal 442

Tiorga Mor ▲ 679

Loch Ailseabhal

Ulabhal ▲ 659

Loch Chliostair

Oireabhal ▲ 662

Abhainn Suidhe (castle, hamlet and river)

Loch Leosaid

B887

LOCH LEOSAVAY

Cleiseabhal ▲ 511

The magnificent Sron Ulladal

The ridge bends to the northwest, and you should follow it downhill for 700m until it is possible to get off the ridge to the northeast without venturing onto the small crags here. Make for a col to the northeast, then climb to the fine little summit of Feadan Dirisgil at 240m.

The route now takes you northwards to **Loch Reasort**, and you can camp anywhere here for the night. However, you'll need to cross the river at **Abhainn Thabhsaigh** tomorrow, and there is a bridge right at the very head of the loch, so it makes sense to make for that point now. Once there, pitch up for the night and enjoy the magnificent wild country at the narrow head of the loch.

DAY 2

Cross the bridge over the Abhainn Thabhsaigh and follow it southwestwards for a while until you can gain the shoulder of Ruidear. Climb up onto the ridge and follow it over a series of rocky knolls to the top of Mullach na Reidheachd at 295m. ▶

From Mullach na Reidheachd head south down to a boggy col with a little lochan, then climb again, first southwards to Gormal Mor, then across the head of a streambed to the north ridge of **Ulabhal** near Muladal (this avoids the steep northeast slopes of Ulabhal). Once on the north ridge turn left and climb, initially over grassy slopes then across a broken rock band, to the summit of Ulabhal at 659m.

Continue southwards down a narrowing ridge to a col, then begin the easy climb up to the summit of **Oireabhal** at 662m. This is another fine summit with views out to St Kilda to the west. Head southwest down the ridge to a col, then over a rocky bump known as Bidigidh at 500m, and down to a col at 425m. The ridge here is quite narrow and gives really good mountain walking before the climb up to the next peak, **Cleiseabhal** at 511m. ▶

From the summit of Cleiseabhal walk west, then northwest down rough slopes into a hanging valley, then follow the stream down to rejoin the power station track. Turn left and follow this down the glen and back to the car.

Mullach na Reidheachd is another great viewpoint for Sron Uladal, while the glen southeastwards has the impressive summits of Uisgneabhal Mor and Uisgneabhal Beag towering over it.

From Cleiseabhal the views open up southwards to the island of Taransay where the reality TV programme Castaway was filmed.

ROUTE 7

South Uist – the Wild Eastern Coast

Number of Days	2
Total Distance	35km (21.75 miles)
Daily Distances	Day 1 – 20km (12.5 miles), Day 2 – 15km (9.25 miles)
Height Gain	Total: 1680m; Day 1 – 940m, Day 2 – 740m
Maps	OS Landranger sheet 22 Benbecula and South Uist
Starting Point	Start at Howmore, also known as Tobha Mor, on South Uist. Park at the youth hostel or near the chapel (grid ref NF756364).

Area Summary

The Outer Hebrides, also variously known as the Western Isles or the Long Island, is a narrow chain of islands 209km long, and lying about 64km off the northwest coast of the Scottish mainland. The southern part of this chain is made up of four main islands, Barra, South Uist, Benbecula and North Uist, with lots of smaller islands scattered throughout the group. South Uist, or Uibhist a Deas, to give it its Gaelic name, is the second largest of the islands in the Outer Hebrides, measuring 35km north to south and 11km east to west.

The geography is divided into a series of north–south strips, each running the length of the island. The west coast has over 32km of spectacular, white shell beaches running continuously down its length, backed by incredible areas of machair and dunes. The whole area is brimming with flowers and wildlife, including corncrakes and otters. East again is a strip containing a vast number of small, freshwater lochans, and a series of dispersed crofting settlements. The eastern side of this strip is marked by the line of the A865, which runs the length of the island. To its east the ground rises to the mountains that run almost the whole length of the eastern side of South Uist. These are dominated by Beinn Mhor at 620m and Hecla at 606m. The pattern is only broken by the deep intrusion into the eastern coast of three sea lochs, from north to south – Loch Skipport (Sgiopoirt), Loch Eynort (Aineort) and Loch Boisdale (Baghasdail). Any east coast settlements are largely confined to the heads of these three lochs.

Route Summary

A walk suitable for those wanting to get away from it all. The route starts at Howmore on the coastal strip on the west coast and follows a track through the beautiful wildflower machair before heading for the national nature reserve at Loch Druidibeag. A path takes you through this area of lochans and moors before you climb to the delightful rocky summit of Beinn Tairbeirt. It then takes you over to the east coast where you start the ascent of Hecla, one of the most distinctive hills in the Outer Hebrides. A wild camp is then found beneath the southern slopes of this great mountain. The route continues on Day 2 by taking you over Beinn Mhor, then back westwards to the machair of the west coast.

Tourist Information
There is a tourist information centre in Lochboisdale on Pier Road (tel 01878 700286). The Outer Hebrides Tourist Board also has a useful website www.vis-ithebrides.com.

Transport
There are two ways of getting to the Outer Hebrides.
Air You can fly to Benbecula (the island just north of South Uist and connected to it by a causeway) from Inverness, Edinburgh or Glasgow. For details of British Airways flights tel 0345 222 111, or visit their website at www.british-airways.com.
Ferry Caledonian MacBrayne ferries (tel 08705 650000) serve Lochboisdale from Oban, and Lochmaddy on North Uist (connected to South Uist via causeways over the island of Benbecula) from the island of Skye. You can also check timetables and book online at www.calmac.co.uk.

Transport on South Uist
It is much easier to get around if you have your own car on South Uist, although it is possible to use the local bus services. Call the Stornoway bus station on 01851 704327 for details or visit www.cne-siar.gov.uk. For car hire get in touch with Laing Motors at Lochboisdale on 01878 700267, or e-mail laingmotors@yahoo.co.uk.

Accommodation and Supplies

For accommodation on South Uist try the Polochar Inn (tel 01878 700215), or the Orasay Inn (tel 01870 610298). The hostel at Howmore is run by the Gatliff Trust, www.gatliff.org.uk. They do not take advance bookings, but rarely turn anyone away! For supplies there are shops that provide all the basics in Lochboisdale in the south of the island.

Overnight Options

Camp at Loch Coradail beneath the imposing south face of Hecla (grid ref NF828333) – this is a lovely spot in which to spend the night. There is also a bothy at Usinish, just down the glen from this loch, maintained by the Mountain Bothy Association, www.mountainbothies.org.uk.

Escape Routes

In this part of South Uist the only habitation is to the west along the coastal strip, so to get back to civilisation from any point of the walk you have to head westwards towards the A865. That said, however, you can pick up the B890 at Loch Sgiopoirt north of Hecla, and also a minor road at Loch Aineort southwest of Beinn Mhor.

DAY 1

From the tiny crofting community at **Howmore** the walk starts by heading west for the coastal track, but first explore this fascinating hamlet.

Howmore has several claims to fame. The most striking is that it is home to one of Scotland's best collections of thatched buildings. The effect is stunning, and it is easy to think you've been transported back in time. There is a remarkable collection of ruined churches here too. It is believed that the original church was built as early as the 600s. Today you can see the ruins of the Teampull Mor, the 'Large Church' or St Mary's, of which only part of the east gable remains. This church probably dates back to the 1200s.

Just west of the village you hit a track amid a wash of machair-covered dunes. Turn right on this track and follow it northwards for almost 2.5km (1.5 miles) to a junction at the northern end of **Loch Stadhlaigearraidh**. Turn right at this

junction and follow the track along the north side of the loch to the village of the same name. Where you come out on the A865, go over the main road onto another track and pick up a path through a gate heading onto the **Loch Druidibeag** National Nature Reserve.

Look for magpie moths in stone walls at Howmore (also known as Tobha Mor)

This superb reserve is an area of contrasts. The wide open spaces of the machair grasslands on the Atlantic coast give way to heather moorland as you walk through the reserve. Quiet lochans provide a haven for the distinctive plants and birds of the Uists, which include the corncrake with its persistent rasping call. Also look out for day-flying short-eared owls, which are regularly seen here. The reserve covers 1677 hectares of wild moorland and mountain.

The route across the reserve is not always obvious, giving it a truly wild feel, although there are posts hammered into the ground that give you an idea of the way to go. The path actually takes you across a triangular plot of moorland that lies right in the middle of Loch Druidibeag itself. Where it not for a narrow connecting spit of land at either end, this would be an island.

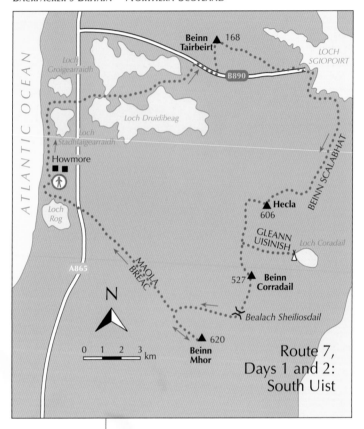

Route 7,
Days 1 and 2:
South Uist

You soon find yourself coming off the moorland onto a narrow road, the B890, just below the summit of Ruabhal.

The collection of buildings and domes on the summit of Ruabal are part of the Ministry of Defence missile range that was built here in the 1960s, and this accounts for the number of 'Danger Area' signs around the west coast of the island on Ordnance Survey maps.

Turn right along the B890 for a short way until it is possible to leave it on the north side and begin the climb over moorland to Glac a' Bhodaich, the low western ridge of **Beinn Tairbeirt.** Gain this ridge and head eastwards along it until you can climb up to the summit of Beinn Tairbeirt, with its OS trig pillar at 168m. ▶

Turn to the southeast and follow the ridge over a few rocky hummocks and down to the road near **Loch Sgiopoirt.** Continue to follow the road out to the coast eastwards, and where it ends you can pick up a path that leads out towards a group of shielings, then onwards around the coast to the little peninsula of Ornais.

Now you can begin the ascent of **Hecla**, one of the finest mountains in the Outer Hebrides. The ascent from here is rough, over rocky bluffs, peat and heather, but the reward is fantastic views all around, and a complete traverse of the Hecla and **Beinn Mhor** ridge.

Climb southwestwards over the ridge of Maol Martaig and up the rugged nose of Beinn na h-Aire. Here the ridge narrows and gives great views down into the deep corries on either side. At **Beinn Scalabhat** the ridge turns to the west and you continue climbing to an intermediate summit at 564m. A short drop into a col to the southwest from here and you're faced with the final ascent to the summit of Hecla ('Hooded' or 'Shrouded Mountain') at 606m.

From the summit head westwards along the ridge for 500m until it is possible to descend southwards to a broad col at the head of **Gleann Uisinish**. Camp either here on the col, or descend into the glen itself to **Loch Coradail** for the night. At the foot of the glen is the **Usinish bothy**, but if you head down to that for the night, you'll have to regain a lot of height to get back on the ridge in the morning.

DAY 2

From the col at the head of Gleann Uisinish you should head southwards up onto a shoulder of Beinn Mhor where you'll find two small lochans. From here a ridge rises in a series of steps up towards the fine summit of **Beinn Corradail**, a rocky peak at 527m. To connect with the ridge up Beinn Mhor you need to descend to the col known as **Bealach Sheiliosdail**,

The views from Beinn Tairbeirt are far reaching, taking in the massive hills of Hecla and Beinn Mhor to the south. Northwards the view stretches over to Benbecula and North Uist.

but a direct descent from Beinn Corradail is steep and rocky. I usually head south for about 600m from the summit, then back to the west across rough ground to the col.

Once on Bealach Sheiliosdail col a broad ridge takes you up westwards to the summit edge of Beinn Mhor. You gain this summit ridge at its northern end, while the highest point actually lies at the southern end. There is a superb ridge walk of just over 1km to the top at 620m. Here you'll find an OS trig pillar and a great view out to sea and the island of Skye.

Once you've enjoyed the views retrace your steps to the point at the northern end of the ridge, then begin the long descent northwestwards to **Maola Breac**. You soon gain the open moorland south of Loch Druidibeag, and once on these easy slopes you can follow a bearing westwards to a track near Loch Dobhrain on the A865.

Turn right on the A865 and go over a bridge over the Abhainn Rog. Take the next left turn along a minor road to Tobha Beag, and follow this through the scattered hamlet and beyond **Loch Rog** to where the road turns sharply to the left. At this point you'll see a track on the right that you can follow to a bridge and a track junction shortly after. Turn right here to return to Howmore and the end of a great two-day walk.

ROUTE 8
Cape Wrath and Sandwood Bay

Number of Days	2
Total Distance	47km (29.25 miles)
Daily Distances	Day 1 – 32km (19.75 miles), Day 2 – 15km (9.5 miles)
Height Gain	Total: 1530m; Day 1 – 970m, Day 2 – 560m
Map	OS Landranger sheet 9 Cape Wrath, Durness and Scourie
Starting Point	The Kyle of Durness Ferry, just off the A838 at Keoldale (grid ref NC377662).
Finishing Point	Kinlochbervie, on the B801 west of the A838 (grid ref NC220564).
Access Note	Cape Wrath is part of a MoD firing range, and is occasionally closed to the public. Telephone 01971 511343 for details.

Area Summary

This wonderful corner of the Highlands epitomises everything that is grand and majestic about Scotland. U⊃ here in the far northwest there are great towering sea cliffs, backed by wild and lonely moors and mountains. Red deer herds gather in otherwise empty corries, and golden eagles hunt through the glens. This area has always been thought of as wild and remote, although over recent years the two main attractions, Cape Wrath itself and Sandwood Bay, have begun attracting more and more visitors. But this does not detract from the feeling of isolation, especially once you've started on the coastal walk south from Cape Wrath. You probably won't see a soul until you reach Kinlochbervie

Route Summary

The route starts with a delightful ferry crossing over the Kyle of Durness, and from there a quiet road walk leads uphill to the cliffs at Clo Mor. The walk follows the coast around to the stunning beach at Kearvaig, then onward along the lane to the lighthouse at Cape Wrath. From there it's southwards all the way, crossing rough moorland and wild cliff tops to the valley of Strathchailleach then down to Sandwood Bay. You then have a choice of routes, one continuing around the coast to Kinlochbervie, the other heading inland up Strath Shinary and across the moor to Kinlochbervie. Both are equally good.

Tourist Information
There is a tourist information centre in Ullapool at the Ullapool Museum and Visitor Centre, 7 and 8 West Argyle Street, tel 01854 612987.

Transport
From Inverness, which is the jumping-off place for anyone heading into the far northwest, you can either drive north or use one of the infrequent buses that serve this wild area. Tim Dearman Coaches operates a bus service from Inverness to Durness via Kinlochbervie (tel 01349 883585, www.timdearmancoaches.co.uk). There is also a post bus that connects Durness to Kinlochbervie (tel 01463 256228).

Accommodation and Supplies
The best place to stay in the Durness area is the Cape Wrath Hotel at Keoldale overlooking the Kyle of Durness, tel 01971 511212, www.capewrath.co.uk. At the end of the walk there is the Kinlochbervie Hotel, tel 01971 521275, www.kinlochberviehotel.com.

There are small shops in Durness and in Kinlochbervie, but no shops en route. It is probably better to stock up in Inverness before heading north.

Overnight Options
There are a number of options for your overnight stay. Ideally you should carry a tent and aim to camp on the coast north of Sandwood Bay. The Mountain Bothies Association maintains a number of bothies in this area. These simple shelters are left open for all hillgoers to use, but please do so responsibly. The bothies are at Kearvaig (grid ref NC293727), Strathchailleach (grid ref NC 249657) and Strathan (grid ref NC 247612). You can join the Mountain Bothies Association at www.mountainbothies.org.uk.

Escape Routes
There is a minor road from the Kyle of Durness Ferry to Cape Wrath, which this route partly follows initially, and which gives a good means of getting back to Durness. Once heading south along the coast the best way out is onwards, or back to this minor road, whichever is nearer. The country to the east is rough and involves a lot of hard walking to reach the A838.

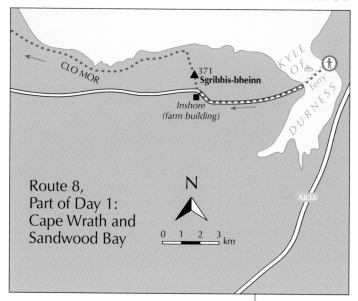

Route 8,
Part of Day 1:
Cape Wrath and
Sandwood Bay

N

0 1 2 3 km

DAY 1

The superb little ferry plies backward and forward across the
Kyle of Durness all day during the summer months. You don't
book, but just turn up at the pier, or ask in the bar at the Cape
Wrath Hotel the night before – the boatman can often be
found in here in the evening!

The last time I was at the Kyle of Durness we watched in
delight from the entrance to the hotel as a dog otter rolled
around on his back in the shallow waters with a big mus-
sel on his stomach.

Once across you should head off along the road. (Note
that there is the option of getting a minibus to take you to
Cape Wrath lighthouse, thereby making this a very short backpack, but if you do that you'll miss out on some superb coastal
scenery around Clo Mor.) The road takes you steeply uphill
then drops down to the shore again at Daill.

The Kyle of Durness

Continue along the road and over a wooden bridge.

The wooden bridge was constructed by the Royal Marines in 1980. Before the bridge the bus carrying passengers to the lighthouse would frequently stall at this crossing over the burn, and passengers had to help push it out.

The tin-roofed building by the side of the road is an old school. Between 1935 and 1938 there were around 35 people living on the cape side, west of the **Kyle of Durness**, and apart from the lighthouse keepers all the men were shepherds working for two local farms. Then there were 10 children attending the school at Achiemore near Daill, although it was last used in 1947.

Continue climbing up the hill from Daill. You enter the 'MoD Danger Area' at the top of this hill (see the note on access at the end of route information box). The road now passes between two lochs, Loch Inshore and Lochan nam Breac Buidhe, before coming to the house at **Inshore** (now owned by the MoD).

Just beyond Inshore the road bends to the left, and here you should leave it and head northwestwards across the moorland to the small hill of **Sgribhis-bheinn**. The going is hard but pleasant, with lots of typical moorland wildflowers to look out for.

While you walk you might see the little buttercup-like flowers of the tormentil. This is a very common plant on moorlands. Tiny blue flowers of milkwort should also be around, and you might be lucky enough to spot insectivorous sundews, which look a little like Venus flytraps, and butterwort, which has pale, yellowish-green star-shaped leaves and a lobed blue flower on a narrow stem. The three common heathers that you will see are ling, bell and cross-leaved heath.

There is an OS trig pillar on Sgribhis-bheinn at 371m, and from here you get great views eastwards along the coast beyond Durness.

Continue over the summit and head down the broad north ridge of the hill, bearing northwest as you lose height down to a boggy col. Head over a little hill at spot height 293m, then down to the cliff top at **Clo Mor**.

The Clo Mor cliffs are the highest cliffs on the British mainland, with a drop of 189m. These Torridonian sandstone cliffs are an important breeding site for seabirds, including fulmars, kittiwakes, puffins, guillemots and razorbills.

Head westwards along the top of the cliffs, losing height as you go until you are overlooking impressive Stack Clo Kearvaig out off the headland. Turn left here and walk down steep slopes to the bothy at **Kearvaig**. Go out along the track leading away from the bothy until you hit a minor road. Turn right here and drop down to cross the Kearvaig river via a bridge. ▶

From the bridge follow the road out to the **lighthouse at Cape Wrath**, turning left at a junction where a track goes down to a jetty on the right.

The yellow-and-black hut before the bridge is a sentry post for the MoD. During exercises sentries are stationed here to stop walkers straying onto the range.

The old buildings by the lighthouse are the remains of a signal station that was first used in 1930. All passing shipping had to signal the station, giving such information as cargo being carried, port of departure and ETA. Looking eastwards from the lighthouse you can see the Clo Mor sea cliffs stretching back towards Durness.

Turning southwards the way now lies across many kilometres of rough country – and all of it wonderful! Follow the coast around to the stacks known as **A'Chailleach**, the 'Old Woman' or 'Witch', and **Am Bodach**, or the 'Old Man'. The route takes you downhill beyond this to cross a stream, then it's a short and easy climb uphill to the top of Dunan Beag, passing two small lochans along the way. Drop down southwards again, to the top end of a narrow ravine giving good views down to the broiling sea below. Then onwards around the coast to the top of the little hill of **Sidhean na h-Iolaireich**, or the 'Hill of the Eagles'.

This really is a good place to see eagles. I have seen golden eagles here on a number of occasions now, and during a recent visit a white-tailed eagle flew by along the top of the nearby cliffs. Golden eagles are, as you would expect, pretty huge, but the white-tailed eagle is bigger still. It looks like a barn door flying overhead!

From Sidhean na h-Iolaireich you can either stay close to the cliff top or head more inland to the eastern side of Loch a' Gheodha Ruaidh. From there a short walk across the moor brings you to the **Strath Chailleach** river. Aim for the bothy at **Strathchailleach**, just over the river, and bear in mind that you may well have to wade or go higher upstream to get across.

DAY 2

From the bothy you can follow the river westwards down to the coast then along to the wide sandy beach at Sandwood Bay. I often cut the corner here and make first for Lochan nan Sac, then westwards to **Sandwood Bay** from there. It

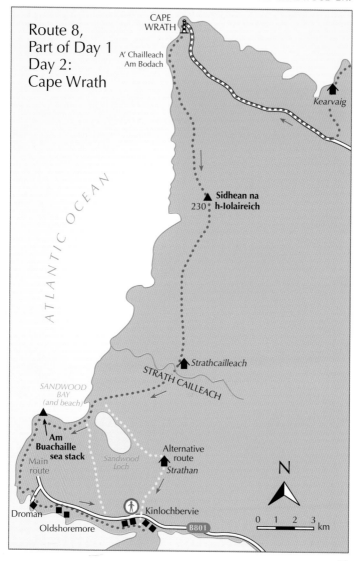

Route 8,
Part of Day 1
Day 2:
Cape Wrath

CAPE WRATH

A' Chailleach
Am Bodach

Kearvaig

ATLANTIC OCEAN

▲ **Sidhean na
230 h-Iolaireich**

▲ *Strathcailleach*

STRATH CAILLEACH

SANDWOOD
BAY
(and beach)

▲ **Am
Buachaille
sea stack**

Sandwood
Loch

Alternative
route
▲ *Strathan*

Main
route

N

Droman

Oldshoremore

Kinlochbervie

B801

0 1 2 3
km

Sandwood Bay looking northwards

really doesn't matter which way you choose to go – that's the beauty of backpacking in these remote areas!

From Sandwood Bay a track leads south via Loch na Gainimh to Blairmore and Oldshore and the road to **Kinlochbervie**. This is the route taken by all the day-trippers, and I prefer to avoid it.

Sandwood Bay is now part of the Sandwood estate, the northern half of what used to be Kinlochbervie estate, and is owned by the John Muir Trust. This estate is perhaps best known for its stunning beaches, wild cliffs and peaty moorlands. The glacially eroded peatland landscape with coastal crofting settlements is characteristic of northwest Sutherland, and unique to Scotland.

Some of the natural features of the estate are considered to be world class – most notably Sandwood Bay itself, bordered by dramatically eroded cliffs, and backed by dynamic sand dunes set in a coastline that curves away gracefully to the most northwesterly point on mainland Britain.

There is a famous sea-stack at the southwestern corner of the bay, **Am Buachaille**, or 'the Shepherd'. It was on this stack that Tom Patey, a well-known figure in Scottish mountaineering, was killed in May 1970 while abseiling from the top, having just made the first ascent. He was 38 years old, and had come to fame initially as a result of the televised film of his ascent of the Old Man of Hoy, with Chris Bonington and others, although everyone within the climbing world knew of him already, well before this event.

It's better to recross the river at **Sandwood Loch** and follow Strath Shinary along the north side of the loch to **Strathan** bothy. Here you'll find a dangerous-looking bridge (think Lara Croft and you'll get the idea!). Cross over, carefully, then head southwards to a group of old shielings at Loch Carn Mharasaid. A track across the moor can then be picked up that takes you into Kinlochbervie, past the school. Turn right for the centre of the village and the hotel.

Another option is to follow the main path from Sandwood Bay to the top of the first slope, then bear right to the cliff top where you get a great view of **Am Buachaille**. Follow the coast around to Droman, then on via a series of lovely bays to **Oldshoremore**. One last section of coastal walking then brings you into Kinlochbervie and the end of this walk.

ROUTE 9
Ben Hope

Number of Days	2
Total Distance	24km (15 miles)
Daily Distances	Day 1 – 17km (10.5 miles), Day 2 – 7km (4.5 miles)
Height Gain	Total: 1160m; Day 1 – 980m, Day 2 – 180m
Maps	OS Landranger sheets 9 Cape Wrath and 10 Strath Naver
Starting Point	Minor road at Kinloch Lodge at the head of the Kyle of Tongue. Head south on the minor road from Tongue, parking sensibly by the roadside (grid ref NC555523).

Area Summary

This wild area in the far north of the Highlands is a world away from most other mountain routes in this book. Sandwiched between Loch Eriboll in the west and the Kyle of Tongue in the east, both huge sea lochs cutting into the landmass from the north, this region, known as the Moine (or 'the Moss'), is one of open spaces and sweeping mountain ridges. The A838 between Durness and Tongue forms the boundary to the north, while southwards the rolling moorland carries the eye to distant Loch Shin. A great area for lovers of wildlife and wild places, this is the place to come to get away from it all.

At the centre of the Moine lies Ben Hope, meaning 'Hill of the Bay'. As Scotland's most northerly Munro, Ben Hope is a superb vantage point, with views south to Ben Klibreck, east to Ben Loyal and west to Cranstackie. Northwards the views are dominated by the wild North Atlantic coast. The usual ascent of Ben Hope from Alltnacaillich to the south is fairly straightforward, and well trodden, but our route takes in the little-known moorlands to the east.

Route Summary

This is the shortest backpacking route in this book, and although a fit hillwalker could do it in a single day, to miss out on

Tourist Information
There is a tourist information centre at the Ullapool Museum and Visitor Centre, at 7 and 8 West Argyle Street, tel 01854 612987.

Transport
From Inverness you can drive north to the area via a number of lovely routes. Perhaps the best, and the one I use most frequently, is via Bonar Bridge, Lairg and Alltnaharra on the A836. This takes you to Tongue, where you should turn left and follow the minor road around the Kyle of Tongue. There is no public transport to the start of this walk.

Accommodation and Supplies
For accommodation you need to be in the Tongue area itself. Top of the range are the superb Ben Loyal Hotel (tel 01847 611216) and Tongue Hotel (tel 01847 611206). Rhian Cottage is also a good, slightly cheaper bet (tel 01847 611257), while budget walkers will receive a warm welcome and comfortable bed at the SYHA in Tongue (tel 01847 611301). You can camp at Kincraig near the post office (tel 01847 611218), or at Tamine on the other side of the bay (tel 01847 601225). There are no shops en route, although you can get some supplies in Tongue. It is probably better to stock up in Inverness before heading north.

Overnight Options
Camp wild at one of the superb mountain lochans to the east of Ben Hope's summit.

Escape Routes
This is such a short route that you are never too far away from the minor roads east or west of Ben Hope. The Moine Path cuts across the range to the north of Ben Hope, and links the minor roads at Kinloch Cottage and the southern end of Loch Hope.

camping high up at one of the lovely lochans below the east face of Ben Hope, and waking to a golden sunrise over Ben Loyal to the east, would be a real loss. Yes, by all means do it in a day, but my advice is to linger over this beautiful mountain.

The route starts at the head of the Kyle of Tongue and takes you along the Moine Path to the rocky north ridge of Ben Hope. Here a little scrambling is called for to get to the top, but this is short lived and you are soon at the cairn. You then head southeast across an open plateau, and down the south-east ridge to the open moorlands and mountain lochans under the east face. A short ridge route then leads to a path that takes you back to Kinloch at Kyle of Tongue. Being short, the route would be suitable for first-time backpackers, and what a great location for your first wild camp. Having said that, you do need a bit of a head for heights to tackle the north ridge of Ben Hope.

DAY 1
Start the walk by crossing the road bridge, which takes you westwards across the Kinloch river. Just beyond, the road turns sharp right while a track goes ahead to Kinloch Cottage.

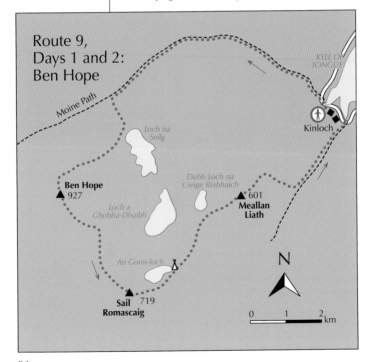

Route 9, Days 1 and 2: Ben Hope

Moine Path

KYLE OF TONGUE

Kinloch

Loch na Seilg

Ben Hope ▲ 927

Dubh Loch na Creige Riabhaich

Loch a Ghobha-Dhuibh

▲ 601 Meallan Liath

An Gorm-loch

△

▲ Sail Romascaig 719

N

0   1   2 km

This is the start of the old, established right of way along the **Moine Path** to Loch Hope.

Ravens frequent the Ben Hope plateau

Walk down this track to the cottage, turn right at the junction, pass behind a small wood and go down to a stream. Cross the stream to another junction and here go straight ahead, climbing slightly to a rise upon which stands an ancient, chambered cairn. The track now contours around and soon crosses the tumbling waters of the Allt Ach' an t-Srathain.

This is a good area to watch for common buzzards hunting over the nearby woods and moors. They usually give away their presence with loud mewing cries, and can be seen gliding in tight circles above the trees.

The path now starts to climb gradually, giving good views behind across the **Kyle of Tongue**. You cross a number of small streams before gaining the broad and not very distinct crest of Druim nan Clair, a long moorland ridge running northwards from **Ben Hope** towards the north coast. ▶

High on your left from here you'll see the imposing bastions of Ben Hope's north and eastern corries. In the foreground lie the small hills of Creig Riabhaich Bheag and Creig Riabhaich Mhor.

The path continues across the moor to the southwest, and you should follow this to where it starts to descend more noticeably towards Loch Hope. Here you'll see a side stream coming down from the corrie between Ben Hope and Creig Riabhaich Bheag – this is the An Garbh-allt. Turn left here and climb up alongside this stream to the loch at its head, **Loch na Seilg**. (As you approach Loch na Seilg you should cross to the west side of the stream, if you haven't done so already.)

Above rises a fine edge, the north ridge of Ben Hope, and this gives some good, easy scrambling, with just one hardish step. From Loch na Seilg you can climb directly up this ridge, and in fact this is the easiest way onto it from this direction.

Once you have gained the ridge it presents no real problems as far as a cairn before a dip to a steep, rocky step. This offers just 10m of quite exposed scrambling, which may seem challenging with a heavy rucksack on your back. It also require a good head for heights, but no technical rock-climbing skill. (There is a well-marked escape route off to the left – to take this you follow a line across the head of the corrie for 30m, gaining a shallow gully that can be climbed to regain the ridge above the 'bad step'.) After the scramble (or the escape route) the ridge gradually broadens to the summit of the mountain at 927m.

> Being the most northerly of the Munros, the views from the summit of Ben Hope are wonderful. To the east and south Ben Klibreck, Foinaven, Arkle and Ben Loyal dominate, while Cranstackie is the obvious peak to the west. Northeastwards, across the Pentland Firth, on a clear day you can see the islands of Orkney, with the hills on Hoy being most noticeable.

Head south from the summit for a short distance, across rocky steps and short, arctic-type flora. A broad ridge to the southeast should be followed down to a col at the head of An Garbh Coire. A little rise over two bumps in the ridge follows, then a steeper descent to the south brings underfoot the small knoll of **Sail Romascaig**, at 719m. From here you can head just north of east down a broad ridge to the southern end of beautiful **An Gorm-loch**, where you can camp for the night.

DAY 2

After packing up camp and enjoying the sun rising over Ben Loyal to the east, you should start the day by heading northeast towards a pair of small lochans. Just beyond these, in the same direction, a rocky ridge begins and you should climb this to the lovely little hilltop of **Meallan Liath** at 601m.

The views westwards into the corries of Ben Hope are superb. From right to left, as you look across the lochs of Loch na Seilg and Loch a' Ghobha-Dhuibh, you will see into the heart of Coir' a' Ghallaich with its hidden lochan. Left of this a broad rocky nose comes down from the summit of Ben Hope to separate the two lochs in the glen below. Left again is steep-sided An Garbh-choire, then left again you'll see An Gorm-loch, where you spent the night.

From Meallan Liath drop down to the east to pick up the continuation of the ridge, leading you in a series of delightful rocky steps to a summit at the northeastern end at 501m.

A very steep but straightforward descent to the east from this top brings a good stalker's track underfoot, and you should turn left along this and follow it downhill to join a bigger track just above the Kinloch river by a wood. Turn left on this bigger track and follow it back to Kinloch Cottage, and the end of this short but memorable backpack.

Red grouse can be seen on the moorland around Ben Hope

ROUTE 10
Inverpolly

Number of Days	2
Total Distance	36km (22.5 miles)
Daily Distances	Day 1 – 16km (10 miles), Day 2 – 20km (12.5 miles)
Height Gain	Total: 1200m; Day 1 – 810m, Day 2 – 390m
Map	OS Landranger sheet 15 Loch Assynt
Starting Point	Car park just east of Inverkirkaig village on 'the mad road' (so called because of the very rough country it crosses) south of Lochinver (grid ref NC085194).

Area Summary
Personally I think this is one of the wildest, and therefore the finest, mountain areas in the whole of Scotland. Huge tracts of open moorland studded with sparkling lochs form the bulk of the interior, and here and there, thrust up like great warts, are majestic mountains with names to match – Suilven, Stac Pollaidh, Canisp, Quinag, Cul Mor and Cul Beag. This is a true paradise for anyone with a deep-seated love of wilderness.

The area is split naturally into three distinct mountain regions, all of which lie just to the north of Ullapool on the west coast. To the left of the A835 and visible from Ullapool are the superb mountain ridges of Coigach, while north of these hills are the peaks of Inverpolly. North and east of Inverpolly, on both sides of the A837 at Inchnadamph, is the interesting area of Assynt. All three areas are well-worth exploring and all are great country for backpacking. You could happily spend weeks here with a tent and sleeping bag and never get bored.

Route Summary
The route starts at the Falls of Kirkaig car park and follows the River Kirkaig eastwards to the falls themselves. Just east from

this point lies lovely Fionn Loch, and the way lies around the loch's northern shores. As you walk around the loch the views northwards are dominated by the huge mountain mass of Suilven, and the route takes you to the top via a steep but short scrambling path. From the summit ridge you head northwards into Glencanisp Forest, where you will find a bothy at Suileag in which to spend the night. The following day sees you head west for the coast at Lochinver, before picking a way through open moorland and rocky knolls back to Fionn Loch and a return to the Falls of Kirkaig.

Tourist Information
There is a tourist information centre at the Ullapool Museum and Visitor Centre, at 7 and 8 West Argyle Street, tel 01854 612987.

Transport
There is no public transport to Inverkirkaig, and the only easy way to get there is by driving to Ullapool and then north from there to Drumrunie. At Drumrunie turn left onto a minor road that heads out towards the coast at Achiltibuie. A couple of miles beyond the Stac Pollaidh car park there's a sharp right turn and you should take this onto 'the mad road'.

Accommodation and Supplies
There are a few accommodation options in this area – try the bed and breakfasts at Ardglas (tel 01571 844257), Davar (tel 01571 844501) or Polcraig (tel 01571 844429), all in Lochinver village. The nearest youth hostel is the spectacularly placed Achmelvich Hostel, just a couple of miles northwest of Lochinver (tel 01571 844480). Also, a little further away, is the Summer Isles Hotel in Achiltibuie (tel 01854 622282).

There are no shops en route, other than at Lochinver near the end of the walk. It is best to stock up in Inverness or Ullapool before heading north to Assynt.

Overnight Options
The Mountain Bothies Association maintains a bothy in this area. These simple shelters are left open for all hillgoers to use, but please do so responsibly. The bothy is at Suileag (grid ref NC149211), and you can join the Mountain Bothies Association at www.mountainbothies.org.uk. There are also numerous wild campsites throughout this superb area, with many small lochans to choose from as great camping spots.

DAY 1

Begin the walk by heading east from the car park to a high gate through a deer fence. There is a signpost here to the **Falls of Kirkaig**. A good track underfoot takes you along the north side of the **River Kirkaig**, initially low down, close to the fast-flowing water, then climbing slightly through wonderful alder and rowan woodland to more open moorland. The path here is good and very easy to follow, winding in and out of rocky outcrops and around heathery knolls. ◄

As you walk eastwards the views gradually open out to the east and south, revealing the rocky outlines of Cul Mor, Cul Beag and Stac Pollaidh.

As you climb above the river it becomes enclosed in a deep gorge, and you can usually hear rumbling notes as it dashes over the Falls of Kirkaig, throwing spray high overhead. A path to the right takes you on a slight detour to the top of the falls, and this diversion is well worth taking for the views down the gorge.

Once back on the main track continue eastwards, enjoying occasional glimpses of the towering western bastion of **Suilven**, rising over the moor to the northeast.

The OS map shows a path cutting a corner off to the north, but it is actually easier to follow the main track around a lovely peninsula where the River Kirkaig flows out of **Fionn Loch**.

Look out for red-throated divers on this loch in summer. They nest in the vegetation of the shallow margins and are much prone to disturbance by humans – please do not attempt to find their nests. Red-throated divers usually raise one chick on inland lochs and lochans high in the hills, the parents often flying to coastal waters to catch fish and bring them back to the chicks on the nest.

Turn to the north and continue along the track, which skirts the edge of the loch. It soon heads northwestwards, and

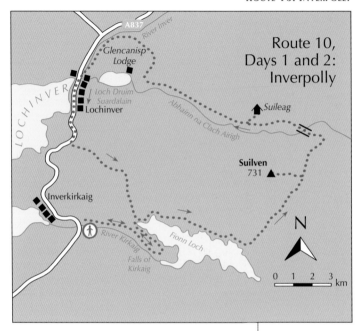

Route 10,
Days 1 and 2:
Inverpolly

seems to be taking you in the wrong direction, as you almost have your back to Suilven. However, to get to Suilven you must first walk around the western end of Fionn Loch, which cuts deeply into the low hills. The track crosses the end of the loch, where a lovely little river flows through from Loch Uidh na Ceardaich. (If the water level is high it is sometimes necessary to cross further up, in which case you should head for a point about midway between Fionn Loch and Loch Uidh na Ceardaich. The river is only a couple of metres across here, and the bottom is sandy.)

Once back on the track you gain height for a short while, moving away from the loch slightly, then crossing a small stream at a lovely little slaty footbridge. The track is now taking you back eastwards towards your goal, and you cross the open slopes of Coire Mor before gaining height again to the north of a little knoll. As you pass between the knoll and the higher ground to the north (the lower slopes of Suilven) there is a cairn and a small path on the left.

This path gives an alternative approach to Suilven, climbing through rocks to start, then leading you on a new path across open moorland towards the western end of Suilven. This path is now marked by cairns and slowly becoming more established, although it can be very boggy underfoot. The main path continues down to the north shore of Fionn Loch, however, and I still prefer this way when I'm backpacking through these hills.

Continue along the main path until you are almost at the eastern end of Fionn Loch, to another knoll on the right, and here you'll find a cairn marking another path on the left. This path is easy to follow, although again it is boggy in places. The path follows the true right bank of a stream to the flat moorlands beneath the obvious col between the two peaks of Suilven. This point on the moorland is where the alternative path previously mentioned joins the main track.

Above you tower the massive ramparts of Suilven – this may seem rather intimidating, but an easy route is possible from this side. As you look up at the mountain you'll notice that there are two distinct summits – Caisteal Liath at the

Suilven

western end and Meall Meadhonach at the eastern. Between these summits lies Bealach Mor, or 'the Big Pass' – the route to the summit is via this col.

From the moorland a path leads to the start of the climb by a group of rocks. Above, you will see a scree slope descending the hillside just to the west of the Bealach Mor. The path takes you up the right side of this scree slope, zigzagging at first until an eroded trench leads out to the Bealach Mor to the right. This path is a little loose and requires some care.

> As you gain the last few metres to the Bealach Mor the majestic outline of the hills of Quinag rise over the wild moorlands ahead of you, framed on either side by the rocks of the summit ridge of Suilven.

A large drystone wall cuts across the ridge at the Bealach Mor, and you should turn left here – westwards – passing through a gap in the wall and continuing along the path to the summit of Suilven. The path here is rocky, but nowhere difficult – just very easy scrambling throughout. You'll soon find yourself on the grassy summit of Suilven, Caisteal Liath at 731m, the top marked by a large cairn.

> Head westwards for a short way for the best views out to the coast at Lochinver. On a clear day you can easily see the Outer Hebrides from here, including the hills of Harris and Lewis.

Return to the Bealach Mor and look for a path on the left, north, side of the hill. This leads down steep scree slopes in zigzags to Loch a'Choire Dhuibh. The path now becomes much easier underfoot, albeit a bit boggy after rain, and you should follow it to a bridge near the outflow of Loch na Gainimh. Do not cross the bridge, but instead take the track on the left, following the river downstream at first, then cutting over a hill to another bridge near Lochan Buidhe. Cross this bridge and turn left, following the rushing waters of the **Abhainn na Clach Airigh**.

After 1km the river turns sharply to the southwest and the path goes straight on to cross a little side stream. Cross this and follow it uphill to the north to the great bothy at **Suileag**. Either spend the night here or find somewhere nearby to pitch your tent.

DAY 2

A much easier day than yesterday's walk. Once you've packed up (and cleaned out the bothy, if that was where you stayed), begin by heading downhill to pick up the main track again above the Abhainn na Clach Airigh. The track here does not follow the river however – it takes a much straighter course than that!

Cross over a col, then contour for a little while until the track takes you down to some small woodlands at **Glencanisp Lodge**. Just before reaching the lodge there's a path on the right that takes you uphill between two woods. Follow this over the small ridge of Druim Suardalain and down to a stream. The path here splits – ignore the one going straight ahead over the stream, but look instead for the one going northwestwards down to a good track alongside the **River Inver**. You will cross the small stream just before your final descent to the River Inver.

Turn left and follow the main track downriver by a lovely series of weirs. Here, woodland shades you overhead and the walk through to the main road at **Lochinver** village is a delight. Once on the main road (the A837) turn left and walk into the village. There are a few shops here, as well as places to eat, and a great visitor centre.

Continue through the village and stay on the road up to the school at Loch Culag. The road leads you around the loch and onwards to the scattered hamlet of Strathan. As you approach the hamlet, look out for a path on the left by the first building. Follow this path eastwards across moorland to a tiny lochan. Just beyond this lochan the path ends and you should follow rough ground to Loch Peallaig. A superb moorland walk takes you over a hill and down to Loch a' Ghlinne Sgoilte. Now head out to the easternmost end of this loch and continue in the same direction through a wonderful gorge to Loch Uidh na Ceardaich. Pass this on its south side and pick up the track that you followed yesterday back to the Falls of Kirkaig and the car park near **Inverkirkaig**.

ROUTE 11

Assynt from Inchnadamph

Number of Days	2
Total Distance	33km (20.5 miles)
Daily Distances	Day 1 – 17km (10.5 miles), Day 2 – 16km (10 miles)
Height Gain	Total: 1420m; Day 1 – 890m, Day 2 – 530m
Maps	OS Landranger sheet number 15 Loch Assynt
Starting Point	You can start this walk from the large car park in Inchnadamph (grid ref NC 251216). Turn right for the Inchnadamph Hotel and you'll find the car park on the right before the hotel. However, starting here necessitates a 2.5km walk along the main A837 at both the start and the finish of this route. It's not a very busy road, and this option may well be preferable to parking on the roadside at the point where the track leaves the road at Stronchrubie Farm (grid ref NC2481930).

Area Summary

As I said in the summary for Route 10, I think this is probably one of the wildest, and therefore to my mind the finest
mountain areas in the whole of Scotland. Vast expanses of
open moorland studded with shining lochs form the bulk of
the interior, and here and there are superb mountains with
names to match – Suilven, Stac Pollaidh, Canisp, Quinag, Cul
Mor and Cul Beag. This is a true paradise for anyone with a
deep-seated love of wilderness.

The area is split naturally into three distinct mountain
regions, all of which lie just to the north of Ullapool on the
west coast. To the left of the A835 and visible from Ullapool
are the mountain ridges of Coigach, while north of these hills
are the peaks of Inverpolly. North and east of Inverpolly, on
both sides of the A837 at Inchnadamph, is the interesting area
of Assynt. All three areas are well worth exploring, and all are
great country for backpacking. You could happily spend weeks
here with a tent and sleeping bag and never be bored.

Route Summary

A short walk south along the road from Inchnadamph (you could drive to the same spot and leave the car there) brings you to a bridge over the River Loanan, from where you climb the mountain known as Canisp. A traverse to the west takes you to Suileag bothy for the night, before returning via the rough and wild moorlands to the north of Canisp and to the south of Loch Assynt. Overall, a short backpacking expedition giving maximum impact over a minimum distance – another route that you could do in a day if you were in a hurry, but why rush such lovely scenery?

Tourist Information

There is a tourist information centre at the Ullapool Museum and Visitor Centre, 7 and 8 West Argyle Street, tel 01854 612987.

Transport

From Inverness, which is the jumping-off place for anyone heading into the far northwest, you can either drive north to Inchnadamph or use one of the infrequent buses that serve this area. Tim Dearman Coaches operates a bus service from Inverness to Inchnadamph, tel 01349 883585, www.timdearmancoaches.co.uk.

Accommodation and Supplies

There are only two options in Inchnadamph – the Inchnadamph Hotel offers rooms and food (tel 01571 822202), while across the river is the Assynt Field Study Centre at Inchnadamph Lodge (tel 01571 822218), offering hostel accommodation as well as camping.

There are several accommodation options to the west of this area – try bed and breakfasts at Ardglas (tel 01571 844257), Davar (tel 01571 844501) or Polcraig (tel 01571 844429), all in Lochinver village. The nearest youth hostel is the spectacularly placed Achmelvich Hostel, just a few kilometres northwest of Lochinver (tel 01571 844480). Also, a little further away, is the Summer Isles Hotel in Achiltibuie (tel 01854 622282).

There are no shops en route. It is better to stock up in Inverness or Ullapool before heading north to Assynt.

Overnight Options
The Mountain Bothies Association maintains a bothy in this area. These simple shelters are left open for all hillgoers to use, but please do so responsibly. The bothy is at Suileag (grid ref NC149211), and you can join the Mountain Bothies Association on www.mountainbothies.org.uk. There are also numerous wild campsites throughout this superb area, with many small lochans to choose from as great camping spots.

Escape Routes
This is pretty wild country, and finding good escape routes isn't easy. South of Canisp you can pick up a stalker's track that runs roughly southeast to northwest from Elphin to Lochinver via Suileag bothy. This is the best option for getting out of the area quickly in either direction, although Elphin is a long way from Inchnadamph, and Lochinver even further! However, those two places are where you'll find civilisation.

DAY 1

Leave **Inchnadamph** and head south on the road (there's only one!) – it isn't terribly busy, but do bear in mind that it is a major A road, and what traffic there is might be going at a fair lick!

The advantage of starting the walk at Inchnadamph, apart from the obvious one of not leaving your car on the roadside for a couple of days, is that there are often red deer down in the glen around here, and you should get good views.

The cliffs above the road to the east are of carboniferous limestone, and riddled with caves, some of which have revealed bones of hyena, bear and lynx. The ridge above the crags is a favourite place for golden eagles to soar on calm days, so keep your eyes peeled.

At a small wood at the southern end of the limestone cliffs beneath Blar nam Fiadhag you'll see a farm down a short track on the right. Go down this to **Stronchrubie Farm** and across fields to cross the River Loanan at a bridge.

Bear left across the rough moorland to a stream, and begin climbing steadily up the side of it, continuing, when

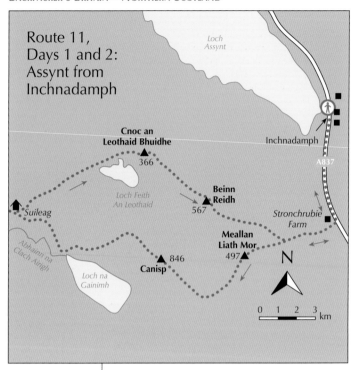

Route 11,
Days 1 and 2:
Assynt from
Inchnadamph

Loch
Assynt

**Cnoc an
Leothaid Bhuidhe**
▲
366

Inchnadamph

**Beinn
Reidh**
▲
567

Loch Feith
An Leothaid

Suileag

Stronchrubie
Farm

Abhainn na
Clach Airigh

**Meallan
Liath Mor**
497 ▲

Loch na
Gainimh

▲ 846
Canisp

N

0   1   2   3 km

the stream ends, to the flat summit of **Meallan Liath Mor** at 497m. The walking here is rough, and provides quite hard going, but the gradient is not too steep and the top is soon reached.

Don't forget to turn round and enjoy the views of Breabag to the east. As you gain height you'll also get great views of the two highest peaks of Assynt – Conival and Ben More Assynt – which lie to the east of the A837 beyond Gleann Dubh above Inchnadamph.

From the summit of Meallan Liath Mor head southwest down to a lochan on a col. Walk around the east side of the lochan and climb southwards for a short distance to reach a ridge at Meall Diamhain. This knoll lies on the superb ridge that leads in a long sweep to the summit of **Canisp** at 846m. The ridge is quite broad, and easy to follow over rocky ground, although you can also climb the open corrie to its north.

The rocks around the summit slopes of Canisp are made of quartzite, giving the hill its name – 'White Hill'.

The summit of **Canisp** is a great viewpoint for the other hills in the area. Being central to the mountains of Assynt, it gives good views in all directions. Starting in the north and moving around clockwise you should see the Quinag hills, Glas Bheinn, Beinn Leoid, Conival and Ben More Assynt one behind the other, then Breabag, the Cromalt Hills, Cul Mor, Cul Beag, the hills of Coigach with Ben More Coigach rising behind Beinn an Eoin, and little Stac Pollaidh, looking just as majestic even when looked down on from this height. Westwards the hills fall away to the coast at Lochinver, but have as the main focal point the mighty ridge of Suilven, which commands your attention. All this depends on good visibility of course!

From the summit of Canisp a steep descent lies down the northwest ridge. This is rocky at first but easy to negotiate. Walk down the ridge to a small lochan at 500m above sea level, then take a bearing southwestwards to pick up a stalker's track above **Loch na Gainimh**.

This track leads down to join another track coming in from the southeast (a good track into the wilderness from near Elphin on the A835). Head northwest on the track to a bridge over the **Abhainn na Clach Airigh** near the outflow of Loch na Gainimh. Cross the bridge and turn right on a path that climbs slightly over a rise then drops back down to recross the Abhainn na Clach Airigh at another bridge.

Cross over this second bridge and follow the path alongside the river to Lochan Buidhe, continuing to a big, left-hand bend in the river. Here the path goes straight ahead to cross a little side stream. Cross this stream and leave the path to climb gently uphill on the right to the bothy at **Suileag**. Either settle in here for the night, or perhaps climb up to the northeast on a good path to camp by lovely Loch Bad an t-Sluic.

Inchnadamph in Assynt

DAY 2

From Suileag a path climbs up alongside the stream and takes you to the eastern end of Loch Bad an t-Sluic. Follow this path to its end at the Allt Loch Coire na Creige. Cross the stream and follow it upstream for a while until it is possible to head northeast to the summit of Sron a' Bhuic at 371m.

The area around Sron a' Bhuic is a superb wild landscape of heathery moorland knolls. There is a sizable herd of red deer in this area, and you might get close views of them as you climb to the summit. Also, keep an eye out for golden eagles – crags on Canisp are favourite perches for these magnificent birds, and a pair usually holds a breeding territory here.

A scattering of beautiful lochans speckles the moor to the northeast of Sron a' Bhuic, and you should head off towards these and onwards to the outflow of **Loch Feith an Leothaid**. Cross the stream here, or a little further down if need be, then head around the loch to its north side. A compact corrie below the summit of **Cnoc an Leothaid Bhuidhe** can be climbed to the summit at 366m.

Backpacking through Assynt

This diminutive top gives unrivalled views across Loch Assynt to the splendid ridges of Quinag to the north, and to the bold rocky outline of Glas Bheinn to the northeast. Southwards, Canisp dominates the view.

A broad ridge slopes down to the southeast from the summit of Cnoc an Leothaid Bhuidhe. Follow this to the north side of the Feith an Leothaid and walk alongside this river for a short way, passing to the south of two lochans (unnamed on the Ordnance Survey maps). To the east the impressive flanks of **Beinn Reidh** rise in rocky steps. Make for the north ridge that overlooks Loch na Beinne Reidhe and follow this to the delightful summit of Beinn Reidh at 567m.

The east ridge of Beinn Reidh is straightforward to descend, although quite rocky, and you should head for the northern side of Loch na Meallan Liatha. Walk clockwise around the loch to its eastern point, then cross rough moorland slopes to the southeast to reach the bridge over the River Loanan at Stronchrubie Farm. Return to your car via the route taken outwards yesterday.

ROUTE 12

The Munros of the Inverlael Forest

Number of Days	2
Total Distance	49km (30.5 miles)
Daily Distances	Day 1 – 27km (16.75 miles), Day 2 – 22km (13.75 miles)
Height Gain	Total: 2520m; Day 1 – 1410m, Day 2 – 1110m
Maps	OS Landranger sheet 20 Beinn Dearg
Starting Point	There is roadside parking at Inverlael on the A835 (T) between Inverness and Ullapool. Follow the road northwards from the Braemore junction until it emerges from the forest on the right (just before the head of Loch Broom on the left) and park in a lay-by here (grid ref NH182853).

Area Summary

The Inverlael Forest forms part of the high land between the west coast at Loch Broom and the east coast near Bonar Bridge. The area encompasses a number of high and remote mountains, six of which are Munros. Southwards the region has the main A835 (T) as its boundary, and here this road passes through the broad valley of Dirrie More.

The area is rough, with lots of exposed rocky summits and slopes, but the higher hills in the region have good access along paths and tracks now well used by Munro-baggers. The Inverlael Forest is still a great place to get away from it all though, especially its eastern fringes, where few people ever go, and here you'll find a good opportunity to relax and forget about the pressures of the outside world.

Route Summary

A walk suitable for those with some experience of mountain walking and camping in remote locations. Although access to the area is straightforward, the hills you'll pass over and the wilderness feel to the whole area mean that you're a long way from help if anything should go wrong.

Tourist Information

There is a good tourist information centre on Argyle Street in Ullapool, tel 01854 612135.

Transport

From Inverness, which is the best starting place for anyone heading into the northwest Highlands, you can either drive north to Inverlael or use one of the regular buses that serve this area. Scottish Citylink runs three buses a day from Inverness to Ullapool, tel 08705 505050, www.citylink.co.uk. Tim Dearman Coaches operates a bus service from Inverness which stops at Inverlae, tel 01349 883585, www.timdearmancoaches.co.uk.

Accommodation and Supplies

There isn't any accommodation at Inverlael other than nearby self-catering cottages. However, on the road from Inverness there's the Braemore Square bed and breakfast (tel 01854 655357, www.braemoresquare.com) near Braemore Junction, and the Aultguish Inn at the eastern end of Loch Glascarnoch, which has bed and breakfast rooms and a bunkhouse, tel 01997 455 254, www.aultguish.co.uk. There are lots of other accommodation options in Ullapool, and the tourist information centre there operates a booking service.

There are no shops en route. You will need to stock up in Inverness or Ullapool before heading into the hills of the Inverlael Forest.

Overnight Options

The Mountain Bothies Association maintains two bothies in this area. These simple shelters are left open for all hillgoers to use, but please do so responsibly. The bothies are at Glenbeg (grid ref NH314835), which is the most useful for this particular walk, and in Choire Mhoir (grid ref NH305887), which is perhaps too far off-route to be ideal, despite its stunning location. You can join the Mountain Bothies Association on www.mountainbothies.org.uk. There are also some great campsites throughout this superb area, including many dramatic wild sites.

Escape Routes

The only feasible option for a route out of the mountains from the high tops is to head west for the A835 (T). From Glenbeg, a low-level route, but one involving a very long walk in the wrong direction, takes you down the glen to Amat Lodge in Strathcarron.

The walk takes you through the forestry plantations of Gleann na Sguaib and onto Eididh nan Clach Geala, the first Munro of the trip. A wild route then follows, over to one of the most remote Munros in Scotland, Seana Bhraigh. From there you head southeastwards to spend the night in Gleann Beag, before heading back to the west over the superb rocky summits of Meall nan Ceapraichean, Cona Mheall and Beinn Dearg. A good track then takes you back to the road at the foot of Gleann na Sguaib. Some of the walk is on good paths and tracks, although the eastern section in Gleann Beag is pathless and very rough.

DAY 1

The approach into this wild and lonely area begins with a straightforward walk up a deeply forested glen. A few hundred metres on the south side of the River Lael, where a bridge takes the A835 over it, there's a track that crosses a meadow and heads off into the forests.

Follow this track eastwards to a bridge over the river. Ignore this bridge and go straight ahead, keeping to the south side of the river. After another kilometre or so another bridge is reached, which again should be ignored. There are a number of forest tracks leading off from this point, and you should just stay close to the river on its south side until the third bridge is reached.

Cross over to the north side here and take a track to the left that climbs through the trees and up onto a ridge above **Gleann na Sguaib** to the south and Gleann a' Mhadaidh to the north. This path gains height very steeply at first until the crest of Druim na Saobhaidhe is reached. You should stay on the track throughout, contouring off the ridge to the north to cross the Allt Glean a' Mhadaidh high up in the corrie.

The path continues alongside the stream, and you should follow this to the top of the slopes and the entrance to Coire an Lochain Sgeirich. The path continues through the coire and on towards distant **Seana Bhraigh**, but for now you should leave it and begin climbing to the little hill above the corrie, unnamed on the OS Landranger maps, but with a spot height at 872m. This hill gives excellent views to

115

Seana Bhraigh to the northeast, and southwards into the Deargs, as this group of hills is collectively known.

Immediately south of this hill is a col that leads you onwards onto the northern flank of **Eididh nan Clach Geala**, the first Munro of the trip. The going is easy from the col, and you'll soon find yourself on the summit looking down at Lochan a' Chnapaich with **Meall nan Ceapraichean** beyond. These are tomorrow's hills.

> The view to the northwest from the summit is superb. The length of Loch Broom leads the eye out towards Ullapool, and you might see the Summer Isles beyond on the horizon. To the southwest the impressive mass of An Teallach commands your attention over the lower hill of Beinn Enaiglair.

Leave the summit of Eididh nan Clach Geala by heading down the grassy slopes to the east to cross a stream. From here head northeast to another unnamed hill, then northwards to where the path through Coire an Lochain Sgeirich comes to an end. This is quite confusing territory, and you should take care to follow a bearing to the north side of Loch a' Chadha Dheirg (grid ref NH 284859). This point is the high pass between Glen Douchary to the north and **Gleann Beag** to the east.

From here Seana Bhraigh is now within your grasp, and all that needs to be done is head northeastwards uphill, skirting around the head of Cadha Dearg, then northwards to the summit ridge of this fine mountain. You'll reach a minor top at 906m, and from there you should head northwestwards down to a col and up the other side to the highest point.

> Seana Bhraigh, at 927m, is one of the most remote Munros, competing with Lurg Mhor above Loch Morar and A' Mhaighdean in the Fisherfield Forest for the title of 'the most distant'. The summit of Seana Bhraigh is a vast plateau at around 914m above sea level, with huge hanging corries falling away on the north side. These corries overlook Coire Mor, which if followed downhill leads to the bothy at Loch a' Choire Mhoir and onwards down Strath Mulzie.

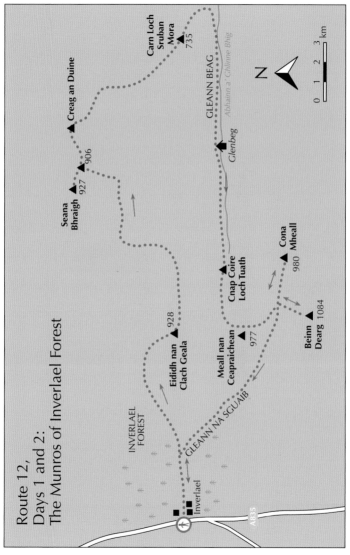

Route 12,
Days 1 and 2:
The Munros of Inverlael Forest

Good stalker's tracks in the Inverlael Forest

This is also good golden eagle country, with a pair often nesting here underneath the rim of the summit plateau.

From the summit return to the southeast top at 906m, then handrail around the rim of the northern corries to **Creag an Duine**, a superb ridge jutting out into the wildest part of Coire Mor. Still handrailing along the coire rim, continue to the southeast, dropping now to cross over streams and up a final rise onto the ridge. Now you should follow rough, open ground to the southeast, picking up a string of small lochans to pass to the west side of Loch Coire Mhic Mhathain (grid ref NH316857). Southeast of the lonely lochan the bare hill of **Carn Loch Sruban Mora** rises easily, and you should climb to its highest point.

The bothy at **Glenbeg** lies to the southwest from here, but the slopes in that direction are rocky, steep and very rough. It is easier to head east to the outflow of Loch Sruban Mora, where a stalker's track is picked up. Follow this track downhill alongside the stream, crossing to the east side about halfway down. The path then cuts diagonally across the hillside to meet a Land-Rover track near a bridge over the **Abhainn a' Ghlinne Bhig** by a weir.

Cross the bridge and walk westwards upstream to where you'll find the bothy just over the Allt a' Chrom-uillt. Either spend the night in the bothy or find somewhere nearby to camp.

DAY 2

The route today lies to the west, over some rough kilometres, before you gain the heights of the Deargs, starting very steeply up behind the bothy. Climb the slopes to the north of the Allt a' Chrom-uillt until you gain the easier ground above the rocky slopes directly behind the bothy. Slowly gain height as you make your way towards **Cnap Coire Loch Tuath** at 884m.

Coire Loch Tuath is a gem. From Cnap Coire Loch Tuath it seems to lie in a hidden fold of the mountains, with just the small streams at the head of the coire feeding it. Below, it flows into Loch Prille, which turns southwards and rushes out to Loch Glascarnoch, and so to Inverness, which this bigger reservoir provides with water.

Walk westwards from Cnap Coire Loch Tuath down to a col, then begin the climb up the northeast ridge of **Meall nan Ceapraichean**. As you gain the summit ridge there's a long, level section before a small rise, then a short descent to a col before the actual summit is reached at 977m. Southeast from the summit of Meall nan Ceapraichean an easy angled ridge leads down to a pair of lochans and a track coming up from **Gleann na Sguaib** to the west. This track provides the means of return to Inverlael, and you could pick it up now and head off for home. However, it would be a shame to come all this way and not climb **Cona Mheall** and **Beinn Dearg**, the two highest Munros of the Inverlael Forest.

First lets look at Cona Mheall. It's an easy ascent from the twin-lochan col – head east to the top of a small knoll, then over this to the col between it and Cona Mheall. A short ascent over rocks then leads to the summit at 980m.

The view to the east from the summit of Cona Mheall is superb. You might just be able to catch a glimpse of the bothy at Glenbeg, while the plateau of Seana Bhraigh fills the view to the north.

Return by the route of ascent to the small knoll, and descend this on its southwest side to a tiny lochan on a col. A vague rib now leads to the summit of Beinn Dearg to the southwest, and has a huge drystone wall running up it. Climb alongside this on its western side, passing through a gap near the top to reach the summit at 1084m. Beinn Dearg's view is supreme. An Teallach rises in massive buttresses to the southwest, and the long line of the Fannichs ridge lies to the south.

Return to the twin-lochan col, where the path comes up from Gleann na Sguaib, and turn westwards down this, zigzagging into the head of the glen. The path is easy to follow, and soon leads down to the forests at the foot of the glen, where you should pick up your outward route and return to Inverlael.

ROUTE 13

Fisherfield and Letterewe

Number of Days	2 or 3
Total Distance	45km (28 miles); 13km (9 miles) extra for the optional Day 3
Daily Distances	Day 1 – 21km (13 miles), Day 2 – 24km (15 miles), optional Day 3 – 13km (9 miles)
Height Gain	Total: 740m; Day 1 – 400m, Day 2 – 340m; optional Day 3 – 970m
Maps	OS Landranger sheet 19 Gairloch and Ullapool
Starting Point	Start in Poolewe at the southern end of Loch Ewe where the River Ewe flows out from Loch Maree (grid ref NG 858808).
Finishing Point	Corrie Hallie on the A832 west of Braemore Junction, just south of Dundonnell (grid ref NH114851).

Area Summary

The Fisherfield Forest is that vast tract of wilderness sandwiched between Dundonnell at Little Loch Broom and Loch Maree. It's a huge area of wild land and rough, rocky mountains, with lots of beautiful lochs and a good network of paths and tracks cutting through it. Many people think of this area as 'the last great wilderness' in Scotland, although like all other regions of Scotland it is anything but untamed by man. Named after the formidable laird who defended the area against both hillwalkers and road builders, the Fisherfield Forest became known as the Whitbread Wilderness.

Apart from the superb walking routes through the glens, there are some great mountains here too. A 'Mhaighdean and Ruadh Stac Mor are often thought of as being the most remote Munros, while Beinn Tarsuinn, Mullach Coire Mhic Fhearchair, Sgurr Ban and Beinn a' Chlaidheimh make for a brilliant ridge traverse. On the north side of the range, the mighty An Teallach, or 'the Forge', ranks among many people's 'favourite' mountains.

Route Summary

This walk takes you on one of the best-known backpacking routes through the region, starting in Poolewe and finishing near Dundonnell. The route itself gives a fine though serious introduction to the area – serious because it is necessary to ford a number of streams and rivers that don't have bridges. The ford over the Abhainn Srath na Sealga near Shenavall bothy, towards the end of the route, is a very serious undertaking, suitable only when the river is low.

Optional Day 3

For those with a little more time to spare, I have suggested an extra day with a base at Carnmore. From here you can tackle the two most remote Munros in Scotland, A 'Mhaighdean and Ruadh Stac Mor, then return to Carnmore for the night before continuing through to Corrie Hallie the following day.

It is possible to complete this walk, including the ascent of A 'Mhaighdean and Ruadh Stac Mor, as a through-route in two days, with a wild camp en route, but with heavy packs this would make both days very long and tiring.

Tourist Information

The nearest tourist information centre is at Gairloch (tel 01445 712130), just west of Poolewe, and there is also a tourist information centre on Argyle Street at Ullapool (tel 01854 612135).

Transport

From Inverness you can either drive north to Poolewe or use one of the buses that serve this area. The Westerbus serves both Poolewe and Dundonnell from Inverness (tel 01445 712255), and Rapsons also runs a service to Poolewe via Dundonnell from Ullapool (tel 01463 710555, www.rapsons.co.uk).

Accommodation and Supplies

There is plenty of choice of bed and breakfast accommodation in Poolewe and Gairloch. Try the Myrtle Bank Hotel (tel 01445 712004) or Bains House (tel 01445 712472), both in Gairloch. Also near Gairloch is the SYHA hostel at Carn Dearg (tel 01445 712219).

In Poolewe you could try the Pool House Hotel (tel 01445 781272) or Mrs MacIver's bed and breakfast (tel 01445 781389). There is also a Caravan and Camping Club site in Poolewe (tel 01445 781249).

At the end of the walk you'll find accommodation at the Dundonnell Hotel (tel 01854 633204), or further down the loch side at the Sail Mhor Croft Independent Hostel (tel 01854 633224).

There are lots of other accommodation options in Ullapool, and the tourist information centre there operates a booking service.

There are a few small shops in Poolewe at the start of this walk, but none en route. You would do well to stock up in Inverness or Ullapool before heading for Poolewe.

Overnight Options
There two bothies in this area. These simple shelters are left open for all hillgoers to use, but please do so responsibly. The best bothy on the walk is at Carnmore (grid ref NG978769), ideal because it is roughly at the halfway point. The bothy is privately owned, stands just downhill from Carnmore Lodge, and may not be available during the stalking season. The second bothy is at Shenavall (grid ref NH065810). Shenavall is maintained by the Mountain Bothies Association as an open, free shelter. You can join the Mountain Bothies Association on www.mountainbothies.org.uk. There are also some great campsites throughout this superb area, including many dramatic wild sites.

Escape Routes
This walk provides the only easy route through the Fisherfield Forest – all other routes are either longer or go over high mountains. If it is not possible to cross the Abhainn Srath na Sealga to get to Shenavall bothy, the only option is to go much further upriver, heading eastwards. This can be a very lengthy detour.

DAY 1
Begin by leaving the A832 on the north side of the bridge over the outflow of the **River Ewe**. Walk southeastwards along the private road that runs parallel to the river on its northeast side. This road becomes rougher at a junction just before **Inveran Lodge**, and you should turn left at this junction and continue out of the woods to a bridge. Cross the bridge and stay on the track to the stalker's house at **Kernsary**, where there is another junction by a bridge.

Go over this bridge and follow the track between the buildings going roughly eastwards to the edge of a forestry

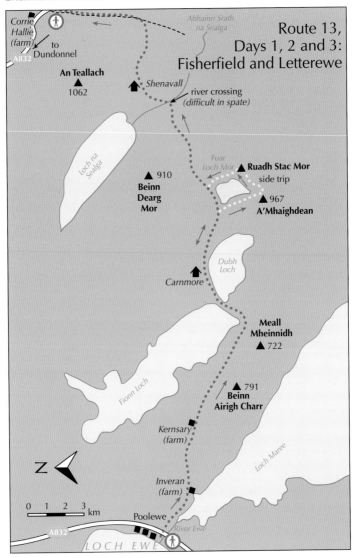

Route 13,
Days 1, 2 and 3:
Fisherfield and Letterewe

Corrie
Hallie
(farm)
to
Dundonnel
A832

An Teallach
1062

Shenavall

Abhainn Srath
na Sealga

river crossing
(difficult in spate)

Loch na Sealga

Fuar
Loch Mor

Ruadh Stac Mor
side trip

▲ 910
Beinn
Dearg
Mor

▲ 967
A'Mhaighdean

Dubh
Loch

Carnmore

Meall
Mheinnidh
▲ 722

▲ 791
Beinn
Airigh Charr

Fionn Loch

Loch Maree

N

Kernsary
(farm)

0 1 2 3 km

Inveran
(farm)

Poolewe

A832

River Ewe

LOCH EWE

plantation. Here again the track splits. The one to the left heads towards **Fionn Loch**, while the one you want to take goes southeastwards into the plantation. This soon comes out of the trees alongside the Allt na Creige, and the going here is rough and boggy. Stay on the path if possible and continue walking in a southerly direction to Loch an Doire Crionaich, which nestles beneath the towering ramparts of **Beinn Airigh Charr.** ▶

Beyond Loch an Doire Crionaich the path drops slightly to the north side of another loch, then crosses the outflow of that loch and turns southwards. The path heads up the glen of Srathan Buidhe to cross the river at a bridge, then goes back northwards on the opposite bank. When the water level is low you can sometimes just wade across here to save the detour round.

The path now skirts beneath **Meall Mheinnidh**, crosses a stream and takes you eastwards around the end of Fionn Loch. Here a causeway separates Fionn Loch from **Dubh Loch**, and you can cross over this causeway to the north side.

These lochs are a favourite haunt of the black-throated diver, or loon as the North Americans call it. These wonderful

Golden eagle in the Fisherfield Forest

The crags on this side of Beinn Airigh Charr are made up of horneblende schist, forming wonderfully sculpted faces.

125

aquatic birds favour large lochs in the Highlands and are among our rarest species. Do not disturb them during the nesting season.

Once on the north side of the causeway follow the path to the lodge at Carnmore. This is private, but you can stay in the stables, which are often used as a bothy, and lie a few hundred metres northwest of the lodge in the direction of Fionn Loch. Camping in this vicinity is often discouraged – if the estate workers see you camping they will usually ask you to move into the stables. Spend the night here and enjoy dusk and dawn over Fionn Loch.

Optional Extra Day at Carnmore

This is a superb, high-mountain circuit over the two most remote Munros in Scotland. You can use Carnmore as a base and do the circuit from there, or continue through towards Shenavall after completing the mountains here.

Leave Carnmore on the track running eastwards from Carnmore Lodge. This climbs steadily across the face of Sgurr na Laocainn to enter a high, hanging corrie through which flows the Allt Bruthach an Easain beneath Carnan Ban. Where the corrie begins to level off you should aim southwards across its mouth to a stream issuing from Fuar Loch Beag. Climb alongside the stream to Fuar Loch Beag. Head southwards onto the rocky ridge, then follow this as a series of steps going southeastwards up to the summit plateau of **A' Mhaighdean**. The summit is at 967m at the south end of the plateau, and you can reach it from the ridge by handrailing along the corrie rim to your right.

The view from the summit of A' Mhaighdean is stunning. To the south the bold outline of Slioch can be seen rising over Lochan Fada, while to the southeast the Munros of Beinn Tarsuinn, Mullach Coire Mhic Fhearchair, Sgurr Ban and Beinn a' Chlaidheimh beckon. This gives yet another option for those with more time and energy. You can traverse these summits down to the bothy at Shenavall in another great day's walking.

Now head northeast from the summit down to a bealach above **Fuar Loch Mor** – the going down to the bealach is straightforward on grassy slopes. A short climb through sandstone crags to the northeast from the bealach will lead you to the summit of **Ruadh Stac Mor** – there is a faint path that finds its way through the crags. Return to the bealach and head down into the corrie on the north side, keeping to the eastern flank below Ruadh Stac Mor. Do not descend all the way to the shore of Fuar Loch Mor, but pick up a stalker's path that takes you northwestwards down to a junction of tracks. The way to the east along the path is the continuation to Shenavall and **Corrie Hallie**, while Carnmore lies down the track to the west.

DAY 2

From Carnmore head east on the track that climbs up into the hanging corrie that holds the Allt Bruthach an Easain. Stay on the north side of the Allt Bruthach an Easain, and walk along the path to the junction of tracks at the western end of Lochan Feith Mhic'-illean. This is the point where the stalker's track comes down from Ruadh Stac Mor.

Stay on the north side of Lochan Feith Mhic'-illean and continue along the path as it descends into Gleann na Muice Beag.

> The view to the north is now dominated by the bulk of An Teallach. The most impressive face of this mountain lies on the other side, overlooking the A832, but it is still a beautiful mountain when viewed from 'the back'.

At the bottom of this slope, where the main Gleann na Muice comes in on the right, join a track coming in from the right. Turn left and follow this northwards alongside the Abhainn Gleann na Muice to the private stalker's bothy at Larachantivore.

The path now heads north for the eastern end of **Loch na Sealga**, but here you should head east over the Abhainn Gleann na Muice to the second river, the **Abhainn Srath na Sealga**. Look for a crossing point and wade over, taking care as you go. This river in spate is particularly dangerous. If in doubt, head upstream, eastwards, until a safe crossing point can be found. Once over the river make for the bothy at **Shenavall**, where you could spend the night if need be.

Looking back from where you have come, you get a great view of Beinn Dearg Mor from Shenavall. This mountain is like An Teallach in miniature, and although it is too small to be a Munro it is nevertheless superb.

A track heads uphill behind Shenavall and takes you around the eastern slopes of **An Teallach**.

An Teallach, or' the Forge', is a wonderful mountain, throwing down rocky pinnacles and towers in all directions. There are few mountains in the world to rival its impressive corries and ridges, despite its lowly height on a worldwide scale.

The path here is easy to follow and takes you over moorland to join a Land-Rover track above Loch Coire Chaorachain. Turn left on the Land-Rover track and follow it downhill in a northerly direction beside the Allt Gleann Chaorachain. After two or more days in the wilderness of the Fisherfield Forest you emerge on the roadside at **Corrie Hallie**.

ROUTE 14

The Applecross Peninsula

Number of Days	2
Total Distance	49km (30.5 miles)
Daily Distances	Day 1 – 37km (23 miles), Day 2 – 12km (7.5 miles)
Height Gain	Total: 1420m; Day 1 –1340m, Day 2 – 80m
Maps	OS Landranger sheet 24 Raasay and Applecross
Starting Point	Park in Applecross at the small car park down by the shore (grid ref NG712446).

Area Summary

This an area of Torridonian sandstone hills, rugged in the extreme as they throw down great faces of horizontal strata to the east, and long, tarn-speckled moors to the west. The Applecross area overlooks the Inner Sound and the islands of Raasay and Skye to the west, while the deep sea loch of Loch Carron forms the border to the south, with its smaller inlet, Loch Kishorn, cutting into the range in the southeast. To the north lie Loch Torridon and the Torridonian giants of Beinn Eighe, Beinn Alligin and Liathach, all well known throughout the hillwalking and mountaineering fraternity. Although Applecross is something of a backwater, it is slowly becoming better known, chiefly thanks to a chapter in Ken Wilson's great rock-climbing book Classic Rock. This chapter covered the ascent of Cioch on Sgurr a' Ghaorachain by Tom Patey and Chris Bonnington.

The Applecross peninsula is cut on its western side by Applecross Bay, where the village with same name lies. The valley here is well wooded and fed by the River Applecross, which comes out of the hills to the east. The two principal hills in the area are Beinn Bhan and Sgurr a' Ghaorachain, both of them too small to be Munros, but both magnificent mountains nevertheless.

Over the southern and western slopes of Sgurr a' Ghaorachain the Bealach na Ba takes the road to Applecross village, and south of the road rises the little-visited summit of Meall Gorm.

Route Summary
The walk starts beside the River Applecross before taking to the long, northwest ridge of Beinn Bhan. The hills of Sgurr a' Ghaorachain and Meall Gorm are then traversed, before the rough moorland crossing to Uags bothy down on the southern

Tourist Information
There are no tourist information centres in this area. The best one for information is at Fort William, in Cameron Square (tel 01397 703781).

Transport
You'll need a car to get to Applecross, the route being from Lochcarron on the A896 to Loch Kishorn, then over the Bealach na Ba road – one of the highest, steepest and windiest roads in Britain.

Accommodation and Supplies
Either stay in the excellent Applecross Inn, which serves good food and superb Scottish real ales (tel 01520 744262), or at the equally pleasant Applecross campsite (tel 01520 744268).

There's a tiny shop in Applecross and a Spar shop in Lochcarron, otherwise it's best to do your shopping in Inverness or Fort William.

Overnight Options
The Mountain Bothies Association maintains a bothy in this area. These simple shelters are left open for all hillgoers to use, but please do so responsibly. The bothy is at Uags, on the southern-most tip of the Applecross peninsula, which, despite its beautiful lochside location, with views out to Raasay and Skye, is possibly not well placed for this particular walk. To use the bothy for this route involves a very long walk on Day 1, and a short walk on Day 2. You can join the Mountain Bothies Association at www.mountainbothies.org.uk. There are also some great campsites throughout this area, including many dramatic wild sites.

Escape Routes
At any point during this walk you can make for the minor road that cuts over the Bealach na Ba from Tornapress to Applecross. The route crosses over this road at the halfway point.

shore of the peninsula. A walk around the western coast back to Applecross village is delightful on Day 2.

This walk is suitable for those with some experience of rough mountain walking. The traverse of the three hills of Applecross is over pathless terrain, much of which is rocky knolls lying between lochans and bog, making for hard going at times.

DAY 1

From the car park in **Applecross** village, begin the walk by heading around the bay to the north. Stay on the minor road above the beach until you reach a bridge over the **River Applecross.**

> The beach here is a great place for wading birds throughout the year. You might see oystercatchers, dunlin, golden plover and redshank. Look out over the bay and you may also see harbour porpoises and possibly common or grey seals.

Cross the bridge and turn right on a track leading alongside the river towards Applecross House. Stay on the north side of the river and continue along the good Land-Rover track into the upper glen beyond Hartfield Adventure School.

Near the summit of Beinn Bhan in winter

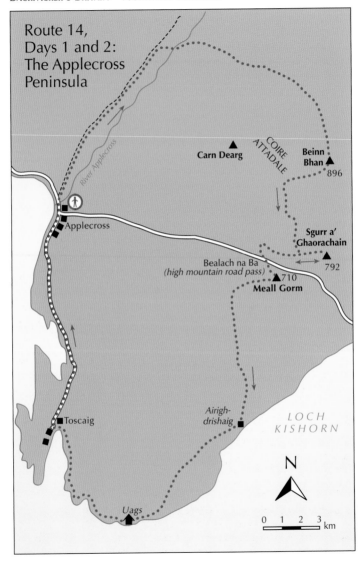

Route 14,
Days 1 and 2:
The Applecross
Peninsula

Carn Dearg

COIRE ATTADALE

Beinn Bhan
896

River Applecross

Applecross

Sgurr a' Ghaorachain
792

Bealach na Ba
(high mountain road pass)
710
Meall Gorm

Toscaig

Airigh-drishaig

LOCH KISHORN

Uags

N

0 1 2 3 km

As you head up the glen keep an eye out for eagles soaring along the ridges on either side. This is a good area for golden eagles, but if you're really lucky you might also catch a glimpse of a white-tailed eagle. These are very rare birds of prey, much larger still even than the golden eagle.

Continue up the glen, known as Srath Maol Chaluim, to on old ruin where the tracks split. The track continuing along the west side of the river goes over a pass to Loch Torridon at Kenmore or Inverbain, whereas you should cross the side stream on your right and follow a track between this and the main river. Again the path splits, the one on the left also going to Inverbain on Loch Torridon, while the one to the right, which you should take, goes up into **Coire Attadale**.

Cross a number of small streams then take to the ridge above, heading eastwards to a tiny lochan high on the ridge. Above the lochan the ridge gets progressively steeper, until it narrows at a knoll at spot height 712m. Continue walking to the southwest down to a little col, then up along the ridge of **Beinn Bhan**, overlooking huge, northeast-facing corries. ▶

Eventually this ridge leads to the high lochan known as Loch na Beinne Baine. Continue beyond this lovely spot, and stay close to the edge of cliffs to your left. Handrailing along this edge will lead to the summit of Beinn Bhan, in a spectacular position at 896m. The summit is marked by a trig pillar set slightly back from the rim of Coire na Poite, one of the best corries in this magnificent range.

The summit of Beinn Bhan has three ridges protruding from it. You've just climbed the northwest one, and this continues down to the southeast to the head of **Loch Kishorn** at Tornapress. The third ridge heads southwest, and this is the way you should go to continue this route.

At first the going is easy, over grassy slopes, and the ridge soon narrows where the head of **Coire Attadale** to the north and Coire nan Arr to the south join. Continue down the ridge as it turns to the west at Bealach nan Arr, then skirt underneath a crag to the southwest, and onto a broad plateau of

These corries are wonderful, especially in winter, when they come into their own as a great playground, with lots of good ice and mixed routes for the climber.

confusing ground made up of hundreds of tiny lochans scattered around a rocky moorland.

The route onwards lies along the rising ridge to the south, and you can use the crags falling into Coire nan Arr to the east as a handrail, along which the going is straightforward. This leads in easy rocky steps to a knoll with a lochan just beyond on the ridge. Follow the ridge beyond this to a radio mast at 776m. But this is not the summit of **Sgurr a' Ghaorachain** – to get there you must head south into a dip, then follow the edge of the huge corrie around to the southeast, then eastwards over rocky knolls to the eastern edge of the ridge where it overlooks Loch Coire nan Arr and the Russel Burn.

Once you've taken in the view from the summit of Sgurr a' Ghaorachain, head back westwards to the point where the ridge opens out, and the rim of the corrie to your right turns to the north. From here continue westwards downhill until you reach the top edge of a long line of sandstone crags. Then keeping this on your left, follow it to the top of the **Bealach na Ba** to the west. The road from Tornapress to Applecross reaches the flat moorland at its top here.

Otters can often be seen near Uags

Cross the road and begin climbing easily to the south, over more rough and rocky terrain. Within 1km you'll reach the trig pillar at the summit of **Meall Gorm**, where there are superb views down the Bealach na Ba to the coast at Loch Kishorn.

Now head westwards across rough ground to a series of three lochans, beyond which a vague ridge is picked up that leads in just over 1km to another lochan. Here the ridge splits, and you should head southwards down to the rocky top of Carn Chailein. Continue southwards down to the path over the burn just above **Airigh-drishaig**. Cross this burn above the buildings, then head westwards around the coast to the bothy at **Uags**, where you'll probably opt to spend the night.

DAY 2

From Uags, start the day by heading westwards along the coast through a small woodland. The coastline here is fantastic and you should follow it northwards towards **Toscaig**.

Watch out for otters hereabouts, as they are fairly common on these western coasts. You'll probably also see seals, and if you're really lucky you might spot a passing minke whale out in the Caolas Mor between Uags and the Crowlin Islands.

Once you come into the little inlet of Loch Toscaig you'll start to see civilisation again, and soon you'll be in the tiny hamlet of Toscaig itself. Here you'll meet the little dead-end road that heads south from Applecross village, and it is a delightful walk northwards along this to Applecross and journey's end.

ROUTE 15

The Fannichs Traverse

Number of Days	2
Total Distance	35km (22 miles)
Daily Distances	Day 1 – 20km (12.5 miles), Day 2 – 15km (5 miles)
Height Gain	Total: 1280m; Day 1 – 1790m, Day 2 – 490m
Maps	OS Landranger sheet 20 Beinn Dearg
Starting Point	Braemore junction is the main road junction on the A835(T) between Dingwall and Ullapool. Start at the junction (there's a car park here, and also a bus turning area where they will happily drop you off and leave you!) (grid ref NH209777).
Finishing Point	Lochluichart railway station on the A832 west of Garve (grid ref NH323625).

Area Summary

The Fannichs was the nearest mountain range to where I used to live, so I'll always have a soft spot for this stunningly wild massif. The range stretches from Fisherfield Forest in the west through to Loch Luichart in the southeast, and has as its northern boundary the A835(T) from Dingwall to Ullapool. The southern boundary is marked by the A832, which branches off the A835(T) at Garve and goes west to Strathcarron. The Inverness to Kyle of Lochalsh railway line also goes through this valley alongside the road.

The Fannich range is one long main ridge with two side ridges, in all containing seven Munros – Meall a' Chrasgaidh, Sgurr nan Clach Geala, Sgurr nan Each, Sgurr Mor, Beinn Liath Mhor Fannaich, Meall Gorm and An Coileachan. To the west of the main ridge, and separated from it by a deep through-glen, there are two more Munros – Sgurr Breac and A' Chailleach. South of the main ridge lies hidden Loch Fannich, with a lonely Munro on its south side – Fionn Bheinn. The eastern end of the ridge rolls away into smaller hills, with only Beinn Liath

Mhor a' Ghiubhais Li being worthy of note as a Corbett (a mountain between 2500 and 3000 feet high).

Route Summary

Although not a long backpacking route – indeed, a fit hill-walker would be able to do this route in a day if she or he wished – this walk is best done over two days with a wild camp along the way, so it is only suitable for those with some experience of mountain walking and camping in remote locations. Although access to the area is straightforward, the hills you pass over and the wilderness feel of the whole region mean that you're a long way from help if anything should go wrong.

The walk takes in the main ridge of the Fannichs, starting at Braemore junction. A good stalker's path leads up to Meall a' Chrasgaidh, the first summit. The adjoining ridge to Sgurr nan Each is followed before retracing your steps, then you head out to Beinn Liath Mhor Fannaich, where you find

Tourist Information
There is a good tourist information centre on Argyle Street at Ullapool, tel 01854 612135.

Transport
Scottish Citylink runs three buses a day from Inverness to Ullapool (tel 08705 505050, www.citylink.co.uk). These stop by request at Braemore junction. Tim Dearman Coaches operates a bus service from Inverness which also stops at Braemore junction (tel 01349 883585, www.timdearmancoaches.co.uk). To return to Inverness you'll need to catch a train from Lochluichart Station on the Inverness to Kyle of Lochalsh line (tel 08457 550033, www.firstgroup.com/sco-trail).

Accommodation and Supplies
The Braemore Square bed and breakfast, tel 01854 655357, www.braemoresquare.com, is near Braemore junction, and the Aultguish Inn is at the eastern end of Loch Glascarnoch – it has bed-and-breakfast rooms and a bunkhouse, tel 01997 455 254, www.aultguish.co.uk. There are lots of other

accommodation options in Ullapool, and the tourist information centre there operates a booking service. There are no shops en route – you will need to stock up in Inverness or Ullapool before heading into the Fannichs.

Overnight Options
Camp wild in one of the many high corries that hold lochans. I often camp at Loch an Fhuar Thuill Mhoir.

Escape Routes
The only feasible options for a route out of the mountains from the high tops is either to head north for the A835 (T), or south for the track to Fannich Lodge, which leads eastwards to Lochluichart and the A832.

a wild campsite for the night. Regaining the main ridge on Day 2, you follow it southeastwards through to the road and railway station at Lochluichart.

DAY 1

Begin the walk by crossing over the A835(T) to its south side at the junction and taking the A832 towards Gairloch. The road takes a big bend to the right, and on this bend, where a plantation comes down to the roadside, there's a track leading uphill through the trees. You should follow this southwards until it comes out of the plantation and you find yourself on open moorland.

The track is an old stalker's route, and easy to follow, albeit a bit boggy in places. Walk southwards until it ends high up beneath the little hill of Creag Raineach Mor at the top of a steep slope. Continue over rough ground to the top of Creag Raineach Mor, where there are good views across the Dirrie More to the Beinn Dearg range. ◀

From the top of Creag Raineach Mor you should head southwest towards the steep ridge leading towards the summit of **Meall a' Chrasgaidh**. The going here is hard with a heavy rucksack, but you soon find yourself coming out at the summit, with the long ridge stretching away to the southeast.

These northern corries of the Fannichs are great for seeing large herds of red deer. The corries on either side of the ridge leading from Creag Raineach Mor often hold lots of stags.

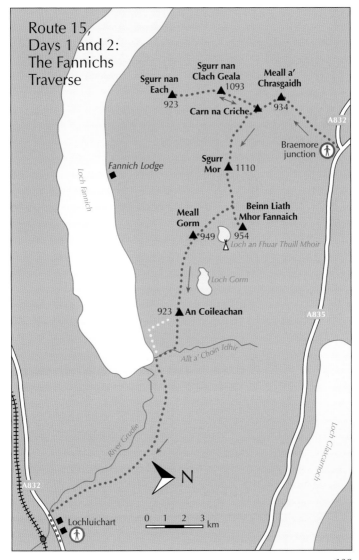

Route 15,
Days 1 and 2:
The Fannichs
Traverse

Sgurr nan Each
▲ 923

Sgurr nan
Clach Geala
▲ 1093

Meall a'
Chrasgaidh
▲ 934

Carn na Criche

A832

Braemore
junction

Fannich Lodge

Loch Fannich

Sgurr
Mor ▲ 1110

Meall
Gorm
▲ 949

Beinn Liath
Mhor Fannaich
▲ 954

Loch an Fhuar Thuill Mhoir

Loch Gorm

A835

923 ▲ An Coileachan

Allt a' Choin Idhir

A835

Loch Glascarnoch

River Grudie

N

A832

Lochluichart

0 1 2 3 km

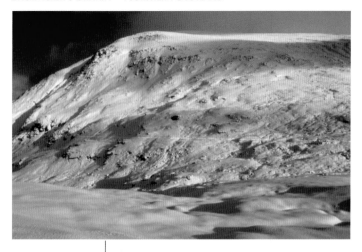

Sgurr nan Clach Geala

The summit of Meall a' Chrasgaidh is a fine viewpoint at 934m. From here you can look down into the large bowl holding Loch a' Mhadaidh to the east, with Beinn Liath Mhor Fannaich rising behind it.

From the summit of Meall a' Chrasgaidh walk south-eastwards down an easy ridge leading to a broad col. Ahead of you rises the minor top known as Carn na Criche, not a Munro, but the pivotal point on the ridge where the north–south ridge of Sgurr nan Clach Geala comes in from the south and the main ridge stretches away to the southeast.

Climb easy slopes until you're almost at the top of **Carn na Criche**, then head over to the southwest to a lochan on a bealach. Climb the northern ridge of **Sgurr nan Clach Geala**, bearing right slightly to the summit trig pillar at 1093m. Continue over the summit, and just east of south, then southwards down to a narrow col. A short ascent then leads over rocks to the fine summit of **Sgurr nan Each** at 923m.

The view from Sgurr nan Each really is superb. You can see right down to Loch Fannich near Fannich Lodge, and across to Fionn Bheinn to the southwest. I was once up by the summit cairn on Sgurr nan Each in winter, sitting on my rucksack for insulation, eating a sandwich, when out of the corrie on the right, and not more than perhaps ten feet away, rose a huge female golden eagle. She hung there on the breeze for what felt like minutes, but was probably only a few seconds, then turned and sailed away without a single wing flap, while I just sat there dumb-struck, realising too late that my camera was in the ruck-sack upon which I sat!

Looking northeastwards from Sgurr nan Each you can see the main Fannich ridge stretching over numerous lumps and bumps towards distant An Coileachan.

From Sgurr nan Each you must retrace your steps over Sgurr nan Clach Geala and down to the lochan on the bealach below Carn na Criche.

The route over to the summit of Carn na Criche is easy angled and straightforward, and from there it is an undemanding slope leading down to the northwest ridge of **Sgurr Mor**, the highest of the Fannich Munros at 1110m. Climb this ridge to the top and enjoy the views along it in both directions.

Sgurr Breac from Sgurr nan Each

To continue to **Beinn Liath Mhor Fannaich** you must first head along the rim of the crags to the southeast. Staying close by this rim leads to a ridge, which you can follow down to a knoll before a bealach is reached below the slopes of Beinn Liath Mhor Fannaich. This col is 2km from the summit of Sgurr Mor. Now easy flanks to the northeast take you up to the top of Beinn Liath Mhor Fannaich, where you get possibly the best views in the entire range.

> Because Beinn Liath Mhor Fannaich's summit is set off the main ridge on its north side, you will find yourself looking back into the great corries on this flank of the ridge. Away to the north the massive bulk of the Beinn Dearg range fills the view.

Once you've taken in the magnificent view you should retrace your steps down to the bealach to the southwest. Continue above the bealach in the same direction, climbing towards the knoll on the ridge of Sgurr Mor. Before reaching the top of the knoll it is possible to contour across to the left onto a broad ridge that lies above the wonderful lochan of **Loch an Fhuar Thuill Mhoir**. Either walk down this ridge, or make directly for the lochan, finding a lovely place here to camp for the night.

DAY 2

After a restful night in the dark bowl holding Loch an Fhuar Thuill Mhoir, you'll be ready for the heights of the main ridge again. Walk around to the south side of Loch an Fhuar Thuill Mhoir and climb southwards up to a col just west of Creachan Rairigidh. The going here is steep, but starting the day from such a high camp means that it's not long before you're back on the ridge.

Turn to the southeast and climb from the col to the top of Creachan Rairigidh. From here an easy angled ridge leads you to the top of the first Munro of the day, **Meall Gorm** at 949m. The going is easy, and the ridge a delight to walk, taking you onwards over a knoll on the ridge and down to a col overlooking **Loch Gorm**. (Loch Gorm is another great place to camp if you decide to go that bit further on your first day, or even better is the tiny lochan high above Loch Gorm and just below this col.)

Now the final Munro lies ahead, and it's an easy ascent to the summit of **An Coileachan** at 923m.

To the southeast a great ridge leads to the edge of Garbh Choire Mor, and from here you have a choice of two routes. You can either head eastwards down to a track alongside the Allt a' Choin Idhir, then turn right and head down to a bridge by the good track through from Loch Fannich, or you can head south around the rim of Garbh Choire Mor, then southwards down to a tiny lochan just above the track from Fannich Lodge. Either way, you should gain the main track that goes along the north side of Loch Fannich and takes you eastwards towards Lochluichart. Follow the track above the **River Grudie**, which is a delight. ▶

The track takes you through woodland and onwards to a bridge. Don't go over the bridge, but instead stay on the north side of the River Grudie, and out to the A832 just west of Lochluichart. Turn left along the road and walk along it for 1.5km to the train station. This is down a short track on the right, signposted from the road.

Look for dippers and grey wagtails on the rocks of the River Grudie, and in summer you should see common sandpipers here too.

Sunset from the Fannich ridge in winter

143

ROUTE 16

Torridon from Shieldaig

Number of Days	2
Total Distance	44km (27.5 miles)
Daily Distances	Day 1 –25km (15.5 miles), Day 2 – 19km (12 miles)
Height Gain	Total: 2070m; Day 1 – 1300m, Day 2 –770m
Maps	OS Landranger sheet 19 Gairloch and Ullapool
Starting	PointStart at Shieldaig at a small car park just east of the hotel (grid ref NG807724). A track leaves the main road (the B8056) here on the left and there is a parking place near to this point.

Area Summary

The magnificent mountains known as the Torridonian Giants are among the very best mountains in Scotland. The three highest, Beinn Alligin, Beinn Eighe and Liathach, are top of the list for many Munro-baggers, and each individually makes for a great expedition. Beinn Eighe and Liathach are not really suitable peaks for backpackers, and this suggested route takes you over Beinn Alligin from a wild camp base where you can leave your tent and other camping equipment. The route heads into the Torridon peaks from the north, through what is known as the Flowerdale Forest. This wild region of mountains, moorland and lochs lies to the west of the A832 alongside Loch Maree, and south of Gairloch. To the south of the region, beyond the Torridonian Giants, the natural boundary is Loch Torridon itself. The hills roll away to the sea in the west at Red Point.

Route Summary

This walk takes you right into the heart of the Flowerdale Forest from Shieldaig on the south shore of Loch Gairloch. It begins on a good stalker's track and follows the Abhainn Braigh to

Loch Gaineamhach before making for the northern slopes of Beinn Alligin. You pitch your tent here then make an afternoon ascent of Beinn Alligin, traversing the Horns of Alligin before heading back to your wild campsite. On Day 2 the route takes you over the superb Baosbheinn ridge and back to Shieldaig through true wilderness country.

The route is suitable for those with some experience of mountain walking and camping in remote locations. Much of it is off beaten paths and tracks, and the going can be hard if you're not used to this sort of thing! That said, this is a walk for anyone with a love of wild scenery and wildlife.

Tourist Information
The nearest tourist information centre is in Gairloch (tel 01445 712130) just west of Poolewe, and there is also a tourist information centre in Ullapool on Argyle Street (tel 01854 612135).

Transport
From Inverness you can either drive north towards Gairloch on the A832 from Garve, then turn off onto the B8056 to Shieldaig, Badachro and Port Henderson, or use one of the buses that serve this area. The Westerbus serves Gairloch from Inverness (tel 01445 712255). Rapsons also runs a service to Gairloch via Dundonnell from Ullapool (tel 01463 710555, www.rapsons.co.uk). If you use these bus services ask the driver to drop you off at the Shieldaig junction from where you'll have to walk to Shieldaig and the start of the route.

Accommodation and Supplies
There is plenty of choice for bed and breakfast accommodation in Poolewe and in Gairloch. Try the Myrtle Bank Hotel (tel 01445 712004) or Bains House (tel 01445 712472), both in Gairloch. Also near Gairloch is the SYHA hostel at Carn Dearg (tel 01445 712219). In Poolewe you could try the Pool House Hotel (tel 01445 781272) or Mrs MacIver's bed and breakfast (tel 01445 781389). There is also a Caravan and Camping Club site in Poolewe (tel 01445 781249).

The Shieldaig Lodge Hotel is conveniently situated right at the start of this walk (tel 01445 741250, www.shieldaiglodge.com).

There are lots of other accommodation options in Ullapool, and the tourist information centre there operates a booking service.

There are a few small shops and a good cafe in Gairloch near the start of the walk, but there are no shops en route. It is best to stock up in Inverness or Ullapool beforehand.

Overnight Options Camp wild at one of the lovely mountain tarns along the route. Ideally you would camp at Loch Toll nam Biast (grid ref NG870619), beneath the northern face of Beinn Alligin, from where you can leave your tent and climb this magnificent mountain.

Escape Routes

There are no obvious escape routes from this walk, other than making for the stalker's track back to Shieldaig. From Loch Toll nam Biast it is possible to skirt around the eastern slopes of Beinn Alligin, and so to the track down into Loch Torridon where you can get help – but bear in mind that this is in the wrong direction if you want to return to Shieldaig.

DAY 1

Begin by leaving the road at **Shieldaig** and following the track over a little stream. The woodland here is made up of lovely old oak trees, and you walk on through these to the open moorland beneath the west face of **Sidhean Mor.** This small hill lies to the east as you walk along the track, and you will be descending those slopes from the summit to end your walk tomorrow. (Tomorrow's route will take you to the Fairy Lochs and a well-known airplane-crash site and war memorial, so ignore the signposts and path leading off up the hill to your left for now.)

Continue along the main track to **Loch Braigh Horrisdale**, a large lake that feeds the Badachro River. The track here becomes a narrower path, but is still easy to follow as you head southeastwards to the banks of the Abhainn Braigh-hor-risdale, the river above the loch.

The path continues beyond an old ruined shieling, then takes a sharp loop to the right to cross a side stream beside some lovely waterfalls. Keep alongside the river on the path for the best views of the falls as you go.

Above the falls the path leads away from the river for a short time, making directly for the western end of **Loch**

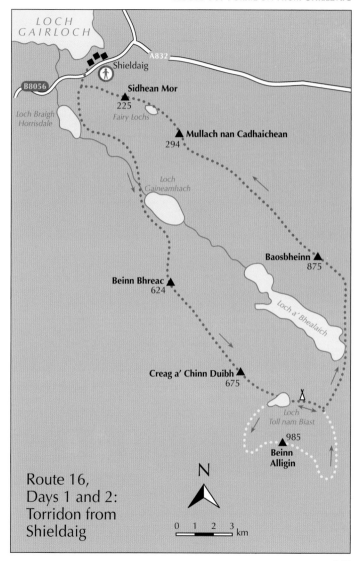

LOCH
GAIRLOCH

A832

Shieldaig

B8056

Sidhean Mor
225

*Loch Braigh
Horrisdale*

Fairy Lochs

▲ **Mullach nan Cadhaichean**
294

*Loch
Gaineamhach*

Baosbheinn ▲
875

Beinn Bhreac ▲
624

Loch a' Bhealaich

Creag a' Chinn Duibh ▲
675

*Loch
Toll nam Biast*

985
▲
**Beinn
Alligin**

Route 16,
Days 1 and 2:
Torridon from
Shieldaig

N

0 1 2 3 km

Gaineamhach. Follow the path to the loch, where you'll find a bridge spanning the river at the loch's outflow. Cross the bridge and squeeze between the main loch and a tiny lochan to your right. The path then takes you around the south side of Loch Gaineamhach.

Just before you reach the eastern end of Loch Gaineamhach you should leave the path and begin to climb easily up the rough slopes to the south. You will soon gain an easy angled ridge that you can follow to spot height 439m, where the ridge becomes more pronounced. Climb up the ridge to a large knoll, then descend into a col before reaching the northern slopes of **Beinn Bhreac**, or 'the Speckled Hill'. These slopes are not too steep, and you will soon find yourself on the summit of this fine little hill at 624m, with the whole of **Beinn Alligin** spread out before you at the far end of the ridge upon which you are standing.

The main summit of Beinn Alligin, Sgurr Mhor, can be seen just to the right of the ridge on which you stand, and your route of ascent will take you up the slopes directly towards this summit.

To the east a good ridge stretches towards Beinn Alligin, first over a minor top, then down to a deep col before the climb up to the top of **Creag a' Chinn Duibh** at 675m (unmarked on OS Landranger maps). Below you to the southeast you will now see the lovely shining levels of **Loch Toll nam Biast**, which is actually a collection of small tarns. Head down to these over easy ground and pitch your tent wherever looks like the best spot – there are lots of really good options to choose from here.

Optional Climb of Beinn Alligin

From your wild camp site at Loch Toll nam Biast you have the option of climbing Sgurr Mhor, the highest summit of Beinn Alligin. **Note** This route follows a scrambling ridge and is recommended only for those with some experience of scrambling and a head for heights.

Begin by heading to the western end of Loch Toll nam Biast. Cross over a stream here and walk southwestwards, gaining height slowly until you are on a broad ridge. Turn to the southeast and climb steeply up this ridge to where it becomes less defined. Continue to the southeast, climbing steeply to the rim of crags overlooking the tangled southern face of this magnificent mountain. Turn left along the rim, walking around the top of the deep defile of the Eag

Beinn Alligin

Dubh, or 'the Black Cleft'. The summit is just beyond this to the north.

From the summit head eastwards down a narrowing ridge. This is rocky and requires a bit of easy scrambling. From a notch a scramble leads over a series of rocky tops, the Horns of Alligin, until the whole ridge turns to the southeast. Do not be tempted into trying to get down directly to the north, but instead follow this ridge down rocky steps to the southeast. You will soon pick up a rough path leading down to the moorland below. Once all scrambling difficulties are behind you, turn to the east and descend towards the Allt a Bhealaich, the river that flows southwards from Loch Toll nam Biast. Turn northwards alongside this river and follow it around the northeast side of the Horns of Alligin. At a collection of lochans the river turns westwards and leads you uphill to Loch Toll nam Biast, where you can spend a delightful night in a truly wild setting.

DAY 2

Begin the day by walking eastwards down the outflow of Loch Toll nam Biast. This leads to a collection of lochans (visited on the return from Beinn Alligin the day before). Head around to the eastern end of these lochans, until you are on the lower slopes of Beinn Dearg, the magnificent mountain east of Beinn Alligin.Contour around the northern slopes of Beinn Dearg to Loch na Cabhaig.North of Loch na Cabhaig you'll see a long ridge rising above **Loch a' Bhealaich**, the large loch that fills the glen to the northwest.

Gain the ridge above Loch a' Bhealaich and climb to the spot height at 707m (grid ref NG882644). The superb rocky ridge of **Baosbheinn** now continues to the northwest, and you should make a start on this by heading just north of west down to a col, then climbing westwards for 400m until you are on a delightful curving arête leading around to the north and a minor top. Westwards again, you'll find yourself on a rocky col just below the main summit of Baosbheinn at 875m. Follow the ridge to the top of this brilliant little peak.

The deep lochs to the west and east give a magical quality to this lovely mountain. Rising from the other side of

Loch na h-Oidhche to the east is the twin to Baosbheinn, Beinn an Eoin. These wonderful hills are good nesting territory for a golden eagle pair, and you might be lucky enough to see them soaring over the ridges.

Continue to the northwest, following the ridge over spot height 800m and on to the end of the ridge known as Creag an Fhithich at 737m. From the end of the ridge you can pick a careful way through the crags to the northwest until you are on the moorland below. Walk northwest across the moor to lonely Lochan nan Leacann Dearga.

West of this delightful spot is a knoll. Walk over to this, then northwestwards again over heaths to a gap in the crags of **Mullach nan Cadhaichean**, from where you can gain that little hilltop. A rough ridge now takes you northwest to an unnamed loch from where you can continue in the same line to the **Fairy Lochs** and the site of a well-known air crash.

In 1945 the B-24H left Prestwick airport on a route that should have taken it over Stornoway, and we can only guess at why it came over the mainland instead. It seems that the aircraft struck the top of Slioch, the huge mountain on the southeastern side of Loch Maree, and lost some bomb-bay door parts. The descent continued until it broke through the cloud base over Gairloch. It circled once round the loch, possibly looking for a place to ditch, and the crew may have decided on the sea loch itself. The aircraft was on the run in when it just failed to clear the rocky spurs by the Fairy Lochs. All crew and passengers were killed. There is a memorial here today, and the site is often visited.

Above the Fairy Lochs lies the summit of **Sidhean Mor**. Gain its top for great views of **Loch Gairloch**, then drop down to the northwest to pick up the track above Shieldaig that you followed yesterday. Turn right and return to the main road where you started.

ROUTE 17

Coulin Forest from Torridon

Number of Days	2
Total Distance	39km (24.25 miles)
Daily Distances	Day 1 – 23km (14.25 miles), Day 2 – 16km (10 miles)
Height Gain	Total: 2470m; Day 1 – 1430m, Day 2 – 1040m
Maps	OS Landranger sheet 25 Glen Carron
Starting Point	About halfway down Glen Torridon between Kinlochewe and Torridon village is the Ling Hut on the south side of the road. There is a car park here (where people park when climbing Beinn Eighe), just west of the bridge over the River Torridon (grid ref NG957568).

Area Summary

Coulin Forest is a glorious mountain range ('forest' here, as in so many other regions of Britain, is an old term for a hunting estate, not one necessarily with trees!), and as I used to run winter skills courses in this area, to my mind it is one of the best places in the UK in which to go looking for that wilderness feeling. It is a much-neglected region, with fine rugged mountains, lovely tumbling burns, hidden corries and remnants of the old Caledonian pine forest – what more could you ask?

The region is sandwiched between arguably grander mountain ranges to the north and south – Torridon in the north and the Achnashellach Forest to the south – all of which just makes these hills even quieter, and the more precious for it. Glen Torridon gives a natural boundary to the north and Strathcarron does the same to the south.

Coulin Forest's mountains are very much individual, and include three Munros and four Corbetts, the best among them being Maol Chean-dearg, Sgurr Ruadh and Fuar Tholl. Coulin Forest has more than just great mountains though – do this two-day route and you'll see what I mean.

Route Summary

From Glen Torridon a short pathless section leads to a stalker's track around Loch Clair, from where you head over Sgurr nan Lochan Uaine, Beinn Liath Mhor and Sgurr Ruadh to an optional ascent of Fuar Tholl. A steep descent then takes you to a crossing of the Fionn Abhainn to the bothy. On Day 2 you traverse Meall nan Ceapairean to Maol Chean-dearg, from where a stalker's track leads over the Bealach na Lice and back into Glen Torridon.

This walk is suitable for backpackers with some experience of crossing rough, open mountain country off the beaten track.

Tourist Information

There is a good tourist information centre in Fort William at Cameron Square (tel 01397 703781).

Transport

There is no bus service to the start of this walk, so it is necessary to drive there. From Inverness make for Dingwall, then follow the A832 westwards towards Gairloch. At Kinlochewe turn left onto the A896 to Torridon.

Accommodation and Supplies

There are a few bed and breakfasts in Kinlochewe and Torridon. Try Cromasaig on the road to Torridon just outside Kinlochewe (tel 01445 760234), or Ben Damph Lodge (tel 01445 791242) just west of Torridon village. There's also the up-market Loch Torridon Hotel (tel 01445 791242) just next door to Ben Damph Lodge.

In Torridon itself you'll find a great youth hostel (tel 01445 791284) and a small campsite. Members of the BMC (British Mountaineering Council) can book the Ling Hut, which is right at the start of this walk. It is owned by the Scottish Mountaineering Club, and for details you should contact their hut custodian, William Skidmore, 1 Kirkton Drive, Lochcarron, Strathcarron, Wester Ross IV54 8UD.

There are small shops in Torridon and Kinlochewe, but you would do better to stock up in Inverness or Fort William before heading north. There are no shops along the route.

Overnight Options
Camp alongside the Fionn Abhainn or at Loch Coire Fionnaraich. There is also a good though small bothy beneath Meall nan Ceapairean, which is maintained by the Mountain Bothies Association. These mountain huts are left open for all to use and are free of charge. You can join the Mountain Bothies Association on www.mountainbothies.org.uk.

Escape Routes
An abundance of stalker's tracks lead through this area, and generally run from north to south, from Glen Torridon through to Strathcarron. They give easy ways out of the hills in either direction.

DAY 1

Begin by walking eastwards along the road for 1.5km, until you are beyond a little plantation on the left. Cross the stream on the right and make your way over rough, boggy moorland to the western end of Loch Bharranch. Walk around the loch on its south side and soon pick up a stalker's track that makes the going a little easier. Follow this track eastwards into the woods at the edge of **Loch Clair**.

There are some lovely trees in these woodlands, most of them Scots pines (or Caledonian pines as they are called locally). The woods are a remnant of the ancient pine forest that once cloaked much of the Highlands. They support a varied array of wildlife, including Scottish crossbills, crested tits, pine marten and the Scottish wildcat. Other trees you'll see here include rowan, birch, alder and holly, all native trees in the Highlands.

The track winds a careful way through the trees, giving views over the loch here and there, until you emerge on a Land-Rover track at Coulin Lodge. Turn right here and walk through the outbuildings to a junction of tracks. Turn right again and follow the stalker's track to the southwest, which soon crosses the tumbling waters of the Allt na Luib. This path climbs steadily through the trees alongside the stream to

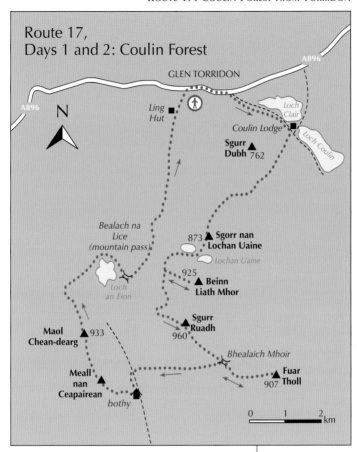

Route 17,
Days 1 and 2: Coulin Forest

emerge high up in Coire an Leth-uillt, beneath the imposing south face of **Sgurr Dubh.**

High up in this coire the path ends and you should take to the open hillside, following the stream to the southwest until you can gain the broad north ridge of **Sgorr nan Lochan Uaine.** The going here is quite rough, and you'll have to pick your way carefully through heathery moors and rocky outcrops. Climb southwards to the summit of Sgorr nan Lochan Uaine.

> The views from Sgorr nan Lochan Uaine are tremendous. You'll find yourself looking over the twin lochs at Lochan Uaine to Beinn Liath Mhor to the south, while the mountains of Torridon are massed to the north.

Carefully drop down to the small gap between the twin lakes at **Lochan Uaine**, then skirt around the westerly loch to its southwestern point. From here climb diagonally to the southwest to a tiny lochan on the western shoulder of **Beinn Liath Mhor**. From here an easy route leads you eastwards to the summit of your first Munro of the trip, Beinn Liath Mhor at 925m. (There is a really nice ridge walk along Beinn Liath Mhor to the east, but you will probably want to leave that for another time, as it takes you in the wrong direction. Just enjoy the views along it from the western summit.)

Return along the ridge to the west, dropping back down to the lochan on the western shoulder. Crags are thrown down to the south, so pick a careful route through them to the southwest, then south down to a small pool on a col (grid ref NG959515).

To the southwest a knoll rises and has another pool on it southwestern side. Climb over the knoll and descend to this second pool. Above this to the southwest you'll see the northwest ridge of **Sgurr Ruadh**. Climb steeply, though thankfully briefly, onto this, passing to the left of a band of crags. Once on the ridge turn left, to the southeast, and follow the arête to a small tarn. Continue up a scree slope then onwards to the magnificent summit of Sgurr Ruadh.

From the summit of Sgurr Ruadh you'll see **Fuar Tholl's** northern corries masked in shade to the south. This route takes you to the summit of Fuar Tholl, an extension that really should not be missed, but you can, if you wish, just cut down into the glen to the west.

Follow the ridge to the southeast for 100m, then descend southwards down rough slopes to Loch a' Bhealaich Mhoir, the large lake on the col between Sgurr Ruadh and Fuar Tholl. A little further to the south you'll find another loch by a knoll,

River crossing in the Coulin Forest

and here you can pick up the path up the western ridge of Fuar Tholl. This skirts above the massive buttresses of the corries on the north side of the mountain, and gives a feeling of exposure. The summit of Fuar Tholl has an OS trig pillar at its top.

Return to the Bhealaich Mhoir along the west ridge, then descend steep slopes to the west down into the glen. The going isn't too difficult down here and you'll soon find yourself at the Fionn Abhainn, which needs care to cross. If in doubt, head northwards to Loch Coire Fionnaraich and walk around this to get onto the western side of the glen. A stalker's path runs through the glen on this western side – once on the path turn southwards and follow the path to the **bothy**.

DAY 2

The path leading up the glen from the bothy bypasses the superb ridge of **Meall nan Ceapairean**, which is well worth climbing. Head uphill to the west from the bothy, climbing up an open gully of heather and rocks to gain the south ridge of Meall nan Ceapairean. Turn right once on the ridge and climb easily over rocky ground to the summit of this fine hill.

To the north, the great cliffs rimming the summit fall into a lovely corrie with the col between Meall nan Ceapairean and Maol Chean-dearg at its head. To get to this col you must first descend to the west, down a ridge that curves around to the northwest as you approach the col.

Above this col a narrowing ridge leads onto the southeast face of Maol Chean-dearg, from where it is an easy though steep climb to the summit at 933m. From here there is a great view over to the east and the mountain traversed yesterday.

Steep scree leads down to the northwest, and you can pick up a broad ridge leading down to a stalker's track above **Loch an Eion**. Once on this stalker's track follow it to the outflow of the loch at its western end. Just north of the crossing of the stream here the track splits. To the left it leads downhill to Torridon village, but to get back to the Ling Hut you need to first contour around the loch to its eastern end, from where the tracks takes you uphill to the **Bealach na Lice**, a high pass lying between Maol Chean-dearg and Meall Dearg. The path over the pass is the through-route from Strathcarron

to Glen Torridon via the Coire Fionnaraich bothy. (This path
also makes a good escape route in either direction if needed.)

Just downhill on the southeast side of the bealach there
is another junction of tracks. Turn left here and contour across
the headwall of the corrie to a short climb up to another col,
the Bealach Ban. This col lies on the northwest ridge of **Sgurr
Ruadh**, just below the ridge you climbed yesterday. You'll find
a little tarn here, around which the path heads to the east.

Just beyond this tarn you should leave the path and begin
the descent into the glen to the north. At first stay on the east
side of a stream, but where this turns to the northwest to
descend to Lochan Neimhe, head northeast to pick up a
stalker's track. This takes you just east of north and down to
the east side of Loch na Frianach. Beyond this loch the track
stays above the eastern side of a stream, passing close to some
beautiful waterfalls, then leading down to the Ling Hut close
to Lochan an Lasgair.

The path passes to the right of the loch, then around the
east side of a little knoll, before crossing the River Torridon at
a footbridge and depositing you on the road through the glen.
Turn left to walk along the road to the car park.

ROUTE 18

Strath Carron Munros from Craig

Number of Days	2
Total Distance	48km (30 miles)
Daily Distances	Day 1 – 24km (15 miles), Day 2 – 24km (15 miles)
Height Gain	Total: 3070m; Day 1 – 1580m, Day 2 – 1490m
Maps	OS Landranger sheet 25 Glen Carron
Starting Point	There's a small car park on the north side of the A890 at Craig between Achnasheen and Loch Carron (grid ref NH039493).

Area Summary

South of the A890 across the road from Coulin Forest lies the mountain fastness of the Munros of Achnashellach. This area takes in many ancient hunting forests, including those of Achnashellach, West and East Monar, Glencarron and Glenuig. This is real wild country, and once you've headed south away from the main road you'll find yourself a long way from anywhere.

There are some great mountains in this area, and this route gives you the opportunity to traverse a number of the best in a two-day route. The walk takes you along long ridges little traversed by people, mainly due to the inaccessibility of it all.

Route Summary

A superb high-level route based around the Munros of the Achnashellach Forest. The walk starts at Craig and follows a good track into the heart of the hills before taking to the tops of Sgurr nan Ceannaichean and Moruisg. It then heads into the depths of Gleann Fhiodhaig before crossing the River Meig and climbing Maoile Lunndaidh, where you'll find a campsite for the night. On Day 2 you traverse the

long mountain ridge westwards ending on the Bealach
Bhearnais. A short ascent over Sgurr na Feartaig takes you
into the Achnashellach Forest, from where good tracks lead
back to Craig.

This walk is only suitable for backpackers with some
experience of crossing rough, open, mountain country off the
beaten track.

Tourist Information
There is a good tourist information centre in Fort William at Cameron Square
(tel 01397 703781), also a small tourist information centre in Lochcarron village (tel 01520 722357), just along the A890 to the west from the starting point.

Transport
There is no convenient bus service to the start of this walk, although Achnashellach
(which is just a few kilometres down the road from Craig) has a railway station
on the Inverness to Kyle of Lochalsh line, www.firstgroup.com/scotrail, tel 08457
550033. To drive from Inverness make for Dingwall, then follow the A832 westwards towards Gairloch. At Garve turn left for Achnasheen, then once there turn
left at the roundabout and take the A890 towards Loch Carron.

Accommodation and Supplies
Not much locally, other than the well-known Gerry's Hostel (tel 01520 766 232,
www.gerryshostel-achnashellach.co.uk), just across the road from the start of
this walk in Craig. There are a few bed and breakfasts in Loch Carron – try the
Rockvilla Hotel and Restaurant (tel 01520 722379) or Bank House bed and
breakfast (tel 01520 722332). There's also a small Spar shop and some places
to eat, otherwise it's best to bring supplies with you.

Overnight Options
Camp wild along the route. The large Loch a' Chlaidheimh on Maoile Lunndaidh
is a good place at about the halfway mark, although it can be a bit bleak here
at times.

Escape Routes
The track through Gleann Fhiodhaig that runs from Craig through to Strath Conan
is a good route, giving a way out of the hills in both directions.

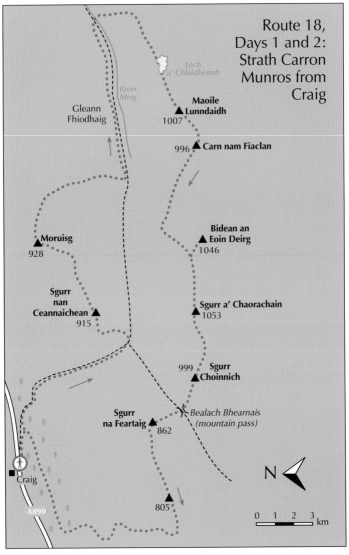

Route 18,
Days 1 and 2:
Strath Carron
Munros from
Craig

Loch
a' Chlaidheimh

River
Meig

Gleann
Fhiodhaig

▲ Maoile
Lunndaidh
1007

996 ▲ Carn nam Fiaclan

Bidean an
▲ Eoin Deirg
1046

▲ Moruisg
928

Sgurr
nan
Ceannaichean ▲
915

▲ Sgurr a' Chaorachain
1053

999 Sgurr
▲ Choinnich

Sgurr
na Feartaig ▲
862

Bealach Bhearnais
(mountain pass)

Craig

A890

▲
805

N

0 1 2 3
km

DAY 1

From the car park at **Craig** walk down to the main road and cross almost directly over to a track that heads down to the railway line at a level crossing. Go over here and follow the track around to the left. It runs parallel to the railway and road for a while then veers off to the right and crosses the River Carron at a bridge.

Just over the bridge there's a junction, and you should go left along the track that climbs uphill to the east of the Allt a' Chonais. You soon emerge from the trees, which here are a mix of lovely Scots pine, larch and spruce. The track now contours away from the river for a short distance, then passes beneath the impressively craggy west face of **Sgurr nan Ceannaichean**, the Munro towards which you are heading. Once beyond the crags of Sgurr nan Ceannaichean there is a little path that cuts the corner off the main track to the left. Either take this path or stay on the main track – it doesn't matter either way, as the two meet up again at an important junction.

Where the path and track rejoin there is another path that climbs steeply uphill to the east of north, making towards the summit of Sgurr nan Ceannaichean. This stalker's track should

Buzzards hunt in Strath Carron

be followed until high in a corrie just below the west ridge of Sgurr nan Ceannaichean. Head up to gain this west ridge, then turn to the east and follow the ridge to the fine summit of Sgurr nan Ceannaichean at 915m.

The view down into Coire Toll nam Bian to the northwest is superb from this ridge walk between Sgurr nan Ceannaichean and Moruisg.

Leave the summit by heading just east of north for 500m, then turn eastwards along the rim of crags falling into the corrie to the north. This leads down to a col, from where an easy ridge takes you up to the east, curving around towards the northeast to a minor top at 854m. ◀

From the minor top at 854m head north to where the slopes open out, and just ahead you'll find the summit of **Moruisg** at 928m. Walk southeast down to a broad col and continue over this to climb up onto another minor top to the southeast. A good stalker's track runs off this top to the south and you should head down the south ridge to pick this up. The track lies on the ridge between Coire a'Chlaiginn and Coire Beithe.

There are some superb corries hanging from both sides of the summit ridge of Sgurr nan Ceannaichean, and these can be good places to see large herds of red deer.

Once on the track the going is easy down to the main track through **Gleann Fhiodhaig**, at a point just east of Glenuaig Lodge. Turn east along the path that runs along the glen – after 6km you'll need to cross over to the south side of the river, so it's worth keeping an eye on the level of water here. It's definitely easier to walk on the path along the north bank, but in spate this river can be impossible to cross lower down, so bear this in mind. ◀

The head of the glen here is one of my favourite places for watching golden eagles. There are at least two eagle territories in this area, so there is a good chance you might see them hereabouts.

Follow the glen downstream for 6km until the ridges of Meall Doir' a' Bhainne to the north and Creag Dubh Bheag to the south both come down into the glen. At this point you need to cross over to the south side of the river and pick up the stalker's track that heads uphill to the south, gaining the northeast ridge of Creag Dubh Bheag before leading to the top of that minor summit by a lochan. Head southwest down to **Loch a' Chlaidheimh**, where you should look for a suitable campsite for the night.

DAY 2

Begin the day by walking around to the south side of Loch a' Chlaidheimh. A ridge rises above you to the south, and you should gain this and turn westwards along it, keeping slightly to the right of rocks to gain the summit plateau of **Maoile Lunndaidh**. The summit itself lies on the north side of a shallow ridge at 1007m.

From the top walk southwestwards down to a narrow nick in the ridge before a small knoll. Climb the knoll and use the rim of crags on your right-hand side as a guide down to the west where another col lies. Beyond this is a minor summit known as **Carn nam Fiaclan**, which you need to cross to gain the west ridge of Maoile Lunndaidh. Descend the west ridge down to a pair of lochans on a low bealach (this is another good option for an overnight camp if you feel like going that bit further the night before).

To the southwest you'll see a vague ridge rising up the middle of the steep slopes of **Bidean an Eoin Deirg** – it has a stream to its left as you look up at it. Gain and climb this ridge, which leads steeply to the left of the summit of Bidean an Eoin Deirg. Turn left briefly to get to the top at 1046m.

The ridge to the west is now an easy walk over stony slopes. Begin along this by descending to the northwest to a high col, then follow the obvious ridge up the broad top of **Sgurr a' Chaorachain** at 1053m. There is an OS trig pillar on the summit. To the north of the ridge the coire headwall is now quite rocky, but the ridge crest above still gives straightforward walking. The scenery here is spectacular, with the huge gulf of these northern corries falling to the Pollan Buidhe far below.

Continue westwards down to a stony col, then climb up the east ridge of **Sgurr Choinnich** to the top of that fine mountain – the summit lies at the western end of a short ridge. Continue to the northwest over a minor top, then descend steeply down the west ridge to a col.

The ground here can be quite confusing, especially in mist. There is another, lower col to the northwest – the **Bealach Bhearnais** – and you must drop down to the northwest to get to it. From the col climb northwestwards directly for the top of **Sgurr na Feartaig** at 862m.

This fine mountain ridge is often ignored by hillwalkers heading for the higher mountains nearby, but it is well worth taking in as part of this backpacking expedition. The way is obvious, and as you drop down from the summit westwards you pick up a path that traverses the ridge. Continue along this to the western peak of the mountain, then keep on the path as it descends westwards to a broad col at a pass.

The paths come to a junction here, with the track to the left heading off down to Bearnais bothy in the south – northwards is your route down into Achnashellach. The path leads down a ridge, then through a rocky nick and down to a narrow col on Carn Mor. A steep descent to the west brings you into the head of Coire Leiridh, then the path traverses high above the eastern flank of the corrie to bring you down into the dark forests of Achnashellach.

Stay on the path throughout, until you reach a major track running east–west alongside the River Carron down in the bottom of the glen. Turn right on this track and walk eastwards, over a bridge over the Allt Coire a'Bhainidh.

Although much of the forest here is planted up with non-native species of fir and spruce, there are some really good examples of Scots pine here too. If you're lucky you might catch a glimpse of crossbills in the treetops, or perhaps even the occasional crested tit.

Continue along the track to a bridge on the left that takes you over the Allt a' Chonais to the junction you passed yesterday just after leaving Craig. Turn left here and follow the track back into Craig.

ROUTE 19
The Head of Strathconon

Number of Days	2
Total Distance	38km (24 miles)
Daily Distances	Day 1 –19km (12 miles), Day 2 – 19km (12 miles)
Height Gain	Total: 1880m; Day 1 – 870m, Day 2 – 1010m
Maps	OS Landranger sheet 25 Glen Carron
Starting Point	There's a small car park at the head of the public road in Strathconon (grid ref NH225519). This is overlooking Loch Beannacharain at its western end. Do not drive beyond the car park, as the road is private from there onwards.

Note The OS Landranger map shows this car park 0.5km further along the road that it actually is.

Area Summary

A fantastic area for the walker and backpacker, often bypassed by those on the way further north to higher mountains, but well worth making a detour to get to. A delightfully quiet Highland glen lies at the heart of the Strathconon Forest, with low mountains and lots of wildlife all around. The hills in the region are never too high, and often rounded and heathery, making for easy going.

Strathconon is sandwiched between the hills of Achnashellach and the Fannichs in the north, and Glen Affric and Glen Strathfarrar in the south, and within easy reach of Inverness. There are a number of Corbetts in this region, with some notable lower hills too, but the Munros have their feet in other glens. At the head of Strathconon, where the public road ends, the glen itself continues right through to Achnashellach via the River Meig, and the bulk of Maoile Lunndaidh dominates the view as you look southwestwards from the car park.

Route Summary

A lovely, wild walk in an area little visited by other walkers. This route is suitable for those with some experience of walking and navigating over pathless terrain, but being short it is a good introduction to backpacking.

The route starts at the head of Strathconon and takes you along the River Meig to a bridge from where you climb up Coire Mhoraigein, which gives you access onto a long mountain ridge to the summit of An Sidhean. You then camp overnight by the shores of Loch Monar, and on Day 2 return via the River Orrin and a traverse of Bac an Eich, which gives good

Tourist Information

There is a large, and very busy, tourist information centre in Inverness, on Bridge Street beneath the castle (tel 01463 234353). You can book accommodation here for a stay in Inverness or further afield.

Transport

There is no bus service to the start of this walk, so you need to drive from Inverness. Head for Ullapool as far as Contin, the turn left at the western end of the village. Follow the minor road around Loch Achilty and onwards to the Loch Meig Dam. Drive over the dam and turn right onto the road into Strathconon. Continue right to the head of the glen where you'll find the car park.

Accommodation and Supplies

There isn't much accommodation in Strathconon, although the comfortable Achilty Hotel is nearby in Contin (tel 01997 421355, www.achiltyhotel.co.uk). It is also very feasible to stay in Inverness the night before and head out to Strathconon early in the morning of your first day's walk. There are no shops in Strathconon either, although Contin does have a small Spar shop and a petrol station.

Overnight Options Camp wild along the route. Somewhere along the northern shore of Loch Monar is usually a good bet, and the views up the loch to its head are superb in the evening sunlight.

Escape Routes

There is a stalker's track running through from the eastern end of Loch Monar to Inverchoran in Strathconon, via the River Orrin and Gleann Chorainn. This is the best way out of the mountains in this area. The stalker's track to the west of An Sidhean, which leads north to the River Meig, can be a good option for an escape route, but at times of spate the river can be difficult and even dangerous to cross.

views down the length of Strathconon. In all, a walk that is a really good backpacking route, or a very long single day for the hardened hillwalker.

DAY 1

Walk westwards along the road from the car park. Go over a cattle-grid, and at a junction follow the track to the left. This passes by a couple of houses, then beneath Scardroy Lodge. Continue along the track to the stalker's houses at **Scardroy**, then across open meadows with a little knoll to your left (now planted with young trees). You should still be on the main track heading up the glen.

> There are very large herds of red deer in this area. Many people now believe that we don't have any pure-blood red deer left in Britain, as they hybridise with the introduced Sika deer, and this is thought to be the cause of the problem. Sika deer are generally smaller than red deer, and their coats turn very dark, almost black, in winter, when they also have spots on their coats. You can often see this in hybrids.

You soon reach a small house at Corrievuic with a junction just beyond. The track to the right heads through the glen to Achnashellach – itself a very fine walk, and a good way of combining this route with the one in the previous chapter. Our way, however, lies over the bridge to the left.

Once over the bridge, head for the ruined house at **Corriefeol**, where there is another junction of paths. Turn right and follow the path alongside the river, heading westwards. After a little over 1km the path turns to the south and begins to ascend steep slopes above a side stream in **Coire Mhoraigein**. Climb up this glen on the path that here is on the east side of the stream. The path leads up to a high col between **Bac an Eich** to the northeast and the long ridge leading to **An Sidhean** to the southwest. Continue right up to the head of the glen until you're almost at this col.

Now leave the path and climb up an open corrie to the south that brings you out onto a very broad ridge on the northeastern flank of **Sgurr Coire nan Eun**. From this ridge an easy

169

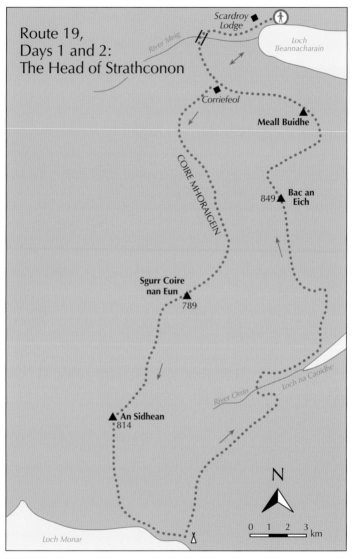

Route 19,
Days 1 and 2:
The Head of Strathconon

Scardroy Lodge

River Meig

Loch Beannacharain

Corriefeol

Meall Buidhe

COIRE MHOR AIGEIN

849 ▲ Bac an Eich

Sgurr Coire nan Eun ▲ 789

▲ An Sidhean 814

River Orrin

Loch na Caoidhe

N

0 1 2 3 km

Loch Monar

slope to the southwest takes you onto a more obvious ridge leading to the summit of this fine little hill at 789m.

> To the southeast, across the deep trench holding the River Orrin, lie the Glen Strathfarrar Munros. This is a popular ridge walk over four magnificent mountains, plus a number of minor tops. The Munros as you look at them from Sgurr Coire nan Eun are, from right to left, Sgurr Fhuar-thuill, Sgurr a' Choire Ghlais, Carn nan Gobhar and, just out of sight, Sgurr na Ruaidhe.

Walk west down easy slopes, then southwest around the head of Coire a' Chrotha to a ridge leading over a broad whale-back. West of here the ridge continues as a great plateau with a slight dip down to a col, the very easy slopes rising to the summit of An Sidhean to the west. The summit lies just north-west of a pair of lochans at 814m.

From the summit, head south down a lovely ridge known as Mullach a' Gharbh-leathaid to a knoll at 690m. Now continue southwards until you pick up a good stalker's track that takes you down to the shores of **Loch Monar**, where the Allt na Cois flows into it. You can either find somewhere around here to camp for the night, or head eastwards along the track above the loch to camp at the outflow of the Allt a' Choire Dhomhain.

DAY 2

East of the Allt na Cois the path splits where it enters the valley formed by the Allt a' Choire Dhomhain. The path going straight ahead continues around Loch Monar to Monar Lodge, whereas the path on the left, going up the Allt a' Choire Dhomhain, leads back towards Strath Conan.

Take the path as it climbs along the western side of the Allt a' Choire Dhomhain, ignoring the branch off to the left, which gains the ridge of Druim Dubh. Your path crosses this ridge further to the northeast, right at the very head of the glen, then drops down to the **River Orrin** at a point 2km above **Loch na Caoidhe**.

Cross the River Orrin to its north side and here you'll pick up a path running through the glen. Turn right along this path

Barn owls hunt in the lower reaches of Strathconon

and follow it to Loch na Caoidhe. The path cuts along the northern side of the loch, and about a third of the way along its length there is another track leaving the main one and climbing steeply uphill to the northeast.

Climb up this track to a high col where you come across another junction. Turn left here along a path that skirts around to the south ridge of Bac an Eich. (If you continue along this track you come out on the col above Coire Mhoraigein, where you started on the climb up Sgurr Coire nan Eun yesterday.)

Once on the south ridge of Bac an Eich you can leave the path and begin the straightforward ascent of this fine mountain. Climb northwards up the ridge directly to the summit. The top is marked by on OS trig pillar at 849m.

Golden eagles are regularly seen from the summit of Bac an Eich, and indeed all along the length of Strath Conan. They change their nest sites annually, and so can be seen in slightly different parts of their territory each year.

From the summit of Bac an Eich you need to descend the steep slopes to the northeast, and this is much easier if you first go northwest for perhaps 300–400m down an easy ridge, then cut back to the northeast to a col between Bac an Eich and **Meall Buidhe**.

The River Meig at the head of Strathconon

Snipe can be seen in the middle reaches of Strathconon

From the col climb eastwards to the summit ridge of Meall Buidhe, turning northwards to gain the top of this superb viewpoint. A lovely walk to the west down a steepening ridge leads you through heather to Corriefeol and the bridge over the River Meig. Cross the bridge and turn right to return to your car beyond Scardroy Lodge.

ROUTE 20
The High Traverse of Glen Affric

Number of Days	3
Total Distance	59km (37 miles)
Daily Distances	Day 1 – 24km (15 miles), Day 2 – 18km (11.25 miles), Day 3 – 17km (10.75 miles)
Height Gain	Total: 3400m; Day 1 – 1790m, Day 2 – 1480m, Day 3 – 130m
Maps	OS Landranger sheet 25 Glen Carron
Starting Point	There's a small car park on the road side in Glen Affric (grid ref NH215242). This is at the point where the road goes over the Abhainn Gleann nam Fiadh by the bridge almost at the western end of Loch Beinn a' Mheadhoin. Park sensibly on the left (south side) of the road in the lay-by.

Area Summary

A very popular area for walkers and backpackers, with some superb mountain ridges, including a number of very good Munros. The glen itself is a national nature reserve, containing an important habitat, in the form of Caledonian pine forest. This lovely area of stunning Scots pines is a unique habitat, upon which rely a number of species endemic to Britain, making a walk here all the more special. There are only a handful of ancient pine woodlands like this left in Scotland.

This wilderness area is sandwiched between Loch Ness and the Great Glen in the south, and the remote lands of the Strath Conan Forest and the Achnashellach mountains to the north.

Route Summary

This is quite a tough route for backpacking, taking in all the Munros on the north side of Glen Affric, and finishing with a stunningly beautiful walk through the forests in the glen itself. The suggested route does this walk in three days, but if you're really fit you might like to do it in two. Much of the route is along mountain ridges, occasionally on paths and tracks, but it can only really be recommended for those with a good deal of experience in mountain walking in Scotland.

On Day 1 you leave the glen almost immediately and make for the eastern-most Munro in this area, Toll Creagach. It's then a long ridge walk westwards over Tom a' Choinich to Carn Eige. After a slight diversion to the summit of Mam Sodhail, you go back over Carn Eige and northwards to Beinn Fhionnlaidh, overlooking lonely Loch Mullardoch, to camp down by the shore of the loch. On Day 2 the walk takes you over Mullach na Dheiragain to Sgurr nan Ceathreamhnan, then eastwards to An Socach. You then descend to the Allt Beithe youth hostel for the night, right at the head of Glen Affric. On Day 3 forest tracks lead you through the glen and back to your car.

Tourist Information
There is a large and very busy tourist information centre in Inverness, on Bridge Street beneath the castle (tel 01463 234353). You can book accommodation here for a stay in Inverness or further afield.

Transport
There is no bus service to the start of this walk so you'll need to drive from Inverness. Head towards Fort William on the A82 as far as Drumnadrochit. Here you should turn right for Cannich. Go through Cannich village to the T-junction with traffic lights to your right and the continuation of the village street to your left. Turn left here and follow the signs for Glen Affric, with a right turn onto the dead-end road at a power station. Follow the road up the glen (perhaps with a brief stop off at the Dog Falls on the way) and park in the lay-by just before the bridge near the western end of Loch Bheinn a' Mheadhoin.

Accommodation and Supplies
There is nothing in Glen Affric itself, although there is a run-down hotel in Cannich, and a nice, basic youth hostel. Contact the SYHA central booking service for information on opening, prices and booking (tel 0870 155255, www.syha.org.uk). There is also an independent hostel next door to the SYHA hostel (tel 01456 415263), as well as a campsite (tel 01456 415364). For hotel accommodation I would recommend the Tomich Hotel (tel 01456 415399), just a short drive southwest of Cannich.

Overnight Options

Camp wild along the route. Somewhere along the southwestern shore of Loch Mullardoch is usually a good place for your first night out, while on your second you can camp near Allt Beithe youth hostel, or stay in the hostel itself. Contact the SYHA central booking service for information on opening, prices and booking (tel 0870 155255, www.syha.org.uk). The Mountain Bothies Association maintains an open shelter at Camban (grid ref NH054184), which is 4km southwest of the hostel at Allt Beithe. Though slightly off this route, it makes for a really useful base for your second night, or if you want to climb some more hills in this area. You can join the Mountain Bothies Association at www.mountainbothies.org.uk.

Escape Routes

The only feasible escape route from anywhere on this walk is to make your way into Glen Affric and pick up one of the tracks eastwards back towards Cannich. You can get down into Glen Affric from most points along the ridge, although as much of it on Day 2 is to the north of the ridge, this makes getting out of the hills in an emergency very problematic. If you're down by Loch Mullardoch and you need to escape, the best option may well be to head west for Killilan on Loch Long, or Morvich in Strath Croe. Do bear in mind, though, that both these routes are very long in themselves, and are in the wrong direction.

DAY 1

From the car park you'll see a track on the other side of the road heading westwards along the northern bank of the Abhainn Gleann nam Fiadh (this is on the north side of the bridge). Take this track and follow it as it curves around to the north through delightful open woodland.

When we think of the ancient forests that once cloaked Britain, we often have a vision of dense and lush woodlands. This was not actually the case – the original woodlands of Britain were often quite open, with a mix of species. Here in the Highlands the species you'd expect to find in a native woodland are Scots pines (the Scots themselves call these Caledonian pines, or even just 'calies'), birch, alder, rowan, and perhaps some

Glen Affric

oak and beech. The woodlands here in Glen Affric are a good example of this, with Scots pines predominating, but a mix of other species present too.

The track takes you up a wonderful Highland glen into the heart of the mountains. Where it starts to turn towards the west, you should look for a junction with a path running off to the northeast into a very broad col between **Beinn a' Mheadhoin** to the southeast and **Beinn Eun** to the northwest. Take this path into the boggy col. Before you reach the stream of Allt Coire an t-Sneachda, climb up rough slopes to the northwest, steeply at first but soon easing off slightly, until you're on the broad, grassy ridge between Beinn Eun and the summit of **Toll Creagach.** Turn northwards and climb up the ridge to the top. The summit is at 1053m and marked by an Ordnance Survey trig pillar.

Head westwards, then slightly south of west down to the ridge with a minor top at the head of Choire Odhair. Go over this grassy ridge and down to the Bealach Toll Easa. Above this, the route onto the next summit, **Tom a' Choinich**, looks quite steep and intimidating. In actual fact it is easy, and a very pleasant way onto the summit. Climb this east ridge to

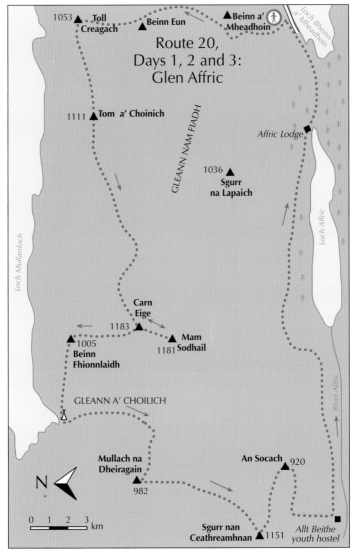

Route 20,
Days 1, 2 and 3:
Glen Affric

1053 ▲ Toll
Creagach
▲ Beinn Eun
▲ Beinn a'
Mheadhoin

1111 ▲ Tom a' Choinich

Affric Lodge

GLEANN NAM FIADH

1036 ▲
Sgurr
na Lapaich

Loch Bheinn a' Mheadhoin

Loch Affric

Loch Mullardoch

Carn
Eige
1183 ▲
▲ Mam
1181 Sodhail

▲ 1005
Beinn
Fhionnlaidh

GLEANN A' CHOILICH

River Affric

N

Mullach na
Dheiragain
▲
982

An Socach ▲ 920

0 1 2 3
km

Sgurr nan
Ceathreamhnan ▲ 1151

*Allt Beithe
youth hostel*

the top, with the summit set slightly to the southwest at 1111m. The continuation is now long and rewarding. The route stays high all the way to **Carn Eige**, giving magnificent views to **Loch Mullardoch** to the north and across to **Sgurr na Lapaich** above **Gleann nam Fiadh** to the south.

Head west down a narrowing ridge and follow it throughout, over numerous bumps and knolls, until you're above Loch a' Choire Dhomhain, which lies on the north side of the ridge 3–4km west of Tom a' Choinich. As you pass Loch a' Choire Dhomhain you come to a junction of ridges. Ignore the one swinging away to the northeast, and instead head southwest along the ridge and up to the summit of Carn Eige at 1183m.

The route to your overnight campsite lies to the north, but for a little more effort you could climb **Mam Sodhail**, just over 1km away to the south. You could probably even leave your rucksack on the summit of Carn Eige, as you have to return this way.

Drop down to the southwest to a narrow nick above Loch Uaine, then up the ridge beyond to the summit of Mam Sodhail at 1181m. Return the same way to Carn Eige.

Head northwest from Carn Eige down the ridge to spot height 917m, then down to a bealach just beyond. Ahead lies the final climb of the day, **Beinn Fhionnlaidh**. An easy ridge takes you up to its summit at 1005m.

Walk northwards along the ridge for a short way, then descend the steep slopes to the northwest, down towards the head of Loch Mullardoch. You can either camp here by the loch, or walk around to the south into the glen and camp there.

DAY 2

Go south from the head of Loch Mullardoch into the very deep and impressive trench of **Gleann a' Choilich** – there is a vague path that stays on the east side of the glen. After 3.5km you need to be thinking about crossing the river, and in spate it may be necessary to go some way beyond this point and return on the other (east) side.

You are aiming for the steep and imposing east ridge of **Mullach na Dheiragain**, which rises to the left of a corrie as you look up at it. Gain this ridge and climb up to some rocks ringing the summit plateau. These are easily bypassed, and you then walk to the right around the rim of the plateau to gain the summit at 982m.

Now a lovely ridge walk awaits. From the summit of Mullach na Dheiragain head southwest along the spine of the ridge, walking down to a col, then over an unnamed bealach overlooking the delightful hidden tarn of An Gorm Lochan to the west. The steep top. The ridge here is quite rocky, but nowhere difficult, and soon leads you down to a summit slopes of **Sgurr nan Ceathreamhnan** now rise via a narrow crest to the southwest. From the bealach gain this ridge and follow it steeply and directly to the summit at 1151m.

> Looking to the southwest from Sgurr nan Ceathreamhnan the view is dominated by the bulk of Beinn Fhada, while to the west the shapely peak of A' Ghlas-bheinn rises above the rough corrie of Gleann Gaorsaic.

From the summit of Sgurr nan Ceathreamhnan head southeast to a ridge, following it eastwards along its narrow crest and down to a cleft. Immediately south from this cleft is a path that takes you directly to the youth hostel at **Allt Beithe**. You can follow this path and be down at the hostel door in half an hour, but for just a little more effort you could continue along the ridge to add another Munro to your tally.

Climb eastwards from the crest to a slight rise on a broad ridge, then continue up steepening slopes to the summit of **An Socach** at 920m.

> From the top of An Socach the views are a little restricted, but you can see right across the head of Loch Affric to the southeast to the delightful rolling heather country around Carn Glas Iochdarach. This lovely little hill has its feet in some of the most wonderful pine forests in Scotland.

From the summit of An Socach you can either retrace your steps back to the cleft on the ridge to the west, then down the path to the youth hostel, or head south on a ridge until easy angled and open slopes on your right lead you down into Coire na Cloiche, where you'll pick up the same path.

Turn southwards and follow this down the corrie to one of the most stunningly located hostels in Britain.

If you're staying at the hostel you'll have time to kick back and relax, but those heading for Camban bothy must first walk down to the banks of the **River Affric** to the southwest. Follow a path that stays on the north side of the river, ignoring another climbing away to the right. Cross two streams and follow the path going southwest, climbing some way above the river after the second stream has been crossed. Camban bothy lies a couple of kilometres up Fionngleann, nestled in between Beinn Fhada on the north side and Ciste Dubh to the south. You'll have to walk back to Allt Beithe to start the walk on Day 3.

DAY 3

After the rigours of the last two days you'll probably be ready for something a little easier, and today you head through Glen Affric itself, enjoying the lovely pine forests as you go.

Begin by heading eastwards along the north side of the River Affric. This is a well-beaten track, often used by people staying at the hostel, or by those going cross-country from west to east or vice versa.

The track is always easy to follow, although it can be a bit boggy after rain. You cross the stream known as the Allt Coire Ghaidheil, and just beyond this ignore the path going down to the river on the right. Continue eastwards over more streams to a little tarn. Beyond this the track climbs slightly to the knoll known as Cnoc Fada, and just beyond this you drop down into a little dip and the track rises over another bump. At the dip between the two there is a path on the left that you should take. This goes northeastwards around the uphill side of Loch Coulavie, and contours at more or less this level across the hillside above Loch Affric. Follow this path into the open pine woods above the northern shore of Loch Affric.

Keep a look out in the treetops for the Scottish crossbill – these chunky looking finches are native only to Scots pines in the Highlands. The male crossbill is reddish-orange and the female is green. Also in the pine trees, but often lower

down and therefore easier to see are crested tits. These are about the same size as a blue tit or coal tit, but are black and white-headed with creamy brown sides. As their name suggests, they have a large crest on top of their heads. Again, you'll only see these birds in ancient Caledonian pines in Scotland.

The Scottish wildcat is a secretive predator

The path keeps high above the loch right to its eastern end, where it eventually drops down to **Affric Lodge**. Ignore tracks going towards the lodge itself, but continue eastwards along the north side of the loch to the end of the public road. All you need to do now is follow the road eastwards for 2km and you'll find yourself back at the car park above the western end of Loch Beinn a' Mheadhoin.

ROUTE 21
Beinn Fhada and A' Ghlas Bheinn

Number of Days	2
Total Distance	35km (21.75 miles)
Daily Distances	Day 1 – 19km (11.75 miles), Day 2 – 16km (10 miles)
Height Gain	Total: 1750m; Day 1 – 930m, Day 2 – 820m
Maps	OS Landranger sheet 33 Loch Alsh, Glen Shiel and Loch Hourn
Starting Point	You can park in Morvich on a side road from the main A87(T through Kintail. There's a campsite here with a visitor centre, and you should leave your car here (grid ref NG961210).

Area Summary

A fairly quiet region of magnificent mountains, including two important Munros. Considering the nearness to the main peaks of Kintail, few people go into this particular area other than by taking the standard Munro-bagger's route up Beinn Fhada. On this walk that approach is used only for the descent at the end of Day 2. You are unlikely to come across any other walkers on this route until then.

Beinn Fhada lies between the very head of Glen Affric, which cuts into the main mountain mass of Scotland from the east at Cannich, and Loch Duich on the west coast near Kintail. To the south of Beinn Fhada is a deep glen with the Five Sisters of Kintail rising on the other side, to its north a high bealach from where a pleasant ridge takes you northwards to A' Ghlas Bheinn.

Route Summary

A short backpacking route that could be done in a single day if you wanted. The going underfoot is not too strenuous either, and good tracks are made use of for the approaches to the hills. Both Munros now have paths appearing on their ridges – testament to the number of feet that Munro-bagging brings to otherwise wild parts of the country.

The route starts up Strath Croe, where forestry tracks lead up onto the northwest ridge of A' Ghlas Bheinn. This ridge is followed to the summit, then a nice descent is taken to the bealach between this peak and Beinn Fhada. The descent continues to the east into the head of Glen Affric, where you can camp, or use the youth hostel, or a nearby bothy. On Day 2 you climb the superb and wild eastern ridge of Beinn Fhada, following a line of cliffs around to the summit plateau. The descent is then back to the bealach passed over yesterday and down into the forests of Strath Croe.

Tourist Information
There's a good tourist information centre in Kyle of Lochalsh down by the harbour (tel 01599 534276).

Transport
Citylink buses from either Fort William or Inverness pass through Kintail (tel 08705 505050, www.citylink.co.uk).

Accommodation and Supplies
There are quite a few accommodation options in the Kintail area, but whenever I'm staying in this region I choose either the cheap option of camping at Shiel Bridge (grid ref NG938186), or the much more comfortable one of staying at Conchra House Hotel on Loch Long near Dornie, tel 01599 555233, www.conchra.co.uk, sales@conchrahouse.co.uk. Other places to stay nearby are Ratagan youth hostel – contact the central booking service of the SYHA, tel 0870 155255, www.syha.org.uk – or the Morvich Caravan Club Site, tel 01599 511354, which is where this walk starts. Tourist offices can give further information on other places to stay locally.

There are a few shops in the Kintail area where you can buy supplies, including a well-stocked petrol station-cum-shop at Shiel Bridge, or you can find small supermarkets in Kyle of Lochalsh just west along the A87(T).

Overnight Options
Camp wild along the route or book into the Allt Beithe youth hostel – contact the SYHA central booking service for information on opening, prices and

booking (tel 0870 155255, www.syha.org.uk). The Mountain Bothies Association maintains an open shelter at Camban (grid ref NH054184), which is 4km southwest of the hostel at Allt Beithe. You can join the MBA on their website www.mountainbothies.org.uk.

Escape Routes
From the Bealach na Sgairne, which lies between A' Ghlas Bheinn and Beinn Fhada, it is a simple matter of heading west on the tracks that lead down Strath Croe. From the head of Glen Affric, Allt Beithe youth hostel or Camban bothy you can go up Fionngleann and over a low pass (361m) that takes you into Gleann Lichd. Good paths lead right over this pass and down the glen to Morvich.

DAY 1

Begin by following the road eastwards from the entrance to the countryside centre at **Morvich**. This soon becomes a track and you should turn left down to the River Croe at a bridge. Cross over the river here, enjoying the view up **Gleann Lichd** as you cross. ◀

As you look up Gleann Lichd from the bridge, the huge ramparts of the Five Sisters of Kintail rise to the right, while the impressively steep slopes of Beinn Fhada are to the left.

From Innis a' Chrotha a path heads north for the south side of the Abhainn Chonaig. Follow this down to the river and turn right, heading up the glen for 1.5km. Look for a path on the left that goes down a cleft to a wooden bridge deep within a beautiful gorge. Cross this bridge to the north side of the Abhainn Chonaig.

Look for dippers and grey wagtails as you cross the bridge. The woodland here is a mix of alder and birch, with the odd rowan thrown in for good measure, and in summer you should see a variety of woodland birds, including redstart, wood warbler and common tits and finches. In winter there are usually siskins and redpolls too.

Pick up the track past **Dorusduain** and follow it northwards through forestry plantations on the west side of a river. Ignore the first track going down to the river on the right, but look out for the second one, 700m beyond Dorusduain. Take this and cross the river. Continue northwards on the track

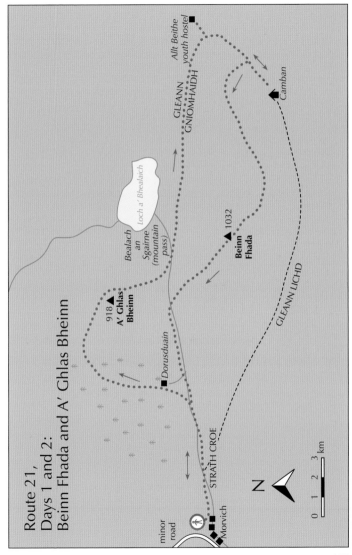

Route 21,
Days 1 and 2:
Beinn Fhada and A' Ghlas Bheinn

GLEANN GNIOMHAIDH

Allt Beithe youth hostel

Camban

loch a' Bhealaich

Bealach an Sgairne (mountain pass)

918 A' Ghlas Bheinn

1032 Beinn Fhada

GLEANN LICHD

Dorusduain

STRATH CROE

minor road

Morvich

N

0 1 2 3 km

alongside the river until you come clear of the trees, where the glen sweeps sharply to the east.

From this corner of the forest you should gain the other side of the deer fence to your right and pick up the steep lower slopes of the northwest ridge of **A' Ghlas Bheinn**. The going is steep at first, but soon eases off once you reach A' Mhuc. Above this the ridge becomes a little rockier and can be followed easily to the summit of A' Ghlas Bheinn at 918m.

On the rocky ridge on the way up, and around the summit, you may be lucky enough to see **ptarmigan**. These high-mountain members of the grouse family are superbly camouflaged against the grey rocks of summits, and in Britain are only found in the Scottish Highlands. They are much easier to see in the Cairngorms National Park than other mountain areas, but I have seen them here on **A' Ghlas Bheinn** on at least five occasions, the last time there being 12 birds in the flock, three males and nine females. In summer they are grey coloured, but in winter they turn white. The birds have feathers on their feet to stop them freezing in the cold temperatures of a Highland winter.

From the summit a lovely little path leads you southwards down an undulating ridge, passing above delightful Loch a' Chleirich, nestled in a quiet fold of the mountain on the west side of the ridge. Continue just east of south, down the ridge to the **Bealach an Sgairne**, a deep cleft lying between A' Ghlas Bheinn and Beinn Fhada.

At the bealach you meet a path that cuts over this rocky pass from west to east. The path to the west gives a good escape route back to Morvich, whereas heading east takes you into some really wild country.

Follow the path to the east, then southeast high above **Loch a' Bhealaich**, and then sloping down to the loch's southern shore. The path now leads into the steep-sided trench of **Gleann Gniomhaidh**. Stay on the path that lies on the north side of the stream as you walk down the glen. Where you reach the bottom of the glen you'll find the youth hostel at **Allt Beithe** just a little further along, on the north side of the infant River Affric.

Either spend the night here, or find an out-of-the-way spot for a wild campsite. Alternatively, you could head up

Fionngleann to the bothy at Camban. To get to Camban, head southwest from the point where you reach the bottom of Gleann Gniomhaidh. There is a path alongside the river here that then cuts up the hillside high above the stream that issues from Fionngleann. Camban lies nearly 3km up this glen.

A' Ghlas Bheinn from Beinn Fhada

DAY 2

Midway between Camban bothy and Allt Beithe youth hostel there is a point where you can leave the track and begin the climb onto the lovely east ridge of **Beinn Fhada**. Begin the day by climbing this ridge and following it to spot height 825m, which is a little knoll overlooking the impressive Coire an t-Siosalaich to the north. Beyond the knoll the ridge drops you into a small col, then you climb up to another minor top at 962m. Again, from here you get superb views down into the corries on the northern side of the range.

Continue heading westwards, gaining more height as you go, and you'll soon find yourself on the eastern tip of a large, high-altitude plateau, as the ridge curves to the north and flatter ground rolls away to the west. This is the wild summit plateau of Beinn Fhada (or 'Ben Attow' to give it its alternative spelling).

The OS map always gives both spellings for Beinn Fhada, implying that the mountain has two different names. This is not actually the case. Beinn Fhada should be pronounced 'ben atta', as 'fh' in this case is silent, and the 'd' is pronounced as a 't'. Ben Attow is merely an English attempt at spelling the name the way the locals pronounce it!

Once on the summit plateau you should stick close to the line of cliffs to your right, handrailing along these in a northerly direction to the summit of the mountain at 1032m. There is a summit shelter here and an OS trig pillar.

The way off Beinn Fhada lies to the northwest, but first, if the weather is good, it is well worth a detour across the plateau to the west, aiming just north of west across open, stony ground down to a high col 1.3km from the summit. From here climb the little peak to the northwest, at 954m, for great views down into the northern corries on this part of this massive mountain.

Now head eastwards, towards the top of the cliffs above Coire an Sgairne. Handrail around these cliffs to the east, getting great views down gullies and chimneys into the corrie itself as you go. Follow the rim of the corrie around, eastwards,

A winter backpack over Beinn Fhada

Mountain hare on Beinn Fhada

then turn northwards to pick up a path along the ridge top. Before reaching the Bealach an Sgairne that you passed over yesterday, the path shoots off to the northwest, zigzagging down through scree slopes into Coire an Sgairne itself. It is much easier to follow the path than to try to get to the bealach from above, as rocky ground bars the way in that direction.

The path leads across the eastern side of Coire an Sgairne, and beneath a fine series of waterfalls where this hanging valley has been cut off by the main valley below, joins the through-route from **Strath Croe** to the west leading over Bealach an Sgairne to the east. Turn left, westwards, and follow the path easily down into Strath Croe.

Note The Allt Coire an Sgairne can be difficult to cross lower down below the waterfalls if the stream is in spate. I often cross above the waterfalls and follow grassy slopes down to the western side of the stream to pick up the path at the bottom.

Once in Strath Croe the path leads down the glen and back over the bridge at Innis a' Chrotha and so back to Morvich.

ROUTE 22
The High Level Traverse of Glen Shiel

Number of Days	3
Total Distance	60km (37.5 miles)
Daily Distances	Day 1 – 22km (13.5 miles), Day 2 – 23km (14 miles), Day 3 – 15km (10 miles)
Height Gain	Total: 4610m; Day 1 – 2270m, Day 2 –1720m, Day 3 – 620m
Maps	OS Landranger sheet 33 Loch Alsh, Glen Shiel and Loch Hourn
Starting Point	Park on the minor road at Ault a' chruinn, just off the A87(T) in Kintail village. This is 750m north of Kintail Lodge Hotel, and is the minor road that leads to Morvich and the countryside centre and Caravan Club campsite.

Area Summary

Without a doubt, the mountains on either side of Glen Shiel, hemming you in as you drive along the A87(T), provide among the very best ridge walks in Scotland, giving the hardened hillwalker the opportunity to 'bag' a number of Munros on either side of the glen. It has to be said that these mountains are probably hardly ever covered by backpackers, and certainly not often in one expedition.

From the west, as you drive alongside Loch Duich, you first see the Five Sister of Kintail rising above the village. Beyond this the road is hemmed in on all sides by huge-looking mountains. Along the ridge the summits continue in a long line beyond the Five Sisters, leading eventually to a deep glen, the An Caorann Beag. At this point the ridge sweeps away to the north towards Glen Affric, and here it is best to make for the Cluanie Inn, which sits beside the A87(T). South of the road and Glen Shiel itself lies, not surprisingly, the South Glen Shiel Ridge, a wonderful outing in its own right, but one that you will complete in its entirety, something that few walkers can claim to have done.

North of the Five Sisters and its continuation the mountains roll on to Beinn Fhada (covered in Route 21) and the Munros of Glen Affric, whereas to the south of the South Glen Shiel Ridge you'll find more tempting peaks in the Glen Quoich and Knoydart regions.

Route Summary

Although this is a must for any keen hillwalker, it is an expedition that should not be undertaken lightly. It is without a doubt the most difficult route in this book, and although it is possible to escape the ridge, you can't do this easily at all points of the traverse.

The route starts by crossing the classic Five Sisters of Kintail from west to east, then, where other walkers head for the glen, you continue along the high ridge over three more Munros before dropping down to the Cluanie Inn for the night. On Day 2 you follow another superb ridge walk, the South Glen Shiel Traverse, to a high and wild campsite along the ridge. On Day 3 the route takes you over Sgurr na Sgine, and gives you the option of a scramble over the Saddle before heading towards Shiel Bridge. The Saddle can be avoided if you do not have a head for scrambling.

Tourist Information
There's a good tourist information centre in Kyle of Lochalsh down by the harbour (tel 01599 534276), and another good one in Fort Augustus for those coming from that direction (tel 01320 366367).

Transport
Citylink buses from either Fort William or Inverness pass through Kintail, tel 08705 505050, www.citylink.co.uk.

Accommodation and Supplies
As I said in Route 21, whenever I'm staying in this region I either go for the cheap option of camping at Shiel Bridge (grid NG938186), or the much more comfortable one of staying at Conchra House Hotel on Loch Long near Dornie, tel 01599 555233, www.conchra.co.uk, sales@conchrahouse.co.uk. Other places to stay nearby are Ratagan Youth Hostel – contact the central booking service of the SYHA, tel 0870 155255, www.syha.org.uk, or the Morvich Caravan Club

campsite, tel 01599 511354, a little further along the road from the start of this walk. Tourist offices can give further information on other places to stay locally.

There are a few shops in the Kintail area where you can buy supplies, including a well-stocked petrol station-cum-shop at Shiel Bridge, or there are small supermarkets in Kyle of Lochalsh, just west along the A87(T).

Overnight Options
On Day 1 it's a real treat to stay at the Cluanie Inn (tel 01320 340238) after a hard day on the hill. You can probably get them to let you camp nearby and still have a good meal at the inn with a few pints of Blaven or Young Pretender before turning into your bag. If you plan ahead you could even drop off your tent and sleeping bag here on the drive through to the start of the walk, so that on Day 1 you'll only have a light rucksack. Just a thought, and of course it does mean you'll have to get to the Cluanie Inn that night!

On Day 2 you'll be camping somewhere along the South Glen Shiel Ridge, which offers plenty of choice. You'll probably find yourself somewhere in the vicinity of Bealach Duibh Leac, between Creag nam Damh and Sgurr na Sgine, but anywhere that suits you will be fine.

Escape Routes
At any point along the route you could pick a careful way down to the A87(T) running through Glen Shiel. This is the main 'Road to the Isles' and always has some traffic, so stick out your thumb and you'll be out of the mountains in no time. It's worth marking a few possible routes down off the ridges beforehand, as some routes are steep and scrambly, and not very good for backpackers! The hardest bits to get are the Five Sisters, right at the start of the walk, and around Maol Chinn-dearg on the South Glen Shiel Ridge. Also, it's worth avoiding heading off the ridge between Sgurr an Lochain and Sgurr Beag, as you'll have to wade the River Shiel in order to reach the road.

DAY 1

Today you take on the challenge of the Five Sisters of Kintail, traversing their length from west to east and finishing by continuing along the ridge and down to the **Cluanie Inn**, where you can have a good meal and a comfortable bed for the night. Begin by following the path up the north side of the Allt a' Chruinn from the minor road just off the A87(T). The path is clear underfoot, but steep at the start of the day. Where the path seems to fade, continue alongside the stream right to the

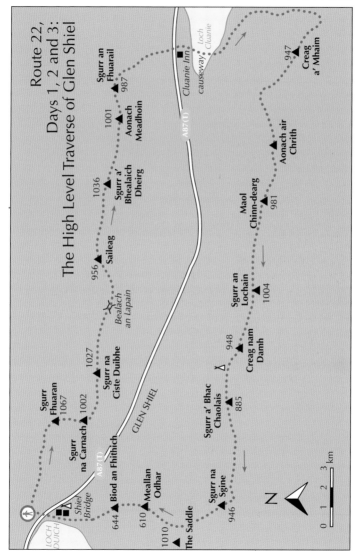

Route 22,
Days 1, 2 and 3:
The High Level Traverse of Glen Shiel

Glen Shiel Munros in winter

top where it begins at a col between Sgurr na Moraich and Beinn Bhuidhe. Once on the ridge turn southwestwards and handrail along the edge of the cliffs to your left until you are on the summit of Beinn Bhuidhe at 869m.

Beinn Bhuidhe marks the start (or more usually, the end) of the Five Sisters (most walkers do the traverse from east to west). The rocky ridge is obvious, and you should follow it to Sgurr nan Saighead, with its fine summit at 929m giving great views down into Gleann Lichd and across to Beinn Fhada to the east.

Head southeastwards down to a col, then pick up a vague path that cuts across the northwest face of Sgurr Fhuaran. This path gains the west ridge of **Sgurr Fhuaran**, and once you're on it you can turn to the east and climb up rocky slopes to the summit at 1067m.

A really fine ridge now takes you southwards. (Do not be tempted to follow the east ridge – although it's a fine walk in itself, in bad weather it has been known to lead people off the main ridge on the wrong side, down into Gleann Lichd, which is a long way to walk in the wrong direction!). A stony col lies between Sgurr Fhuaran and Sgurr na Carnach, and from the col it is easy enough to gain the summit at 1002m.

The way now leads you down steep slopes to the south into a deep col, and from there you can climb the superb northwest ridge of **Sgurr na Ciste Duibhe.**

The name Sgurr na Ciste Duibhe translates as 'Peak of the Black Chest', and it has a wonderful summit with fine views in all directions, including a particularly good view of the South Glen Shiel Ridge.

The ridge now leads you down to the east, into yet another col, before the climb up to Sgurr nan Spainteach at 990m.

Sgurr nan Spainteach translates as 'Peak of the Spaniards', from the Battle of Glenshiel in 1719. A small group of Jacobites had come ashore on Loch Duich at **Eilean Donan Castle**, supported by 300 Spanish soldiers. They were set upon by an army of Hanoverians and chased into Glen Shiel. Gaining the uphill advantage on the slopes of what is now Sgurr nan Spainteach, it looked promising for the Jacobite force until the Hanoverians had the idea of setting the hillside alight. The Jacobites and their Spanish comrades where forced to hastily retreat up the peak as the heather burned around them – some may even have summited!

Beyond Sgurr nan Spainteach the ridge drops more gently to a grassy col, known as the **Bealach an Lapain**, from where you should climb the easy ridge to the summit of **Saileag** at 958m.

Onwards towards the east the ridge continues, and gets a bit narrower and more rocky as you approach **Sgurr a' Bhealaich Dheirg.** You'll reach a drystone wall ('drystane dyke' if you're a Scot!) that leads along a northeast ridge, off the main ridge, and the summit lies 100m along this northeast ridge. Follow the wall along the narrow ridge to this splendidly exposed summit at 1036m.

Just one more twin-peaked mountain to end the day! Return to the main ridge and follow easy slopes down to the southeast where the ridge splits. Make sure you go eastwards down to a deeper col, from where you can pick up the continuation ridge rising in rocky steps to the summit of **Aonach Meadhoin** at 1001m. The top lies on a small, level plateau and is marked by a cairn.

Eilean Donan is near
the start of Day 1

There is a minor top to the northeast of Aonach Meadhoin that must be traversed before you head for the pub. Follow the ridge, which is quite narrow at times but nowhere difficult, to the northeast. The top of the twin peak to Aonach Meadhoin is known as **Sgurr an Fhuarail** at 987m. An excellent route down to the southeast takes you along a lovely ridge over a little knoll at 864m, then down heathery and grassy slopes to the Cluanie Inn at the western end of **Loch Cluanie**.

> The Cluanie Inn is an old coaching inn on the Road to the Isles. It was here that Dr Johnson stayed and first had the idea of keeping a journal of his travels.

DAY 2

The Cluanie Inn stands beside a small loch at the western end of Loch Cluanie. This is really part of the larger loch, but has been separated from it by a short causeway and bridge. Begin the day by heading east for a short way on the A87, and just beyond the buildings of the Cluanie Inn you'll find the track leading southwards over this bridge. This is a good track and makes getting to the base of **Creag a' Mhaim** relatively straightforward. Follow the track all the way around to the eastern pass that leads through to Loch Loyne.

From here rough slopes lead up onto the southeast ridge of Creag a' Mhaim, but you can pick up a good stalker's path. This is excellent once you've gained it, and leads easily to the summit of this fine eastern outpost of the South Glen Shiel Ridge. The summit is at 947m, and lies right on the edge of the northern cliffs, from where there is a good view across to yesterday's hills.

Pick up the path along the northwestern ridge of Creag a' Mhaim and follow it down to a col above Coireachan Gorma (meaning 'the Blue Corries'). An easy ridge then takes you up to the top of Druim Shionnach at 987m.

The ridge continuing westwards is never hard to follow, as there is now an eroded path all the way. Pass over the minor tops at 938m, then into a col before **Aonach air Chrith**. The ridge is now a little rockier and takes you to the summit at 1021m. Narrower now, but never difficult, the ridge takes you over **Maol Chinn-dearg** (981m) to Sgurr an Doire Leathain, at 1010m.

> The view southwards from here is across Glen Quoich to the Munros of Gleouraich and Spidean Mialach to the east, and Sgurr a' Mhaoraich to the west. Between the two you'll see Loch Quoich.

The next summit is **Sgurr an Lochain** at 1004m, a fine conical peak giving good views in all directions. Next go downhill to Sgurr Beag at 986m. A low bealach lies between this peak and the final Munro on the South Glen Shiel Ridge at the head of Am Fraoch-choire, 'the Heather Corrie'.

From the bealach an easy ridge leads to the summit of **Creag nam Damh** at 918m. A lovely ridge walk to the west takes you in 2km down to the Bealach Duibh Leac, where you will probably be ready for somewhere to camp. A steep path zigzags down slopes on the north side of the bealach, leading into a fine corrie where I've camped a number of times, or in good weather why not camp on the bealach itself? You'll get great views in the morning if you point your tent door towards the east.

DAY 3

From the Bealach Duibh Leac an easy ridge undulates to the summit of **Sgurr a' Bhac Chaolais** at 885m, from where you should drop down to the west to a col before the steep slopes of Sgurr na Sgine. Climb up towards the summit cliffs of **Sgurr na Sgine**, and outflank the cliffs by heading southwestwards to bypass the crags and gain the easy south ridge of the mountain. Follow this ridge directly to the top at 946m.

Descend to the northwest, then northwards to a col where a fine crescent curves around to Faochag to the east. From this col make your way down rough slopes to the northwest to a lower col with a small lochan, known as the Bealach Coire Mhalagain. From the bealach the impressively steep slopes of **the Saddle** rise above you.

The only good way onto this fine mountain from this direction is a narrow scramble known as the Forcan Ridge. It is possibly not the best place for the backpacker, although it is nowhere very difficult. You can reach the Forcan Ridge to the northeast of the Bealach Coire Mhalagain, above a drystone wall. A stiff climb gains the ridge from where the narrow crest leads westwards to the summit at 1010m. This is a truly magnificent expedition, but you need a head for heights to tackle it.

If it's not for you, it's probably best to head northeast from the Bealach Coire Mhalagain, following the line of the drystone wall, to pick up a good stalker's track that leads over **Meallan Odhar** at 610m. Just north of this little hill the path shoots off into the glen on your right, leading to the road a long way short of **Shiel Bridge**. Better instead to continue northwards over the easy and undulating terrain of **Biod an Fhithich** at 644m. This ridge forms a really nice end to the walk, and can be followed right down to the campsite at Shiel Bridge, thereby finishing a complete traverse of the rim of the glen. From Shiel Bridge a short walk along the road leads back to Ault a' chruinn.

ROUTE 23
Shiel Bridge to Glenfinnan

Number of Days	5
Total Distance	71km (44 miles)
Daily Distances	Day 1 – 16km (10 miles), Day 2 – 12km (7.5 miles), Day 3 – 13km (8 miles), Day 4 – 10km (6.25 miles), Day 5 – 20km (12.25 miles)
Height Gain	Total: 2310m; Day 1 – 760m, Day 2 – 210m, Day 3 – 560m, Day 4 – 360m, Day 5: 420m
Maps	OS Landranger sheets 33 Loch Alsh, Glen Shiel and Loch Hourn, and 40 Loch Shiel
Starting Point	Shiel Bridge, on the A87(T) between Glen Moriston and Kyle of Lochalsh (grid ref NG937187).
Finishing Point	Glenfinnan railway station, off the A830(T) between Fort William and Mallaig (grid ref NM899810).

Area Summary

This route passes through a number of important mountain regions of the northwest Highlands.

From Glen Shiel, where the Five Sisters tower above the glen, the route takes you through the mountains south of the glen. Loch Duich cuts deep into the land mass from the Kyle of Lochalsh, and the mountains here are popular with hill-walkers and sightseers alike. South of Glen Shiel the hills are less visited, until you drop into the head of Loch Hourn. This is another vast sea loch, cutting into the hills from the Sound of Sleat between the mainland and the Isle of Skye. The hills of the Knoydart peninsula rise magnificently to the west of this region, while the quieter wilderness of the Barrisdale Forest lies to the east.

This route passes between Knoydart and Barrisdale, cutting across the grain of the land to Loch Nevis, another important sea loch. Wilder country lies ahead as the walk goes first to Loch Arkaig, a huge freshwater loch running west to east, then a high pass is crossed to gain the long glen leading through to Glenfinnan on the West Highland railway line. This fantastic walk takes in all of these wonderful mountain tracts, cutting across via mountain passes and lovely lochsides.

Route Summary

This is a good route for those new to backpacking, or anyone who wants to really get to grips with some of the finest wilderness country in the western Highlands. The whole route can be done in three days, but I've divided it into five to allow for a more relaxed trip – you can of course take as long as you like! There are good paths and tracks for most of the way, with other route-finding being concerned mainly with following a glen in the right direction – it's quite hard to go wrong on this route!

On Day 1 you leave Glen Shiel and head over a pass between the mountains known as the Saddle and Sgurr na Sgine, then a track is picked up that leads you down into Kinloch Hourn. On Day 2 you follow what has been called one of the greatest coastal walks in the world. The scenery along Loch Hourn really is stunning, and you follow a good path westwards to Barrisdale where you can camp for the night. On Day 3 a good track takes you high above the glens to the Mam Unndalain, a pass between Luinne Bheinn and Sgurr a' Choire-bheithe. A shortcut is then taken to pick up a path down Glen Carnach and around the head of Loch Nevis to the bothy at Sourlies.

A walk over the Mam na Cloich Airde on Day 4 leads through to Glen Dessary, where you can stay at A' Chuil bothy near the western end of Loch Arkaig. Day 5 takes you off the beaten track a little as you cross a high pass to gain the last downhill stretch into Glenfinnan, finishing the walk at the memorial to Bonnie Prince Charlie on the shores of Loch Shiel. A wonderful walk, and one not to be missed.

Tourist Information

You'll find a good tourist information centre in Kyle of Lochalsh down by the harbour (tel 01599 534276), another good one in Fort Augustus, for those coming from that direction (tel 01320 366367), or at Cameron Square in Fort William (tel 01397 703781).

Transport
Citylink buses from either Fort William or Inverness pass through Kintail and will drop you off at Shiel Bridge (tel 08705 505050, www.citylink.co.uk). There are trains from Glenfinnan through to Fort William and onwards to Glasgow, tel 08457 550033, www.firstgroup.com/scotrail.

Accommodation and Supplies at the Start of the Route
Camping at Shiel Bridge at the start of this walk is a good option (grid ref NG938186), or there's the much more comfortable choice of staying at Conchra House Hotel on Loch Long near Dornie, tel 01599 555233, www.conchra.co.uk, sales@conchrahouse.co.uk. Other places to stay nearby are Ratagan youth hostel – contact the central booking service of the SYHA, tel 0870 155255, www.syha.org.uk, – or the Morvich Caravan Club site (tel 01599 511354) a little further along the road from the starting point. Tourist offices can give further information on other places to stay locally.

There are a few shops in the Kintail area where you can buy supplies, including a well-stocked petrol station-cum-shop at Shiel Bridge, or you can find small supermarkets in Kyle of Lochalsh, west along the A87(T).

Accommodation and Supplies at the End of the Route
From Glenfinnan it's a good idea to head for Fort William, where you'll find lots of places to stay and eat. I highly recommend Myrtle Bank Guest House just south of the town centre (tel 01397 702034). There's also Berkeley House, which is also a pleasant place to stay, tel 01397 701185, e-mail berkeleyhouse67@hotmail.com.

Overnight Options
On the first night you should ask at one of the farms at Kinloch Hourn for permission to camp nearby. Barrisdale, on Day 2, has a campsite and bothy, for which there is a small charge (take some change to pay for this – just a couple of pounds per person). On Day 3 you can use the bothy at Sourlies, or camp nearby. Day 4 has the bothy at A' Chuil in Glen Dessary, or you can head around into Glen Pean where there is another bothy. On Day 5 you reach Glenfinnan and your onward train to Fort William, but if you would like one more night in the wilds before heading for civilisation, there is a bothy at Corryhully, 5km short of Glenfinnan, where you can spend the night and end the walk the following morning.

Escape Routes
On such a long and complicated route means of escape in an emergency are
many, but I will summarise the options, starting from the north and working
southwards.

- At Kinloch Hourn there is a road head with a few farms and cottages
  where help is available. There is a post bus service to Kinloch Hourn,
  and local people will be able to advise on this.
- From Barrisdale the easiest way out is by heading back to Kinloch
  Hourn. Another option is to head over the Mam Barrisdale, a high pass
  that leads easily through to Inverie in Knoydart. A long walk in the
  wrong direction, but with a pub at the end! You'll need to catch a ferry
  from Inverie to get out to Mallaig and the West Highland railway line.
- From Sourlies bothy the easiest way out is over the high pass, the Mam
  Meadail, which also leads to Inverie in Knoydart.
- From Glen Dessary you can walk out to Strathan at the head of Loch
  Arkaig where you may be able to get assistance in calling for a taxi from
  Fort William.

DAY 1

From **Shiel Bridge** head around to the little petrol station on
the A87(T) and go around the back and into the campsite.
Walk to the back of the campsite where you meet a track going
up the glen. This is a delightful way to start the walk, but where
the track goes down to cross the river at a bridge you should
head southeastwards and gain the ridge on the east side of the
glen. Once on the ridge follow it to the south over **Biod
an Fhithich** at 644m and on to **Meallan Odhar**, a rocky little
bump at 610m.

A path leads southwestwards to a drystone wall and on
to a broad col, the **Bealach Coire Mhalagain**. On the bealach
there is a small lochan amid stunning rocky scenery.

> The mountain to your right here is the Saddle, a fine peak
> that is popular with Munro-baggers. The rocky ridge you
> can see is the Forcan, a superb scramble for those with a
> good head for heights. To your left, south of the bealach,
> is Sgurr na Sgine, another lovely Munro.

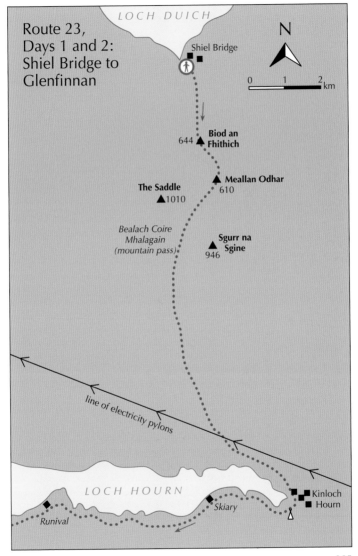

Route 23,
Days 1 and 2:
Shiel Bridge to
Glenfinnan

LOCH DUICH

N

Shiel Bridge

0   1   2 km

Biod an
Fhithich
644

Meallan Odhar
610

The Saddle
▲1010

Bealach Coire
Mhalagain
(mountain pass)

Sgurr na
Sgine
946

line of electricity pylons

LOCH HOURN

Kinloch
Hourn

Runival

Skiary

205

Glen Barrisdale

Cross over the pass and head down the other side, south-westwards at first, then curving to the south to gain a path. Follow this downhill to a junction of paths, and here you can cut off a corner by continuing down across the Allt a' Choire Reidh to pick up another path heading just east of south towards a line of electricity pylons (looking very out of place here in the 'wilderness' of the Kinloch Hourn Forest). Once at the pylons the path runs beneath them in a southeasterly direction, and leads easily through to **Kinloch Hourn** where you should spend the night.

DAY 2

This is, without a shadow of a doubt, the most beautiful section of the entire route, and should not be rushed. Wherever you spent the night, you should begin by heading down to the tarmac road that ends at a small car park on the south side of the river. Follow the road westwards until it becomes a track, then follow this along the shores of Loch Beag, the small cove at the head of Loch Hourn. As you walk you'll notice how well built is the path underfoot. ◀

Along this section of the loch keep an eye out for siskins, coal tits, treecreepers and, in summer, wood warblers.

A short way from Kinloch Hourn the path takes you uphill slightly to cross the Allt Coire Mhicrail at a substantial wooden bridge. Beyond this is **Skiary**, a lonely cottage down on the

Many of the stalker's paths through these hills leading towards Knoydart were built by an engineer called **James Watt**. He came to Scotland from Rhodesia under a bit of a cloud, and wanted to take up work somewhere out of the way. He was successful in getting a contract from the estates to build a network of paths linking the main glens in Knoydart, and this he did with just two other men.

shore of Loch Hourn. The path stays a way above the loch shore for quite a while until you reach the crossing of the Allt a' Chamuis Bhain. Once across this little stream the path climbs up and over a knoll before bringing you back down to sea level at **Runival**. The way is now well wooded with a delightful mix of native trees – there are some great old Scots pines here, along with rowan, alder and birch. ▶

The path continues westwards, moving close to the shore near Caolas Mor, or 'the Big Narrows', in the sea loch. Beyond Caolas Mor the path climbs again to a point low down on the northern spur of Carn Mairi. As you gain the last rise the view opens out over **Barrisdale Bay**, a large area of soft, yellow sand, with the magnificent ridges of Ladhar Bheinn rising beyond.

Caolas Mor is a good place to see common seals, while on the shingle banks in summer you might catch sight of the delicate-looking arctic terns that nest here.

Loch Hourn and Barrisdale Bay

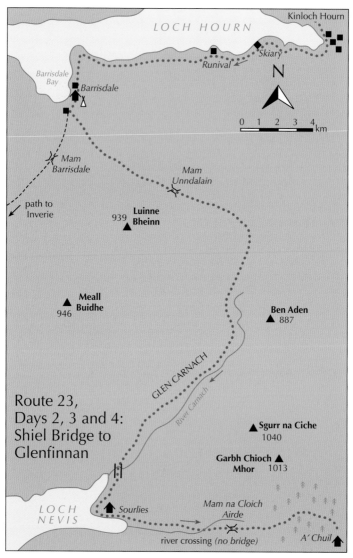

LOCH HOURN

Kinloch Hourn

Skiary

Runival

Barrisdale Bay

Barrisdale

N

0 1 2 3 4 km

Mam Barrisdale

Mam Unndalain

path to Inverie

Luinne Bheinn
939 ▲

Meall Buidhe
▲
946

Ben Aden
▲ 887

GLEN CARNACH

River Carnach

Route 23, Days 2, 3 and 4: Shiel Bridge to Glenfinnan

Sgurr na Ciche
▲
1040

Garbh Chioch ▲
Mhor   1013

LOCH NEVIS

Sourlies

Mam na Cloich Airde

river crossing (no bridge)

A' Chuil

208

Ladhar Bheinn is the highest mountain on the Knoydart peninsula, and is occasionally climbed from Barrisdale. If you allowed an extra day you could climb it from a base here. The route goes up Coire Dhorrcail, then onto the ridge of Druim a' Choire Odhair, which leads in rocky steps to the summit at 1020m. Return via the same route.

Ladhar Bheinn from Barrisdale Bay

Follow the path southwards into Barrisdale, which is little more than a lodge, stalker's house, bothy and bunkhouse. The campsite is by the bothy, just before the bridge over the River Barrisdale.

DAY 3

Begin the day by crossing the bridge over the River Barrisdale to its west side. Follow the track southwards, passing the white house, and shortly after take a path on the left that crosses the river and snakes up towards the Mam Unndalain.

Climb up along the path, which initially takes you through beautiful, open woodlands of Caledonian pine trees. Above this the way is more open, and soon leads to the little nick in the skyline that is the Mam Unndalain. Follow the path over the pass into new territory.

The views on the way up to the **Mam Unndalain** are superb, with the towering mass of Luinne Bheinn ahead on the right. This is a fine Munro, and another peak well worth climbing if you've got time. From a base at Barrisdale you can follow this route to the summit of the Mam Unndalain, then pass crags on the right and follow a ridge that soon takes you via a good path to the summit. To traverse the mountain you can head westwards from the top to pick up a path down a steep slope on its northwestern side. This leads to a broad col, and you can shoot off down to the west to a line of rusty old fenceposts. Turn right and follow these to the top of another pass, the Mam Barrisdale. A good track crosses the pass, and if you turn right and follow it to the northeast you'll soon find yourself back at Barrisdale.

If you were to stay on this path it would take you eastwards via Lochan nam Breac to the head of Loch Quoich. Fine though this is, this route will not get you to **Glenfinnan** easily. Instead, once over the pass you should stay on the path for 500m, then bear southwards downhill to the river in the glen below. On the north side of the river, pick up a path. Turn right, westwards, and follow this path, passing some lovely waterfalls and a delightful camping spot below a dark cliff.

Continue through the glen to the old ruined houses at Carnach. Here you need to cross the **River Carnach** via an old rustic wooden bridge. (A sign warns that the bridge is dangerous – but perhaps using it is better than wading the River Carnach?) Once on the south side of the river, head westwards along the shore and around to the head of **Loch Nevis**.

Loch Nevis and Loch Hourn are lovely names typical of the views the old Highlanders had of natural features in the landscape. Loch Nevis means the Loch (lake) of Heaven, while Loch Hourn translates as the Loch of Hell. The two lochs lie on either side of the Knoydart peninsula, giving rise to a popular saying among the locals that living on Knoydart falls somewhere between heaven and hell!

The path to the head of Loch Nevis is difficult to find, and if the tide is high you might have to go across the boggy ground just inland. (This is often a pretty wet affair, though, and has led to it becoming known by the groups I have led here for 'Wilderness Scotland' as the Bog of Despair – you have been warned!)

Once around the headland you can either stay on the shore, if the tide is out, and follow it around to the bothy at **Sourlies**, or, if the tide is in, you'll need to climb uphill and over a rocky knoll before dropping down to the shore.

Sourlies is a fantastic place to spend the night, and you can either camp or sleep inside. The mussels from the rocks at the headland make a fine supplement to an evening meal here.

DAY 4

From Sourlies a path heads along the shore for a short way to the east, then follows the north side of the river to a short climb and a bridge over a stream with a series of waterfalls. Follow this path easily until you are right up in a little corrie. Here you must cross the river, which at times can be in full flow, and is dangerous. Generally it is just a case of wading across, but if you are in doubt it is safer to wait until the level has dropped – even if this means camping close by until the rain stops! You might also try continuing along the north side until east of Lochan a' Mhaim, where the stream rises.

Contrary to popular belief – and let's face it, everyone seems to have their own ideas about how to cross a river – **the safest way to cross a river** is to take off your boots and socks, put your boots back on again, roll your trousers up and, facing upstream (face downstream and the water behind your knees will buckle your legs), wade carefully across. Once across, empty out your boots, put your socks back on again, and stride off with only slightly damp feet. Going barefoot should be avoided, as boots will protect your feet against moving boulders and rocks, and from sharp stones. This is no place to get your feet crushed or cut!

The path now leads along the south side of Lochan a' Mhaim, then brings you into a valley facing eastwards, and the headwaters of Glen Dessary. Walk eastwards down the glen until you reach a forest, and just before the forest there is a junction of tracks. I usually opt for the one to the left, because it stays above the line of trees and you get better views as you walk, although the one to the right can also be taken into the woods – both lead to **A' Chuil** bothy.

From the left-hand track you walk until clear of the trees, where you'll see a bridge down on the right. Walk over to this, leaving the track to do so, and cross the river. The other track, that went through the trees, lies just above the bridge to the south. Follow the track southwards, then southeastwards to A' Chuil bothy, where you can spend the night.

DAY 5

Once you've packed up at A' Chuil it's time for the longest section of the route. Head east along the forest track that skirts the lower slopes of Monadh Gorm. At the eastern end of this little hill there's another track that branches off to the left and goes down to Strathan. Ignore this and continue round to the right, then head west for another kilometre until you come to a little path on the left that heads down to the **River Pean**, where you'll find a bridge.

Cross the bridge and follow the path southwards towards **Gleann a' Chaorainn**. The going here is easy and the scenery spectacular, with the shapely peak of **Streap** dead ahead at the top of the glen. The pass you are aiming for is the low point just to the right of Streap, and you climb up gradually, following the stream throughout. When at last you reach the pass, which is not too high at 471m, Streap rises steeply to your left and **Sgurr Thuilm**, a superb Munro, to your right.

Head off down the glen, walking in a southwesterly direction. This glen is straightforward, and you'll soon find yourself crossing the river at the bottom and joining the track down to **Corryhully** bothy.

Don't forget to look over your shoulder at the view every once in a while. From the path near Corryhully the mountains throwing up steep flanks behind you are Sgurr nan Coireachan to the northwest, Sgurr Thuilm to the north, and Streap to the northeast.

From Corryhully (the only bothy I know with an electricity meter and pay box for the lights!) the path goes to the

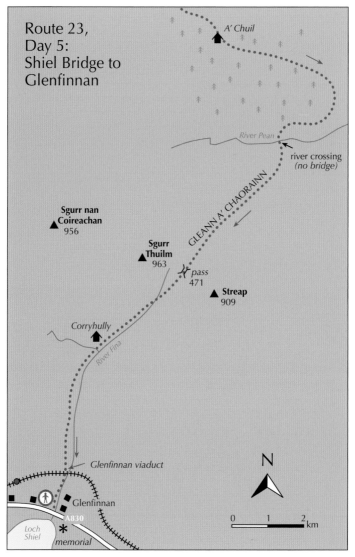

Route 23,
Day 5:
Shiel Bridge to
Glenfinnan

A' Chuil

River Pean

river crossing
(no bridge)

Sgurr nan
Coireachan
956

Sgurr
Thuilm
963

GLEANN A' CHAORAINN

pass
471

Streap
909

Corryhully

River Fìna

Glenfinnan viaduct

Glenfinnan

A830

Loch
Shiel

memorial

N

0   1   2
km

The mountains of Knoydart

south close to the **River Fina**, and you soon see the **viaduct** taking the Fort William to Mallaig railway line (better known these days as the line of the Hogwarts Express in the Harry Potter films!).

Evening storms clouds over Glenfinnan

This is good eagle country. I've regularly watched golden eagles on Fraoch Bheinn, the mountain to the west of the glen, and Mike Tomkies, a well-known wildlife photographer, lived for many years down the glen south of Glenfinnan, on the banks of Loch Shiel. Here he studied golden eagles as well as red deer and Scottish wildcats.

The Glenfinnan memorial marks the spot where Bonnie Prince Charlie raised his standard in 1745, and so marked the beginning of the Jacobite uprising of that year. With an Army of just 200 Highlanders, the young Prince waited here for Cameron of Loch Shiel to bring his men to join the uprising. Cameron did finally decide to join the Prince, bringing 800 men, which persuaded other clan chiefs to follow suit.

Finish the walk by having a look at the visitor centre, then head west along the road for the train back to Fort William.

215

ROUTE 24
The Mountains of Knoydart

Number of Days	2
Total Distance	42km (26 miles)
Daily Distances	Day 1 – 19km (12 miles), Day 2 – 23km (14 miles)
Height Gain	Total: 3510m; Day 1 – 1540m, Day 2 – 1970m
Maps	OS Landranger sheet 33 Loch Alsh, Glen Shiel and Loch Hourn
Starting Point	Inverie, the small village on Loch Nevis on the west coast of the Knoydart peninsula (grid ref NG766000).

Area Summary

Knoydart is often referred to as 'the last great wilderness', something that it most definitely is not. This wonderful peninsula juts out between Loch Hourn and Loch Nevis on Scotland's western seaboard, and has some of the best walking on offer in Britain. But like all other landscapes in Scotland, it is not a 'wilderness' in the true sense of the word – it has very much been made by man – although it is still one of the wildest places in the country, and until fairly recently only the hardened hillwalker would be found there. This is certainly not true today, as scores of walkers pour in every day in summer.

All of Scotland's major walking holiday companies offer trips here, and it is also very popular with the hunting, shooting and fishing fraternity. The false sense of wilderness has been heightened by the marketing ploys of various business in the region – the Old Forge pub, with its 'Britain's Remotest Pub' signs, branded merchandise and website should give you an idea of what to expect. Remote it certainly is in one sense, but bear in mind that you can get here in just over 20 minutes on a fast boat from Mallaig!

Having said all this, I certainly wouldn't shun the place. I think it's a great area of mountains and moorland, with superb scenery all around, stunning wildlife and wonderful people. I usually spend half a dozen or more weeks in Knoydart each summer myself, running walking holidays, and often visit in the depths of winter too, when no other walkers are around, and all the bar and hotel staff who flock here during the summer have backpacked off to some other, warmer corner of the globe. Personally, I'd always plump for a winter visit, when it really does feel remote, and there's a good chance that you might not get out and homeward bound on any boat if the weather turns rough.

The other thing that visitors often don't realise is that Knoydart is actually part of the mainland – not an island at all, even though most people arrive by boat!

Route Summary

A stunning walk over rough mountains, giving fine views of Kintail, Skye, Rum, Eigg, and southwards towards Ben Nevis. This is a high-mountain route suitable for those with some experience of mountain walking – some of the ridges that are traversed are narrow, although do not involve any difficult scrambling.

A few years ago this was pretty much uncharted territory for the general walker, but now things have changed, and all the mountains have eroded paths appearing along their ridges. That is not to say that you should go here without much planning – the walking is hard, the mountains are remote, and help is a long way off in case of emergency.

The walk starts in Inverie and takes you immediately onto the tops via a rough route onto Sgurr Coire Choinnichean, the marvellous pointed peak that rises above the village. A long ridge route takes you around to the summit of Ladhar Bheinn, the highest peak of the Knoydart peninsula, before you walk down into Coire Dhorrcail and the shores of Loch Hourn for a camp at Barrisdale. On Day 2 you take a well-worn track up to the Mam Barrisdale, a high pass between Barrisdale and Inverie, and climb Luinne Bheinn from there. A rocky ridge then takes you to the third Munro of your trip, Meall Buidhe. A steep descent to the Mam Meadail leads to the final section of the walk, a wonderful undulating ridge where few walkers tread. You'll end up on the summit of Beinn Bhuidhe before picking up a little-used descent into Inverie.

Tourist Information

There is a good tourist information centre at Mallaig, down by the harbour (tel 01687 462170), and a bigger one at Cameron Square in Fort William (tel 01397 703781).

Transport

Trains from Fort William and Glasgow go on to Mallaig, tel 08457 550033, www.firstgroup.com/scotrail. To get to Inverie from Mallaig you'll have to catch the ferry (you can walk in from the east, but it takes 2 days to get there!). Bruce Watt currently runs a ferry service on the MV Western Isles, but this is due to be taken over by the CalMac Loch Coruisk Ferry when the new pier is finished. Contact Bruce Watt on 01687 462320, or CalMac on 01687 462403.

Accommodation and Supplies

There are just a few options in Inverie for accommodation. The Pier House hotel is excellent, offering good seafood and comfortable rooms (the staff are friendly too!), and you often need to book well in advance (tel 01687 462347). Another good option if you want self-catering is Torrie Shieling, a very comfortable independent hostel just outside the village (tel 01687 462669). Cheaper is the Knoydart Foundation Hostel (tel 01687 462242).

Without a doubt, for me at least, the best option for accommodation is at Doune. Here you'll find one of the best restaurants in Scotland, offering fantastic seafood such as Doune Bay crab, Knoydart venison or Doune Bay langoustines. Next door is the Stone Lodges, also offering very comfortable accommodation, and all this in a very remote, sheltered bay overlooking the Sleat Peninsula on Skye. They'll even arrange for you to be picked up by a private boat from Mallaig, and can arrange a boat into Inverie, or anywhere else in the area. The only downside is that you must stay a minimum of three nights, but what a way to enjoy this wonderful mountain and sea area. Booking is essential – tel 01687 462267, www.doune-knoydart.co.uk.

Overnight Options

Either camp or use the bothy at Barrisdale. There is a small charge for either, with an honesty box in the bothy. Please take change for this (prices may vary, but usually around £2 to camp and £3 to stay in the bothy). The bothy has electric lighting and basic toilet facilities.

Escape Routes

There are good tracks leading over the Mam Barrisdale and the Mam Meadail, both high passes giving good access through the mountains. These two routes are the best ways of getting back to Inverie from various points along the walk.

DAY 1

Starting from the pier at **Inverie** walk northwards along the road for a short way, beyond the Knoydart Foundation office and the pub. Turn right just beyond the pub onto a track that climbs gradually through forest. Bear left at a new wooden chalet-type house, and continue on the obvious track to a deer fence and gate leading onto open moorland.

Go through the gate and leave the track. Take to the open moorland to the east of the track, initially following the edge of the forest, then continuing up through rough slopes to gain an open, flat area below the east ridge of **Sgurr Coire Choinnichean.**

This eastern slope of Sgurr Coire Choinnichean is a great place to familiarise yourself with the **wild flowers** and **plants** of the Scottish moorlands. You will begin by walking through the low shrubs of scented bog myrtle – this is a lovely plant with somewhat citrus-smelling leaves, and in early summer the smell can be strong and quite far-reaching. Legend has it that Highlanders used to rub it onto exposed skin to keep midges away – it might work, but given that wherever you find bog myrtle you also find plenty of midges, it seems unlikely! It also turns your skin yellow when you rub it on, so be warned!

Other plants growing here include devil's-bit scabious, lousewort, milkwort and bog asphodel, as well ling and bell heather, sundews and butterwort.

Once on the flat area head southeast to the top of a huge landslip – this is the top edge of a gorge that leads down to a track above Inverie House. Walk around the top of the gorge and climb the southeast ridge of Sgurr Coire Choinnichean. This is rocky in places, but nowhere difficult, and you soon find yourself on the summit of this superb Corbett at 796m.

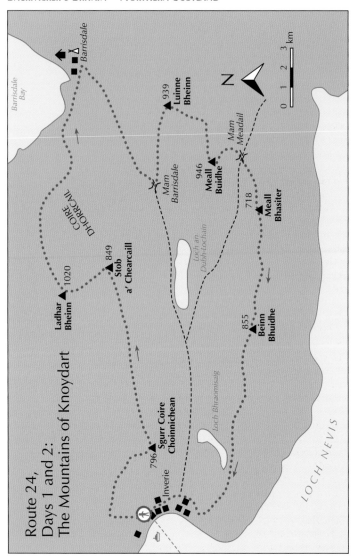

Route 24,
Days 1 and 2:
The Mountains of Knoydart

The view from the summit of Sgurr Coire Choinnichean is extensive. You can see right over the Sleat peninsula of Skye to the west to the ragged outline of the Black Cuillin. The islands of Rum and Eigg are also in good view from here.

The ridge of Sgurr Coire Choinnichean heads eastward and is obvious, leading into a little col then to a second top before broadening out. The summit of Stob an Uillt-fhearna can be visited easily, or you can bypass this by a contour on the south side. You need to regain the ridge at Mam Suidheig and continue over a number of knolls before the rocky hill just west of spot height 758m.

Go over the top of this hill and into a rocky gully just south of the top. This gully leads down to a rocky hollow with the ridge just south. Gain the ridge at a col and follow it to the superb crest of Aonach Sgoilte. The ridge of this leads in a fine position to the top of **Stob a' Chearcaill**, whose summit is set back along the ridge to the northeast, and well worth visiting. From the summit head northwestwards down an obvious path to a col, the Bealach Coire Dhorrchail.

The glen to your right here is Coire Dhorrcail, a truly wild place. You'll be descending into it later in the day, after visiting the summit of Ladhar Bheinn, and throughout the rest of the walk you should keep your eyes open for golden eagles. This corrie is a favourite hunting ground for the local pair.

From the Bealach Coire Dhorrchail the path takes you up a steep and rocky face, easy though exposed, to the summit of a fine little peak at 858m. From this top you can see the rest of the route up **Ladhar Bheinn**. The path leads the way. Drop into a col then tackle the last ascent to the top.

The ridge is quite open at first, and leads you to a low band of rock. The obvious rock 'steps' that the path seems to lead to are usually very wet and horrible – there is a much easier short scramble to the right. This is exposed, but nothing more than a single high step up, and a very short slab of rock. From here the ridge narrows, but is easy to follow. The top has three ridges – the one you've just climbed, another to the northeast and a final ridge heading off to the northwest. The summit lies a short way along this northwest ridge and is

On Ladhar Bheinn's summit ridge

marked by a cairn at 1020m. The OS trig pillar lies further along this ridge at 1010m.

From the summit of Ladhar Bheinn, which means 'the Claw' or 'Hoof Mountain', head back to junction of the three ridges and scramble easily along the northeast one. You start this by a fairly steep descent, then a very narrow section that has a good path along its top. There is no scrambling, but again the ridge is exposed.

Continue over the summit of Stob a' Choire Odhair at 960m, then down to a broad col. From here you can either descend to the upper reaches of **Coire Dhorrcail** to the southeast, or continue on the ridge. The path continues along the ridge, then cuts down steep slopes to the southeast to rejoin the other route in Coire Dhorrcail.

There is a group of old shielings in Coire Dhorrcail that are hard to find, but which tell us that this corrie was used by the Highlanders of old as a summer pasture for their cattle. It must have been a well-protected place then, as the entrance to the corrie from the valley below is narrow and rocky, and all approaches to the corrie from above are hard and exposed.

Red deer below Luinne Bheinn

Walking in Coire Dhorrcail

Cross the stream once in the corrie and pick up a track on the south side. This leads through some wonderful alder and birch woodland to a well-built zigzagging track. Follow the track eastwards, downhill to the southwestern corner of **Barrisdale Bay.** The track crosses a stream at the bottom of the hill, then leads you across the saltflats to the southeast. A bridge takes you over the River Barrisdale to the bothy and campsite where you should spend the night.

DAY 2

From the campsite at Barrisdale walk to the bridge over the River Barrisdale and follow the obvious track to the southwest. This passes the 'White House' and brings you to a junction. Ignore the turning to the left and continue along the main track, climbing gradually and crossing a number of small streams via new wooden footbridges. This track is the main through-route from Barrisdale to Inverie, so you may well have other walkers heading past you as you climb. The path takes you to the top of the high pass between Barrisdale and Inverie, the **Mam Barrisdale** – there is a small cairn marking the top of the pass, which is obvious anyway.

From the top of the Mam Barrisdale you should leave the path and head southeastwards across boggy ground to pick up a line of fenceposts. Follow these posts for 700m, then strike up the hillside to the east to a col between Bachd Mhic an Tosach and **Luinne Bheinn**. The climb to the summit of Luinne Bheinn from here looks steep and intimidating, but if you head over the col to its southeastern corner you will pick up a vague path leading up a short scree slope. This path soon improves and takes you easily to the short summit ridge of Luinne Bheinn. Walk eastwards along the short ridge to the top of Luinne Bheinn at 939m.

> The views northwards from the summit of Luinne Bheinn are excellent – you can see right down into Barrisdale Bay where you spent the previous night. The rocky ridges of Ladhar Bheinn look particularly impressive from here, while the view over to Meall Buidhe, your next summit, to the southwest, is one of a vast corrie dominated by rock.

To the east of the main summit of Luinne Bheinn is another, minor, top at 937m. Walk over to this summit and pick up a path on its south side that leads down a scree-filled gully to a col. From here there is a good path leading around, up and over numerous little rocky bluffs to the minor top of Meall Coire na Gaoithe n-Ear. Beyond this peak you drop down to the deep col of Bealach Ile Coire, and then to the start of the ridge up Meall Buidhe. The path takes you safely up this ridge, bringing you out at spot height 942m, which lies a little east of the main top. Turn right along the main ridge to gain the summit at 946m.

Once you've visited the summit, head back to spot height 942m. From here there is a steep descent down to the pass at Mam Meadail – a vague path leads downhill through numerous short crags, and it is better to follow this, which winds its way down to a point just east of the highest point of the pass.

The Mam Meadail is the main pass between the head of Loch Nevis and Inverie, and has a good track between the two. The quickest return to Inverie from here is to head westwards along this path, but to continue along this route you should climb the knoll to the south of the pass at spot height 610m. This is now pathless terrain and the going is quite rough in places. You climb to the summit of **Meall Bhasiter** at 718m, then turn westwards and follow the ridge down to the Mam Uchd. There is a big, boggy hollow just north off the ridge, regularly used by red deer as a wallow.

Climb up the rocky slopes to the west by keeping to the south side of the ridge and you soon find yourself on the summit of **Beinn Bhuidhe** at 855m. An OS trig pillar marks the highest point on a little rocky ridge.

Continue westwards from the summit, over a minor top at 786m, and down to the Bealach Buidhe. It is possible to descend northwards down into the corrie from here and so gain the path through Gleann Meadail back to Inverie. However, you can continue over the next top, Sgurr Coire nan Gobhar, and down to the southwest to the head of a stream that leads down to lovely **Loch Bhraomisaig**. (Here you might be lucky enough to see red-throated divers, a rare waterbird of upland lochs.)

At the western end of Loch Bhraomisaig is a short stream connecting it with another loch. Cross this stream and head just west of north to the head of another stream, which leads down the eastern slopes of A' Chruach to the southeastern corner of Inverie Bay. This slope is steep, but if you zigzag to the left you'll pick up an easier way down.

Once down at sea level pick up a track leading around Inverie Bay to Kilchoan. From here follow the track over the bridge and on into Inverie village.

ROUTE 25

Skye – the Black Cuillin Lochs and Bealachs

Number of Days	2
Total Distance	40km (25 miles)
Daily Distances	Day 1 – 24km (15 miles), Day 2 – 16km (10 miles
Height Gain	Total: 1640m; Day 1 –1270m, Day 2 – 370m
Maps	Ordnance Survey Landranger sheet number 32 South Skye covers the route, but for greater clarity in the Black Cuillin, Harvey's Superwalker map to Skye and the Cuillin is highly recommended.
Starting Point	Start this walk at the Sligachan Inn at the junction of the A85 and the A863 (grid ref NG486298). You can park in the car park at the hotel.

Area Summary

The Black Cuillin of Skye are mountaineers' mountains. All of the peaks on this fantastic rocky ridge require scrambling skills to reach their summits, and most need more than that! To get to the tops of most of them you need to be a rock climber – there are no walking routes. Even such peaks as Sgurr nan Gillean at the northern end of the ridge, which has 'Easy Route' marked on the map, requires careful use of hand and foot holds and a good head for heights to gain its top.

That said, these are without a doubt the most magnificent mountains in Britain. The rock here is gabbro, a grainy rock giving superb friction when climbing and scrambling over it, and for the most part exposed to the elements and the eye – there's no vegetation on the ridge itself apart from alpine flowers growing here and there in crevices.

The Black Cuillin (you should never put an 's' on the end of Cuillin – it's plural already) is shaped like a crescent, with the outside edge facing west and the inside facing east. This eastern side is split by a major ridge, Druim nan Ramh. This ridge forms two big corries on this eastern side of the main ridge – the Harta Corrie to the north and Coir-uisg to the south.

The deep valley of Glen Sligachan separates the Black Cuillin from Blaven and the peaks of the Red Cuillin to the east, and Glen Brittle separates it from the lower hills of Minginish to the west. To the south is the sea, with two great sea lochs – Loch Scavaig and Loch Brittle – cutting into the hills. The northern boundary of the Black Cuillin is the moorland that rolls away to the A863 and the A850.

Route Summary

This is a challenging walk that looks easy on the map! The start up Glen Sligachan is very straightforward via a good path leading over a pass down to the northern shore of Loch Coruisk. From the northwestern end of this loch you have to climb over the ridge of the Black Cuillin via a high pass. The way is pathless and very rocky, taking you over exposed slabs of rock that can lead to steep ground if you go the wrong way. From the pass similar terrain leads you down into Coir' a' Ghrunnda, from where you pick up a path leading across moorland to Glenbrittle. The route from Glenbrittle back to Sligachan on Day 2 is straightforward, and follows first a minor road then a good track.

This is not a walk to be undertaken lightly. You must know how to look after yourself in the mountains, and be able to read fine detail from the map. (Note Compasses in the Black Cuillin are affected by the magnetic rock and can't be relied upon.) The terrain here is so steep and rocky that the maps – even the very best ones – look cluttered and are quite hard to read accurately. Contours are missing where the gradient is steep, and much of the time in the higher parts of these mountains you'll be walking over pathless ground.

Tourist Information

The tourist information centre in Portree is on Bridge Street and can book accommodation for you on Skye (tel 01478 612137). There is also a good tourist information centre in Kyle of Lochalsh, down by the harbour (tel 01599 534276), and another at Cameron Square in Fort Augustus (tel 01320 366367), or in Fort William (tel 01397 703781), for those coming from that direction.

Transport
Citylink buses from either Fort William or Inverness to Portree pass by the Sligachan Inn and will drop you off there (tel 08705 505050, www.citylink.co.uk).

Accommodation and Supplies
There are lots of accommodation options in Portree, from hotels, guest houses and bed and breakfasts, to hostels and campsites. Give the tourist information centre a call for advice (tel 01478 612137). You can also camp across the road from the Sligachan Inn, or stay at the inn itself (tel 01478 650204). This is a great way to experience the true magic of the Cuillin.

Overnight Options Camp at the official site in Glenbrittle for a small fee, or book into the youth hostel, which lies a little further northwards along from the road head – to contact the central booking service of the SYHA tel 0870 155255, or via their website at www.syha.org.uk.

Escape Routes
Under no circumstances should you attempt to cross the Black Cuillin ridge at other points than those recommended unless you are a seasoned mountaineer with experience of rock climbing. This is dangerous terrain, and people do get into difficulties. Before crossing the ridge the only reasonable escape route is to backtrack to Sligachan, the way you've walked in, and once over the ridge and down into Glenbrittle you can probably thumb a lift out if necessary, though the walk on Day 2 is quite straightforward.

DAY 1

From the **Sligachan Inn** head out onto the A863. Cross over this road, to the east, and then cross the old road bridge to the east side of the River Sligachan. Here you'll pick up a good track that heads southwards. (As you walk southwards keep a look out for red deer, which are often to be seen here-abouts.)

The view as you head southwards from Sligachan is fantastic. To your right you see the northern bastions of the Black Cuillin, Bruach na Frithe, Am Basteir and Sgurr nan Gillean. Just to the left of the glen dead ahead is the imposing cone of Marsco, a fine peak in the Red Cuillin, while to your left are Glamaig and Beinn Dearg Mhor.

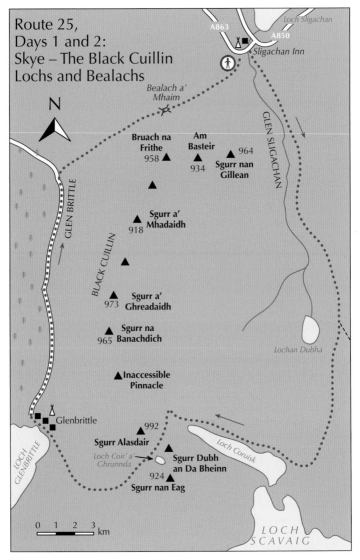

Route 25,
Days 1 and 2:
Skye – The Black Cuillin
Lochs and Bealachs

N

Loch Sligachan

A863
A850
Sligachan Inn

Loch Sligachan

Bealach a' Mhaim

GLEN SLIGACHAN

Bruach na Frithe
958

Am Basteir
934

964
Sgurr nan Gillean

GLEN BRITTLE

Sgurr a' Mhadaidh
918

BLACK CUILLIN

Sgurr a' Ghreadaidh
973

Sgurr na Banachdich
965

Lochan Dubha

Inaccessible Pinnacle

Glenbrittle

992

Sgurr Alasdair

Loch Coir' a' Ghrunnda

Loch Coruisk

Sgurr Dubh an Da Bheinn

924
Sgurr nan Eag

LOCH GLENBRITTLE

0 1 2 3 km

LOCH
SCAVAIG

After 3km cross a stream (ignore the paths going eastwards from here – these lead up Marsco). Continue up **Glen Sligachan** to the south, soon moving back towards the main river as you walk along the western lower slopes of Marsco. You soon reach a lovely pool, known as **Lochan Dubha**, away to your right across the moor. Just beyond this you come to a junction in the path, and here it is important that you go right, continuing southwards up to a pass. (The route to the left goes downhill into the glen and leads you away from the Black Cuillin in the direction of Elgol.)

Heading southwards the route initially skirts the side of the glen, then climbs quite steeply to a pass at just over 300m. From this pass there is a tremendous view to the southern end of the Black Cuillin.

At the pass the path turns to the southwest and you descend to Loch a' Choire Riabhaich. You'll need to cross this stream to the north side lower down, so if it looks as though the water level is high, it might be better to cross higher up the slope. At the bottom of the slope, on the shore of **Loch Coruisk**, you can usually cross the stream right down on the shore of the loch. This is much easier than scrambling across the wet rocks just above – I regularly see people taking a dunking here!

The Black Cuillin from Loch Coruisk

Backpackers enjoying Loch Coruisk

Head westwards along the northern shore of Loch Coruisk, passing the huge boulders left by a massive landslide a couple of years ago. Just beyond this you'll come to a lovely little open woodland of birch, holly, rowan and alder. This is as good a place as any for a lunch break!

Continue to the end of Loch Coruisk, where the stream pours in from higher up in the corrie. Here you're faced with another river crossing, and although the path on the OS map shows that you can go right up into the glen for 1.5km to cross there, with normal water levels you can cross pretty much anywhere along this section of the river. Continue westwards up into the corrie for 1km (from the western end of the loch) to where a stream comes down the hillside to the south.

Climb uphill alongside this stream, easily avoiding rocky outcrops by going round them. High up in the corrie you'll come to a pool that gives the corrie its name, Coir' an Lochain. Walk round to the southern tip of this lochan, and from there head southwestwards uphill to the pass at Bealach Coir' an Lochain.

This pass lies between the impressive peaks of **Sgurr Dubh an Da Bheinn** to the southeast and Sgurr Thearlaich to the northwest. You can leave your rucksack on the pass and easily head southeastwards to the summit of Sgurr Dubh an

Da Bheinn at 938m. This is a fine peak on the main Black Cuillin ridge, and is straightforward from the pass. Return the same way to the pass.

Do not be tempted to try to climb Sgurr Thearlaich to the northwest. The infamous Thearlaich Dubh Gap (pronounced 'chellach doo') lies a little way along the ridge in that direction, and calls for an abseil descent and 'Very Difficult'-grade rock climbing to get out.

From the Bealach Coir' an Lochain, steep scree slopes lead down to the southwest to Loch Coir' a' Ghrunnda, and you should pick a careful route down to the northern side of this.

The descent from Coir' a' Ghrunnda involves careful route choice, as there are huge slabs of rock falling from the mouth of the corrie. Initially you should follow the stream issuing from Loch Coir' a' Ghrunnda. Follow this down onto a lower shelf where the rock slabs begin, then carefully descend on the northern side of the stream. The slabs here are not too steep, and you can head just west of south for a short way before going back towards the stream. There are a few cairns built here to mark the safest route.

Once lower down in the corrie the way becomes easy, and on the western side of the mouth of the corrie you'll pick up a path. Follow this path westwards at first, then across moorland to the northwest and down into **Glenbrittle**. As you enter the tiny hamlet you pass through the campsite where you might be spending the night. For the youth hostel you need to continue along the road, first going around the bay, then heading northwards up the glen. You'll reach the hostel 2.5km from the campsite.

DAY 2

Start by heading along the road, as described above, to the youth hostel. From there you should continue up the road to a bridge leading across the River Brittle to its west side. Go over the bridge. You are now walking with the dense forests of the **Glen Brittle** plantation to your left. ▶

Continue along the road for another 1.6km from the road bridge, and where it turns left, and begins to climb uphill through a broad firebreak, you'll see an obvious track heading to the

As you walk up Glen Brittle the great wall of the Black Cuillin rises to your right, and you look up into the huge bowls of the corries on this western side of the range.

233

Looking for the correct route over the Black Cuillin

From the pass, if you look southeastwards, you'll see the massive rock faces of Am Bhasteir and the pinnacle ridge of Sgurr nan Gillean.

northeast across the moor below the lower edge of the forest. Take this track, which soon begins to climb in tight zigzags, to a cairn and a tiny lochan at a pass, the Bealach a' Mhaim. ◀

Continue over the pass and stay on the path as it leads easily down into Coire na Circe. The path now follows the course of the Allt Dearg Mor and takes you back to the Sligachan Inn.

ROUTE 26
Skye – the Red Cuillin

Number of Days	2
Total Distance	28km (17.5 miles)
Daily Distances	Day 1 – 16km (10 miles), Day 2 – 12km (7.5 miles)
Height Gain	Total: 2870m; Day 1 – 1680m, Day 2 – 1190m
Maps	Ordnance Survey Landranger sheet number 32 South Skye
Starting Point	Start this walk at the Sligachan Inn at the junction of the A85 and the A863 (grid ref NG486298). You can park in the hotel car park, but will need to return from Broadford by bus to pick up your vehicle at the end of the walk.
Finishing Point	This is a linear walk finishing in Broadford on the A850 (grid ref NG641235).

Area Summary

The Red Cuillin tend to be neglected by walkers. This is a shame, as this wonderful mountain range offers great ridge walking and magnificent views all around. If it wasn't for the fact that they are overshadowed by the Black Cuillin just across Glen Sligachan to the west, these hills would be swarming with people. This is no bad thing, of course, as it means that you can come here for a couple of days and probably not see another person until you hit the bright lights of Broadford at the end.

The Red Cuillin are the range of scree-girt hills that lie to the east of the Black Cuillin. They include a number of important summits, including two Corbetts, but no Munros, which also goes towards explaining why they are generally ignored.

Route Summary

This walk starts by heading up Glen Sligachan as far as the Allt na Measarroch, which is then followed to a high col on Marsco. There is the option of climbing Marsco, although this

Tourist Information

The tourist information centre in Portree is on Bridge Street and can book accommodation for you on Skye (tel 01478 612137), as can the one in Broadford (tel 01471 822361). There is also a good tourist information centre in Kyle of Lochalsh, down by the harbour (tel 01599 534276), another in Fort Augustus for those coming from that direction (tel 01320 366367), or one in Fort William (tel 01397 703781).

Transport

Citylink buses from either Fort William or Inverness to Portree pass by the Sligachan Inn and will drop you off there. They also stop in Broadford at the end of the walk (tel 08705 505050, www.citylink.co.uk).

Accommodation and Supplies

There are lots of options in Portree, from hotels, guest houses and bed and breakfasts, to hostels and camp sites – give the tourist information centre a call for advice (tel 01478 612137). Right at the start of the walk you can also camp across the road from the Sligachan Inn, or stay at the inn itself (tel 01478 650204). At the end of the walk there are lots of options in Broadford, including the youth hostel – contact the central booking service of the SYHA, tel 0870 155255, www.syha.org.uk. The tourist information centre in Broadford can also advise on accommodation (tel 01471 822361).

There are shops in Broadford and Portree, but not at Sligachan or anywhere on the route.

Overnight Options

Camp wild in Strath Mor – the southern end of Lochain Stratha Mhoir is a good place (grid ref NG563253)

Escape Routes

It's an easy matter to head northwards for the A850 from pretty much anywhere on this route. It's never more than a few kilometres to get there, and there is always some traffic on this main road through the island.

can be avoided by a contour to another high col. The route then lies over Garbh-bheinn, the highest mountain on the route. The fine summits of Belig and Glas Bheinn Mhor are then traversed before a campsite is found in Strath Mor to the east.

On Day 2 the low hill of Beinn na Cro is climbed before the much higher Beinn Dearg Mhor and Beinn na Caillich are traversed. There is then a short walk over the moor to pick up the lane into Broadford.

This route is suitable for anyone with the ability to navigate over rough terrain without paths. The going is never too difficult, and the route takes you into some beautiful corners of Skye.

DAY 1

From the **Sligachan Inn** head out onto the A863. Cross over this road to the east, and go over the old road bridge to the east side of the River Sligachan. Here you'll pick up a good track that heads south. After 3km you come to a point where the main track crosses a small stream. This is the Allt na Measarroch, and you should follow it uphill, leaving the main track behind. There is a faint path on the north side of the Allt na Measarroch, although this is boggy at first. Higher up it becomes much more obvious and easy to follow.

> The slopes of Marsco to your right, on the south side of the Allt na Measarroch, are a popular place for red deer. There's a small hanging valley high up under the summit, and from the path leading upstream small groups of hinds can often be seen there.

You soon reach the high pass known as **Mam a' Phobuill**, which lies between **Marsco** and Ciche na Beinne Deirge. From here the route contours to the southeast, but for a little more effort you can climb Marsco itself. Both routes are described here.

To climb Marsco you should head southeast for 800m, ascending slightly as you go, and crossing a stream above a series of small waterfalls. From here you find yourself on a broad ridge above Coire nan Laogh, where there are old fenceposts that can be followed onto the southeast ridge of Marsco. The route is quite steep but not difficult, and follows grassy slopes and the odd short scree slope. Once on the southeast ridge of Marsco you should turn to the northwest and climb easily to the narrow ridge that leads to the summit.

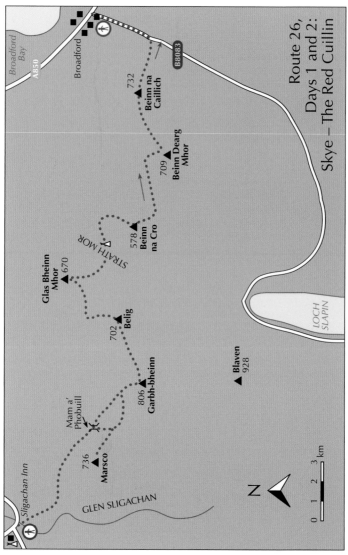

Route 26,
Days 1 and 2:
Skye – The Red Cuillin

The view from Marsco is excellent, taking in the Black Cuillin to the west and Blaven (Bla-Bheinn on the OS map) to the southeast. Southwards you can see across Loch Scavaig to the island of Rum in the distance.

From the summit of Marsco retrace your steps back down the southeast ridge, continuing beyond the point where you gained the ridge. You soon find yourself at the low col between Marsco and **Garbh-bheinn**.

If you don't want to climb Marsco you should start by following that route for the first 800m until well past the stream above the waterfalls. You can then contour across grassy slopes above Coire nan Bruadaran to the col between Marsco and Garbh-bheinn.

To the east you'll see a perfect little dome of a hill at 489m. Climb this via its western side, then descend to the southeast into a col. Here the rock underfoot changes from the red granite of the Red Cuillin to the rough gabbro of the Black Cuillin.

The north ridge of Garbh-bheinn is rocky, but not difficult, and once on the summit ridge turn left to reach the top at 806m. The northeast ridge is rocky and quite narrow at the top, but again not difficult. Lower down it becomes broader and easier, although it is still bouldery in places. You soon reach the low col known as Bealach na Beiste, which lies between Garbh-bheinn and **Belig**, the next peak on your route to the northeast. Bouldery slopes of scree lead to the summit of Belig at 702m.

From the summit of Belig you should follow the north ridge steeply downhill for almost 1km. It is then possible to head eastwards across a wild and lonely bowl to the bealach that lies between Belig and **Glas Bheinn Mhor** (don't be tempted to go for the bealach directly, as the way takes you over crags). From the bealach an easy ridge leads to the summit of Glas Bheinn Mhor at 570m. ▶

Head back to the bealach and from there descend the scree slopes to the east to the flat land to the south of Lochain Stratha Mhoir. I often camp in the strath here, although it can be something of a challenge to find a bit of flat, dry ground to pitch the tent.

The view from Glas Bheinn Mhor is dominated to the northeast by the island of Scalpay, a lovely vision across the channel of Loch na Cairidh.

Climbing Marsco with Garbh-bheinn and Belig behind

DAY 2

From your campsite you should start the day by heading south-eastwards, climbing diagonally across the slopes towards the summit of **Beinn na Cro**. The going here is rough, but the summit, at 572m, is soon underfoot.

Follow the delightful south ridge of Beinn na Cro, with great views across **Loch Slapin**, until it is possible to descend to the east into Strath Beag. Climb straight up the other side from the bottom of the strath, gaining the north ridge of **Beinn Dearg Mhor** well above the crags of Creagan Dubh. Turn southwards and climb the easy ridge to the summit at 709m.

Just east of the summit a ridge curves away to the north-east, descending in a narrow arc to a bealach above Coire Reidh. The summit of **Beinn na Caillich** lies just above to the east, and the top is easily reached from the bealach.

From Beinn na Caillich drop down to the southeast, then head eastwards across the moor below to a bend in the tarmac lane that ends at Coire-chat-achan near the River Broadford. Once on this lane head eastwards to its end, then pick up a path that crosses the river and soon turns south to make for the **B8083** just south of **Broadford**. Turn left on the road and follow it into Broadford, where the walk ends.

Looking out to the Red Cuillin

ROUTE 27
Skye – the Trotternish Ridge Traverse

Number of Days	2
Total Distance	54km (33.5 miles)
Daily Distances	Day 1 – 31km (19.25 miles), Day 2 – 23km (14.25 miles)
Height Gain	Total: 2810m; Day 1 – 1980m, Day 2 – 830m
Maps	Ordnance Survey Landranger sheet number 23 North Skye
Starting Point	Start in Portree at the square in the centre of town (grid ref NG483435).
Finishing Point	Finish in Uig down by the pier (grid ref NG385636).

Area Summary
Until a few years ago the Trotternish Ridge was Skye's last big secret. Walkers invariably would head for the Black Cuillin, and those with an adventurous streak might find their way into the Red Cuillin, but it was rare indeed to see anyone on the Trotternish hills. Things have changed – coachloads of tourists head up into the Storr Sanctuary every day, and it is the same at the Quiraing at the northern end of the ridge. However, this does not detract too much from the enjoyment of walking this route – all the hills on either side of the Storr and the Quiraing are still as quiet as ever, and you can get a real sense of being away from it all.

The Trotternish peninsula is the long, north-to-south running arm of land at the northern tip of the island of Skye. This peninsula has a main road running around the coastal strip, which is also where the villages are. The hinterland is a wonderfully wild area of bizarre hills – almost completely grassy and gentle on their west side, but impressively craggy to the east. From the road north of Portree it looks almost as if this crag is just one very long escarpment. This is magnificent walking country, and on a good day you get superb views across the islands of Rona and Raasay to the east towards the mainland. To the west you can see the Outer Hebrides.

Route Summary

The walk begins by heading north out of Portree along the A855. You soon take to the hills though, and climb the long ridge to the summit of A' Chorra-bheinn. The ridge continues to the summit of the Storr, and leads you onwards over many minor tops to Beinn Edra. This is a good place to camp for the night.

On Day 2 you continue northwards along the undulating ridge, crossing the minor road just before the Quiraing. Once above the massive pinnacles at the Quiraing you head westwards along the ridge of Creag Collascard and then down into Uig.

The walk is suitable for those with some experience of hill walking, although it is not too tough. The going underfoot is generally grassy, with a bit of heather and rocky terrain, and some of the sections of the ridge have a path to follow.

Tourist Information

The tourist information centre in Portree is on Bridge Street and can book accommodation for you on Skye (tel 01478 612137). You'll also find a good tourist information centre in Kyle of Lochalsh down by the harbour (tel 01599 534276).

Transport

Citylink buses from either Fort William or Inverness to Portree also continue to Uig where this walk ends (tel 08705 505050, www.citylink.co.uk).

Accommodation and Supplies

There are lots of options in Portree, from hotels, guest houses and bed and breakfasts, to hostels and campsites. Give the tourist information centre a call for advice (tel 01478 612137).

There are shops in Portree and Uig at each end of the walk, but nothing during it.

Overnight Options

I usually camp somewhere around the Bealach Uige to the north of Beinn Edra (grid ref NG444642), although there are countless other possibilities along the ridge, with some great high lochans just off the ridge to the east that make wonderful campsites, although some of these can be difficult to get to, because of the escarpment.

Escape Routes
You can get off the Trotternish Ridge at many points, but beware of the cliffs that run intermittently along the east side. Some of these are huge, and need a long detour to get around, but if you pick a sensible route you can always get down to the A855 in that direction. The terrain to the west is gentler, but it is a little further in that direction to the A87.

DAY 1

From the square in the centre of **Portree** head east to the main road above the harbour. Turn left along this and follow it out of town (signposted to Staffin). After 2km you pass the Portree campsite on the left at a minor road going to Torvaig. Just north of here you can leave the A855 on the left and climb around the little rocky bluff of Creag an Fhithich. This is the start of the long **Trotternish Ridge**, and you won't descend off this until you get to Uig later tomorrow.

The ridge of Creag an Fhithich leads easily to the first low hill on the ridge, Pein a' Chleibh at 293m (marked as 292m on the Landranger maps), and it is beyond this that the walking starts to get really interesting.

> Across the Sound of Raasay to the east you should be able to see the hummocky moorland of the northern part of the island of Raasay. Further south along this island you'll see the flat-topped hill of Dun Caan, the site of an ancient hill fort.

The ridge takes you down into a little col just northwest of the summit of Pein a' Chleibh, and above this the route onto **A' Chorra-bheinn** is quite rocky. Make directly towards the summit, avoiding the odd rocky outcrop as you go. The summit is a fine place for a break at 459m.

> From the top of A' Chorra-bheinn descend for a short way to the north and climb just east of north to reach the cliffs ringing the eastern side of the Beinn Mheahonach plateau. Follow these cliffs as a handrail around to the summit, marked as **Ben Dearg** at 562m. Steep scree slopes are descended to

Keep an eye out for **white-tailed eagles** while walking along the ridge. Although these massive raptors had been wiped out in Britain, there have been a number of reintroductions onto the island of Rum in the Small Isles, and these are now doing very well, spreading across the western seaboard of Scotland. The coastal cliffs of Skye are a well-known breeding habitat for these huge birds of prey.

White-tailed eagles, also erroneously but popularly called sea eagles (there is another, different species of eagle that goes under that name), are our biggest bird of prey, having a wing span even greater than that of the golden eagle. Female white-tailed eagles can have a wing span up to 2.5m, while the male is a little smaller.

the northeast, then easy ground leads you gently downhill to the first gap on the ridge, the Bealach Mor, or 'the Big Pass'.

Keeping the cliffs to your right, climb northeastwards and follow the edge of the void around until you're above the lovely little tarns known as Lochan a' Bhealaich Bhig. Just beyond this point, where you are directly above the lochans, you drop into the Bealach Beag. where a small stream finds its source. This is in a little bowl, and you can skirt around this to the west to avoid having to descend right into it. Climb northeastwards again, up very steep grassy slopes, until you can gain the wonderful south ridge of **the Storr**.

The Storr is the main peak of the **Trotternish Ridge** at 719m. To the east the cliffs continue, and here, detached from the main escarpment, you'll see a number of fantastic pinnacles, including the huge **Old Man of Storr**, a great fang of rock with a summit at 535m. Walkers can't get onto its top though – and it is difficult enough even for rock climbers.

This is another good place to look out for white-tailed eagles, as well as golden eagles, common buzzards and ravens. In summer you might here the piping call of the ring ouzel up here too. This is the mountain variety of the common blackbird, and it is similar to the blackbird apart from having a white chest. It lives only in mountainous regions, and in Britain is a summer-only visitor. It nests on crags and bouldery scree slopes.

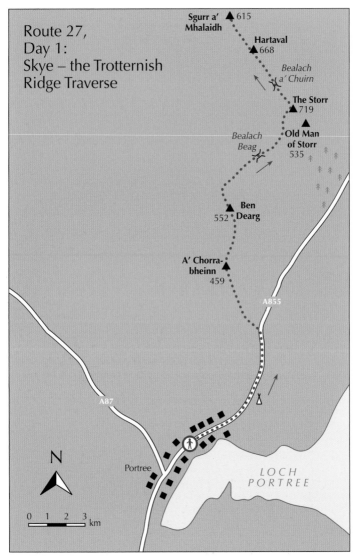

Route 27,
Day 1:
Skye – the Trotternish
Ridge Traverse

Sgurr a' Mhalaidh ▲ 615
Hartaval ▲ 668
Bealach a' Chuirn
The Storr ▲ 719
Old Man of Storr ▲ 535
Bealach Beag
Ben Dearg ▲ 552
A' Chorra-bheinn ▲ 459
A855
A87
Portree
LOCH PORTREE

N

0 1 2 3 km

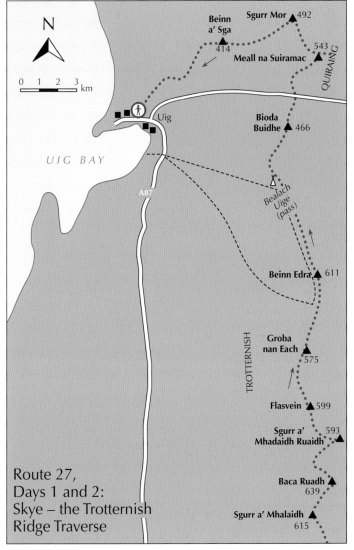

Route 27,
Days 1 and 2:
Skye – the Trotternish
Ridge Traverse

Looking south along the Trotternish Ridge from the Quiraing

North of the Storr a ridge descends into the moors above Rigg. As you don't want to go down this subsidiary ridge you should aim northwestwards from the summit trig pillar, towards the **Bealach a' Chuirn**. The going here is easy and not too steep.Beyond the Bealach a' Chuirn a short rocky slope takes you to the fine summit of **Hartaval** at 668m.

Carrying on from Hartaval the ridge bends first north-wards, then around to the northwest as you descend to Bealach Hartaval. The next hill on the traverse is **Baca Ruadh** at 639m, with its smaller top of **Sgurr a' Mhalaidh** crossed just before you get to the main summit.

Set off the main ridge slightly is a superb promontory known as **Sgurr a' Mhadaidh Ruadh**, and you can get onto this by following the edge of the escarpment around in a big curve, first going northwest, then over to the northeast. The summit stands at 593m, and being set forward on the eastern side of the main ridge there are good views along the escarpment, particularly northwards towards the distant **Quiraing**.

Head back along the promontory to get back on the main ridge, then turn right and climb up to Creag Liath at 609m. Beyond lies the Bealach na Leacaich before the dome-like

top of **Flasvein** at 599m. Along the switchback northwards you drop down into Bealach Chaiplin then onto **Groba nan Each** at 575m. Northwards again, the two cols known as Bealach Amadal and Bealach Mhoramhain are separated by an unnamed bump at spot height 579m. From Bealach Mhoramhain you are now at the base of the summit ridge of **Beinn Edra**, the second main peak of the Trotternish Ridge. An easy ridge has a path that leads up to its summit at 611m, where you'll find an OS trig pillar.

The path continues northwards, keeping the cliffs close by to your right. You'll probably be thinking of camping soon, so keep your eyes peeled for a good spot. At the Bealach Uige there is fresh water at the head of the Lon Airigh-uige, just off the ridge to the west.

The mighty cliffs of the Quiraing

DAY 2

A short and easy climb starts the day as you ascend north-westwards to the top of Druim na Coille at 321m. Continue along the ridge as it dips to Bealach nan Coisichean. Here you are faced with a steep, uniform slope ahead. Keep the edge of the escarpment to your right and climb the short slope to the summit of **Bioda Buidhe** at 466m.

Beyond Bioda Buidhe the ridge descends yet again, this time to the only road pass on the Trotternish Ridge. A minor road cuts over the ridge here from **Uig** in the west to Staffin in the east, and if necessary this offers an easy escape route. However, it would be a shame to take it, as you've nearly completed the ridge traverse. From the pass a good path heads off northeastwards, and usually has a long stream of tourists plodding towards the Quiraing.

Ignore this path, as it just goes under the cliffs. Instead, head just east of north, across grass and bilberry slopes to gain the top of the cliffs again. You go around the cleft of Maoladh Mor, then skirt the cliffs to get the best views at the amazing pinnacles of the Quiraing. These have wonderful names such as the Prison, the Needle and the Table. ◀

The Table is so flat that it used to be the pitch for games of shinty!

Once you've walked around the cliffs to have a good look down on the rock formations and the hundreds of people who will probably be milling about, make your way to the domed summit of **Meall na Suiramach** at 543m, where you'll find another OS trig pillar.

Easy slopes of grass lead northwestwards for **Sgurr Mor**, and from there onwards it's a change of direction. Turn to the southwest and walk over to **Beinn a' Sga** at 414m, crossing a stream to get to this flat summit. Head west a short way to the top of a cliff, then turn southwestwards and handrail along it to a fine gorge holding the stream known as Lon nan Earb.

Cross the stream and walk westwards to Creag Sneosdal above lovely Loch Sneosdal. Another OS trig pillar is passed at Suidh' a' Mhinn at 350m, then you turn southwards to gain the ridge of Creag Collascard. Follow this ridge to the little knoll of Reieval.

The view from Reieval is blocked to the east by the grassy slopes of the Trotternish Ridge, but westwards it is marvellous, leading your eye to the long chain of the Western Isles. Northwestwards you'll pick out the small island group known as the Shiants, the subject of an interesting book by Adam Nicholson. Entitled Sea Room, it describes the history of these fascinating islands, and how Adam came into their possession.

From Reieval follow the broad southwest ridge, passing a tiny lochan, and soon hit the A855 just above the village of Uig. Follow the road downhill into the village and you've completed a magnificent traverse of the Trotternish Ridge.

Backpackers near the summit of the Prison

251

ROUTE 28

Exploring Raasay

Number of Days	2
Total Distance	51km (31.5 miles)
Daily Distances	Day 1 – 28km (17.5 miles), Day 2 – 23km (14 miles)
Height Gain	Total: 930m; Day 1 – 620m, Day 2 – 310m
Maps	Ordnance Survey Landranger sheet number 24 Raasay, Applecross and Loch Torridon
Starting Point	Start at the pier at East Suisnish on Raasay – this is the only access point to the island on the regular ferry from Sconser on Skye. To get there you must first travel to Skye and then catch the regular CalMac ferry to Raasay (grid ref NG554340).

Area Summary

Raasay lies in the Inner Sound, with Skye to the west and south and the mainland to the east. It is separated from Skye by the Sound of Raasay, which is 3km wide to the west, where Portree nestles in its harbour and the Trotternish Ridge rises to the north of that island, but less than 1km wide in the south at 'the Narrows'.

Raasay is about 20km long, north to south, and about 5km wide. The southern part of the island is made up of low hills of Torridonian sandstone, while the northern part is largely gneiss. An oddity here is that there are large expanses of good loam between 200m and 300m above sea level, which indicates that the island pretty much escaped glaciation. This accounts for the very varied flora to be found here, particularly on the eastern side of the island.

The highest hill on Raasay is Dun Caan, a flat-topped mound that gives extensive views all around.

Route Summary

This walk covers much rough ground, but is never too difficult, even for fairly inexperienced backpackers. Although a lot of the walking on the first day is off paths and tracks, the going underfoot is easy, being over grassy slopes with occasional heather patches. On Day 2 the walk follows Callum's Road, now with a good, hard surface, then tracks.

The route starts by heading for the east coast and follows this to the old settlement at Hallaig. From there you climb Dun Caan, then follow the escarpment on the east side of the island right through to the most northern point, where you'll be able to find somewhere to pitch your tent for the night.

On Day 2 you head south, following the easy road to the Alan Evans Memorial Hostel, then tracks through Raasay Forest lead you back to the pier.

Tourist Information

The tourist information centre in Portree, on Skye, is on Bridge Street and can book accommodation for you on Skye (tel 01478 612137), as can the one in Broadford (tel 01471 822361). You'll also find a good tourist information centre in Kyle of Lochalsh, down by the harbour (tel 01599 534276).

Transport

Citylink buses from either Fort William or Inverness to Portree pass by the ferry terminal at Sconser and will stop there, tel 08705 505050, www.citylink.co.uk. The ferry to Raasay is operated by Caledonian Macbrayne (tel 08705 650000), or visit their website at www.calmac.co.uk.

Accommodation and Supplies

On Skye there are lots of options in Portree and Broadford. Give the tourist information centres a call for advice (numbers above). There are shops in Broadford and Portree, but not on Raasay.

For accommodation on Raasay you can book into the Isle of Raasay Hotel (tel 01478 660222, www.isleofraasayhotel.co.uk), or use the delightful SYHA Alan Evans Memorial Hostel, tel 0870 0041146, or contact the central booking service of the SYHA, tel 0870 155255, www.syha.org.uk.

Overnight Options

Either camp wild right at the northern tip of the island, or anywhere else en route.

Escape Routes

At any point on this route you can make your way to Callum's Road, which runs along the western side of the island. This takes you southwards back to civilisation.

DAY 1

From the pier at **East Suisnish** turn right, eastwards, and follow a minor road around the coast to **Eyre Point**. Walk down onto the shore and continue northeastwards towards **Fearns** (at high tide it may be necessary to walk through the woods above the shore).

The shoreline is a good place to look out for otters. They are often seen here, and a flat, calm sea gives the best opportunity for spotting on, splashing about in the water. They are much more difficult to spot on land, but you might be lucky.

There's a small stream to cross coming down through the woods before you reach the scattered dwellings at Fearns.

Pick mussels for supper from the shore of Raasay

The woods here are a great place to see some of the typical birds of Raasay. In summer look out for finches, tits and warblers, while you might see dippers in the fast-flowing streams.

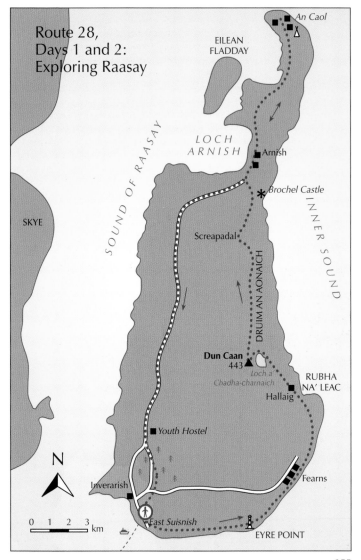

Route 28,
Days 1 and 2:
Exploring Raasay

EILEAN
FLADDAY

An Caol

*LOCH
ARNISH*

Arnish

SOUND OF RAASAY

* *Brochel Castle*

INNER SOUND

SKYE

Screapadal

DRUIM AN AONAICH

Dun Caan
443

*Loch a
Chadha-charnaich*

RUBHA
NA' LEAC

Hallaig

Youth Hostel

N

Inverarish

East Suisnish

Fearns

EYRE POINT

0 1 2 3
km

Once over the stream head uphill to another minor road at South Fearns. Turn right along this and follow it to its end beyond North Fearns. There is a good track here that contours around to a point just above the little headland of **Rubha na' Leac**. From here the path goes westwards for a short way, then splits. Take the path on the right that heads towards the old crofting community of **Hallaig**.

From Hallaig you can climb up to the northwest through ancient flower meadows to the starker moorland around **Loch a' Chadha-charnaich**. Climb up a gully to the northwest of this loch and you are just northeast of **Dun Caan**, the highest point of the island. A delightful little path begins on the

For a long time the island of **Raasay** avoided the Clearances that were going on all over Scotland. Landowners were sympathetic – Macleod of Raasay used up his fortune in the 1830s trying to help the islanders when other communities were suffering with the potato famine.

When George Rainy bought the island for 35,000 guineas in 1843, he too was initially sympathetic. For a while he genuinely tried to improve life on the island, but when this began to fail he turned to sheep farming and the evictions began. The population dropped from over 600 to 400, and continued to decrease until Baird & Co bought the island in 1912 to extract iron ore. This brought jobs, and the population stabilised at around 200.

Hallaig was one village that was lost to the Clearances. It must have once been a lovely place to live, though of course with its hardships too.

northwestwards side of the little peak, and leads easily to the summit.

Raasay was visited by Johnson and Boswell in 1773 during their tour of the Hebrides, and it is said that Boswell danced a reel of pleasure on the flat top of Dun Caan – almost certainly accompanied by one of the famous pipers from the island.

The summit stands at a lowly 443m, but is widely regarded as one of the finest viewpoints on Scotland's western seaboard.

From the summit head back down the path to the moorland to the northwest. The path goes off to the west, but you should aim to the northeast and cross easy moorland to the top of a long line of cliffs that fringe the eastern side of the island. Here the going is not too difficult, and you can use the cliff-top edge as a handrail to guide you northwards to **Druim an Aonaich**. ▶

Beyond Druim an Aonaich there is a huge gully cut by a stream coming from the slopes of Beinn a' Chapuill. Head westwards to get around this, then turn to the northeast and descend the steep slopes on the north side of the stream to the abandoned shielings at **Screapadal**.

It is at Druim an Aonaich that many of the rare plants of the island can be found. There are unusual forms of saxifrage, orchids, ferns and mosses hiding in crevices on the cliffs.

Screapadal was the scene of the worst of George Rainy's clearances. The village and surrounding area were immortalised in the poems of Scotland's arguably greatest poet, Sorley Maclean, who was a Raasay man.

At Screapadal you pick up a path that leads northwards through woodland.

Raasay is the only island in the Hebrides that still has a good population of pine martens. This member of the Mustelid family, which also includes otters, badgers, weasels and stoats, lives in wood and rocky places, and this woodland is ideal for them. You may see signs in the form of scat on rocks, but you'd have to be very lucky indeed to catch a glimpse of these mainly nocturnal animals.

The path becomes a track and takes you uphill slightly to join a minor road. Turn right on this and you'll soon be above **Brochel Castle**.

Continue northeastwards on the main road, passing close by Loch Beag, then skirting the western coast of this most northerly peninsula of Raasay. The road ends at **Arnish**, where a small community once lived. This road is known as Callum's Road.

Beyond Arnish a track continues, first to Torran where the school used to be – it closed in 1960 – then onwards to a junction of paths. Ignore the one going northwestwards to

Brochel Castle was built in the 15th century by the MacSwans, but became better known as the stronghold of a band of pirates, the MacLeods of Lewis. The last known inhabitant was Iain Garbh, who died in 1671. The castle is in a splendid position, sitting on a sheer pinnacle of rock overlooking the east coast, and used to stand three storeys high.

Eilean Fladday, and instead climb up to the east and skirt around the eastern slopes of Beinn na h-Iolaire (you can make a short diversion to climb this smashing little peak). Now heading northwards you pass Lochan gun Ghrunnd, which makes a fine wild campsite, then come to **An Caol**, the scattered shielings at the northern tip of Raasay.

DAY 2
Begin the day by retracing your steps southwards to Arnish and Callum's Road. Follow the road to Brochel Castle, then onwards to the junction with the path leading down to Screapadal. Ignore this path this time and continue along the road. It's a very quiet lane and makes for good walking, with spectacular views westwards to Skye's Trotternish peninsula, and southwestwards into the Red Cuillin and the northern end of the Black Cuillin.

Follow the road all the way to a junction where the lane swings off sharply to the right, well beyond the small crofts at Balmeanach. At the junction take the left lane, heading initially southwestwards to a series of small pools on the roadside.

Here I have twice seen red-throated divers during the summer. These large waterbirds are only found on high lochans in the summer, and when calling to each other let out an eerie wailing noise, which is why the North Americans call them loons.

Just south of the pools you pass the SYHA **youth hostel**, and then enter the woodlands around the main settlement on Raasay – the village of **Inverarish**. Continue through the

delightful woodland to a T-junction and turn left over the river. Turn right on another track immediately and follow this alongside the river down to the coast. This lane leads to a junction, where you should continue southwestwards around Suisnish Point to the pier at East Suisnish.

Skylarks are common Raasay

ROUTE 29
Discovering Rum

Number of Days	2
Total Distance	35km (22 miles)
Daily Distances	Day 1 – 23km (14.25 miles), Day 2 – 12km (7.75 miles)
Height Gain	Total: 1700m; Day 1 – 1520m, Day 2 – 180m
Maps	Ordnance Survey Landranger sheet 39 Rum, Eigg and Muck
Starting Point	Start at the new pier at Kinloch. To reach Rum you have to catch a ferry from either Mallaig, with Caledonian MacBrayne, or from Arisaig, with Arisaig Marine.

Area Summary

Rum (or Rhum, as you persistently see it in some literature) is a diamond-shaped island that lies off the west coast of Scotland. It covers an area of about 10,700 hectares and measures only about 13km between its extreme points.

The highest mountain on the island is the fine summit of Askival at 812m. Other notable mountains in the Rum Cuillin include Barkeval, Hallival, Trallval, Ainshval and Sgurr nan Gillean. This mountain group lies in the south of the island, while to the west are the wonderful, but lower, summits of Ard Nev, Orval and Bloodstone Hill. The north and east of Rum are made up of low hills and moorland, with some substantial forestry around Kinloch village on the east coast. Kinloch is the only settlement on the island, although there are a few bothies, and the deer-monitoring-teams building at Kilmory on the north coast.

Rum is one of the four islands that make up the Small Isles group, the others being Canna, Eigg and Muck. The group lies off the western coast from Mallaig.

The island of Rum has been run as a national nature reserve since 1957 and forms part of the UNESCO Man and Biosphere (MAB) programme. The inhabitants are employees (and their families) of Scottish Natural Heritage, which owns the island.

Route Summary

Rum is one of my favourite islands. There's something about visiting this special place that makes you feel privileged to be there. Perhaps it is that the island used to be quite hard to explore, as the owners, Scottish Natural Heritage, used to ask you to write to the warden for permission to stay on the island, and few people bothered. Nowadays it's a much more relaxed affair – you just turn up on the ferry and everybody greets you!

This walk takes in the very remote hills on the western side of the island, but you start by getting up close and personal with the Rum Cuillin. These rugged mountains are quite tough for walking, and not really the type of terrain suitable for the backpackers, so on this route you'll ascend the two most northerly hills in the group, to give you a feel for this magical mountain mass, then head off westwards for the wilds of the furthest-flung hills.

The walk begins with an ascent of Hallival at the head of Glen Harris. You then traverse over to Barkeval to descend westwards and pick up a track on the rough moorland beneath Ard Nev. This summit is then reached via the south ridge of the mountain before you traverse over to the top of Orval. A circuitous route takes you around the high cliffs that skirt Orval's summit plateau to the west, then you walk beneath these cliffs on a good path to make an ascent of Bloodstone Hill. A rough walk down into Glen Guirdil takes you to the bothy on the west coast for the night.

On Day 2 you follow the coastline northwards for a short way before hiking up beautiful Glen Shellesder and through to the Kinloch Glen.

Tourist Information

The tourist information centre in Mallaig is down by the harbour (tel 01687 462170), and there's also a bigger one at Cameron Square in Fort William (tel 01397 703781). Good information on the Small Isles can be found on the tourist board's website www.visitscotland.com.

Transport

Trains from Fort William and Glasgow go on to Mallaig and stop at Arisaig too, tel 08457 550033, www.firstgroup.com/scotrail. For CalMac ferries contact their central booking department, tel 01687 462403 or visit www.calmac.co.uk. For the boat trip from Arisaig on the MV Shearwater contact Arisaig Marine, tel 01687 450224, www.arisaig.co.uk.

Accommodation and Supplies

There aren't many options on Rum itself. You can camp down on the shore near to the old pier, which is very pleasant, or stay in the hostel in Kinloch Castle, which is also very fine (tel 01687 462037). There is a small shop over on the other side of the Kinloch River beyond the castle, which is good fun and friendly, but it only has a limited supply of stock. It is best to bring your own food with you from Mallaig.

Overnight Options

You can use the bothy at Guirdil, which is maintained by the Mountain Bothies Association. These mountain huts are left open for all to use and are free of charge. You can join the Mountain Bothies Association on www.mountain-bothies.org.uk. This bothy is in a lovely position beneath the huge northern ridge of Bloodstone Hill, and has a superb view out to the island of Canna (grid ref NG319014).

Escape Routes

The main track from the southwest coast of Rum at Harris through Kinloch village is the best option for getting out of the hills quickly in an emergency. You can reach this good Land-Rover track from anywhere on this route.

DAY 1

From the new pier on **Loch Scresort** walk westwards on the track by the shore. You'll pass the old pier, which is still in use, and a couple of houses before coming to the imposing front of **Kinloch Castle**.

As you approach the castle you pass over a rather substantial bridge, and as soon as you're over, before reaching the castle itself there's a footpath on the left-hand side. Follow this path alongside a stream and through the woods. You soon come out onto the open hillside beside the tumbling waters of Allt Slugan a' Choilich. The path is obvious and easy to follow, at least until you are high up in Coire Dubh. ◀

Once in the upper corrie you should head southwestwards for the low point on the main ridge, the Bealach

Look out for eagles here. Golden eagles regularly hunt over the ridges enclosing the corrie, particularly on the Meall Breac side.

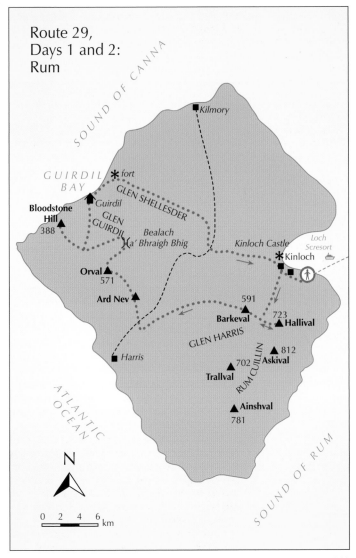

Route 29,
Days 1 and 2:
Rum

SOUND OF CANNA

■ *Kilmory*

*GUIRDIL
BAY*   ✳ fort

GLEN SHELLESDER

**Bloodstone
Hill** ▲   ▲ *Guirdil*
388   GLEN
GUIRDIL   *Bealach
(a' Bhraigh Bhig*   *Kinloch Castle*   *Loch
Scresort*

✳ Kinloch

Orval ▲
571

Ard Nev ▲   591
▲
Barkeval   723
▲ **Hallival**

GLEN HARRIS

■ *Harris*   ▲ 812
Askival

702
▲
Trallval   RUM CUILLIN

ATLANTIC
OCEAN   ▲ **Ainshval**
781

N

SOUND OF RUM

0 2 4 6 km

Bairc-mheall. As you near the bealach the view ahead opens out into the spectacular bowl of **Glen Harris**, with the jagged peaks of the **Rum Cuillin** arranged around its head to your south and east.

The rock on the island of **Rum** is mainly granite, so when the Bulloughs, the wealthy Lancastrian family who owned the island in the latter half of the 19th century, decided to build the luxurious pleasure dome of **Kinloch Castle** they brought in the sandstone from Annan – no expense spared. Seclusion and privacy were paramount to the Bulloughs, who invited high-powered guests to their glittering parties, and guns were often fired at approaching boats to discourage unwelcome visitors. The castle was mysteriously abandoned after one lavish party, and the family never returned, leaving wine in the cellars and musical instruments in the stands in the gallery. You can visit the castle at appointed times when tours are conducted.

These peaks are great for those without heavy backpacks, but you do need a good head for heights to traverse the ridge in its entirety. However, you can climb the first peak quite easily from the Bealach Bairc-mheall. Turn left and follow rough stony slopes to the summit of **Hallival** at 723m.

The next peak on the ridge beyond Hallival is **Askival**, at 812m the highest mountain on the island. Beyond that the ridge drops to Bealach an Oir, then there's a traverse of a really rocky peak, **Trallval** at 702m. Once over that, the ridge takes scramblers on to the summit of **Ainshval** at 781m. However, the best route for backpackers from Hallival lies westwards, towards the wilderness hills on the west coast of the island. (Here you'll find more golden eagles, plus there's a really good chance that you'll see white-tailed eagles too.)

Head back to Bealach Bairc-mheall, and from there go westwards to the fine summit of **Barkeval** at 591m. Descend just north of west down alongside the Allt Cul a' Mhill to the southern end of beautiful Long Loch. From here go west towards a track by a small plantation underneath the eastern facade of **Ard Nev**, your next summit. Ard Nev is a fine mountain rising from the moorland around Glen Harris. Here you'll probably see lots of red deer, and there's always a chance of more eagles.

The Nature Conservancy Council (NCC) bought Rum in 1957 in order to study the breeding habits of the red deer there. This work is ongoing today, by the now renamed Scottish Natural Heritage (SNH), and although much of this research is carried out at the northern end of the island near Kilmory, there are lots of deer to be seen elsewhere too.

The Rum Cuillin from the ferry

Head southwards down the track for a short distance until you can easily walk westwards over the moor to climb the low knoll known as Ard Meall. From here a fine ridge leads northwards to the summit of Ard Nev at 556m.

Leave Ard Nev's top by heading down grassy slopes to the northwest into a narrow col, then walk westwards uphill to the flat summit plateau of **Orval**. The summit, at 571m, is marked by an OS trig pillar to the southwest.

As you leave Orval's top, by heading north across the plateau, you get great views westwards to **Bloodstone Hill**, and across the **Sound of Canna** to the island of the same name. Skirt around the top of a rocky gully, then walk just east of north into a dip and up a slight rise on the other side. Beyond this is a steep descent along a rocky ridge, which should be

Backpacking up Orval

followed carefully down to **Bealach a' Bhraigh Bhig**, with the fine little peak of Fionchra rising on the other side.

Once at the Bealach a' Bhraigh Bhig, pick up a good stalker's track. Turn left on it and it takes you back to the south-west, right underneath the imposing western crags of Orval. The view here looking up really is impressive, as huge pinnacles of rock tower over the path.

The path itself is straightforward, and a joy to follow. It skirts high around the headwall of Glen Guirdil, and you should follow it to a broad col known as Bealach an Dubh-bhraigh, which lies between Orval and Bloodstone Hill. The path then continues to the northwest, leading to the fine summit of Bloodstone Hill at 388m.

The view from **Bloodstone Hill** over towards Canna is superb, and on a clear day you can see much of the Outer Hebrides too. The name of the hill comes from the green, almost serpentine, rock that is found here. It used to be used to make arrowheads and axe heads, and these were shipped around Europe.

Bloodstone Hill today is one of the very best places in the Hebrides to see the **white-tailed eagle**. These huge birds of prey – even bigger than the golden eagle – were first reintroduced to this island in the 1970s. They were extinct in Scotland by 1917 (around 1898 in Ireland and 1794 in England), but by 1975 the NCC had begun to reintroduce birds from Norway. The first British chick was successfully reared by a wild pair on Rum in 1985.

Numbers are still not high though – around 30 breeding pairs to date – but birds have moved further afield and set up territories on the islands of Skye, Mull and the Outer Hebrides, and some can be seen on the mainland. They are regularly seen on all four of the Small Isles. The 2003 breeding season for white-tailed eagles was the most successful since the reintroduction scheme began, with a total of 26 chicks fledging during the summer.

Sitting on Bloodstone Hill you can often watch these birds soaring by, while if you know someone with a boat, that is also a wonderful way to watch them from below.

Once you've had a good, relaxing eagle-watch, retrace your steps down to Bealach an Dubh-bhraigh. From the bealach there is some rough tussock grass to cover before you reach the bothy beneath Bloodstone Hill. Head northwards down into Glen Guirdil, crossing the stream to its north side. Here you'll pick up a vague path that takes you downstream to the **Guirdil Bothy**, which lies right down on the shore in **Guirdil Bay.**

> You'll be spending the night at the bothy, which gives you ample time to watch for eagles on Bloodstone Hill. Also keep an eye out for the wild goats that live down by the shore here. A search in among the rocks on the shore will turn up lumps of green bloodstone too!

DAY 2

Begin the day by climbing back up Glen Guirdil a short way – say 200m. From here you'll see a little knoll to the north-east, just above the coastline. Pass to the right of this and pick up a good path that leads via a shallow wade over a stream into **Glen Shellesder**.

> Where the Glen Shellesder burn tumbles over a cliff into the sea below, you'll see a flat-topped mound overlooking the cliffs. This is the site of an Iron Age fort. It is well worth exploring, although there's little to be seen today.

On the north side of the Glen Shellesder burn is a track that leads up the glen. This is obvious underfoot, if a little boggy in places.

> As you head up Glen Shellesder keep a sharp lookout for golden eagles on the ridge to the north – I've often seen them here. This is also the edge of the main red-deer monitoring area, so you'll probably see herds of them here too. Many have ear tags to aid individual identification, but despite this, do remember that these are wild animals.

The tracks takes you right up to the head of the glen to a broad, boggy col, then down the other side to the top edge of a small plantation. Turn right here and follow the path down to a main Land-Rover track in the glen below. Turn right and follow this track into the head of Kinloch Glen. Here the track comes in from Glen Harris on the right – make sure you go left at this junction!

The Guirdil bothy

Manx Shearwaters nest in the Rum Cuillin.

Walking down into Kinloch Glen is a delight. The track here is good underfoot, so you can afford to take in your surroundings as you walk. The view across Loch Scresort leads the eye out to the mainland across the Sleat peninsula on Skye. On clear days you can pick out some of the Knoydart peaks, including Ladhar Bheinn and Sgurr Coire Choinnichean.

As you near **Kinloch** village you enter the woodland that surrounds the shores of **Loch Scresort**. Follow the track through the woodland to a major junction. Turn left for the small shop, right for Kinloch Castle and the pier, or go straight ahead to walk on a loop by the shore that leads back around to the castle. Spending a little time exploring Kinloch, and perhaps having a look inside the castle if there is a conducted tour, is a fine way to end this walk on the island of Rum.

ROUTE 30

Through Cona Glen

Number of Days	2
Total Distance	38km (24 miles), or 50km (32 miles) for the longer alternative
Daily Distances	Day 1 – 25km (15.5 miles), Day 2 – 13km (8.5 miles), or 26km (16.5 miles) for the longer alternative
Height Gain	Total: 1370m (1920m); Day 1 – 1210m, Day 2 – 160m, or 710m for the longer alternative
Maps	OS Landranger sheet 41 Ben Nevis and Fort William for the start of the walk, and sheet 40 Mallaig & Glenfinnan – Loch Shiel for the second half
Starting Point	Fort William, down by the pier for the Camusnagaul Ferry across Loch Linnhe (grid ref NN099738).
Finishing Point	Glenfinnan railway station, off the A830(T) between Fort William and Mallaig (grid ref NM 899810).

Area Summary

Across Loch Linnhe from the busy hillwalking hotspots of Glencoe and Fort William you'll find the hills of Ardgour pleasantly quiet and relaxing. Few people bother to come here – there are no Munros this side of the loch! Ardgour itself is part of the large peninsula that forms this massive chunk of the western Highlands. Other parts of the peninsula are also well worth exploring, and include the regions of Sunart, Moidart, Ardnamurchan, Kingairloch and Morvern. This is one of the finest areas of Scotland for the hillwalker, and one you should certainly explore time and again.

The western boundary is taken by Loch Linnhe, the huge sea loch that stretches from Fort William southwestwards out to the sea near Mull. Northwards from Ardgour is Loch Eil, itself an extension of Loch Linnhe. To the south is the Sound of Mull, while to the west is Loch Shiel, the long loch that runs southwestwards from Glenfinnan. Over Loch Shiel lie Sunart and Moidart, fabulous areas in their own right.

Although there are no Munros in this region, there are some great lower hills to climb, including some very rugged Corbetts. The best known of these are Garbh Bheinn of Ardgour, and Beinn Resipol over in Sunart.

Route Summary

This walk starts with an ascent of a rough and rugged Corbett, Stob Coire a' Chearcaill. From there you follow a long ridge down into the Cona Glen, then pick up a track through this wild and vast valley. The walk takes you right up into the head of the glen where you will camp for the night.

On Day 2 you have a choice of routes. You can either climb over a pass to the north, then down the other side to the A830 just outside Glenfinnan, or you can climb to a high mountain pass and traverse the little-visited Corbetts of Sgurr Ghiubhsachain and Sgorr Craobh a' Chaorainn before dropping down to the A830. Both ways are tremendous, but the mountain route gives fine views over Loch Shiel to the mountains of Moidart and Sunart, and is recommended in anything like good weather.

The route itself is quite difficult, considering the low stature of these hills, and you do need a good idea of how to navigate to do the high-level route. Having said that, the daily distances are short, and the main track through the Cona Glen and over to Glenfinnan is easy to follow, being suitable for anyone who loves wild country.

Tourist Information

The tourist information centre in Fort William is on Cameron Square (tel 01397 703781). Here you can get up-to-date advice on accommodation, trains and ferries, as well as other things to do in the Fort William area.

Transport

Fort William is on the main west coast railway line from Glasgow to Mallaig, and that is without a doubt the best way to get there. The scenery along the route is spectacular to say the least! It is also the best way to get back to Fort William from Glenfinnan at the end of the walk, as Glenfinnan is on the same line. Contact Scot Rail, tel 08457 550033, www.firstgroup.com/scotrail.

The walk actually starts on the west side of Loch Linnhe at Camusnagaul (grid ref NN095751). To get there you'll have to catch the delightful passenger ferry (no cars) run by the Lochaber Transport Forum under the banner of the Highland Council (tel 01397 709011). (Note There is no Sunday service on this crossing.)

Accommodation and Supplies
There are lots of options in Fort William, from the biggest hotels down to the tiniest of bed and breakfasts, plus hostels and campsites too. I always stay at the Myrtle Bank Guest House just south of the town (tel 01397 702034). There's also Berkeley House (tel 01397 701185), which is a pleasant place to stay, e-mail berkeleyhouse67@hotmail.com.

In Glenfinnan there are few options, but it is easy to jump on the train back to Fort William for the night. Having said that, there are two good hotels in Glenfinnan – the Prince's House Hotel (tel 01397 722246) and the Glenfinnan House Hotel (tel 01397 722235). Both of these are worth a try. There are no guest houses or bed and breakfasts in Glenfinnan.

For shopping your only option is Fort William, where you'll find everything you could possible need for a few days in the hills. There are lots of shops, supermarkets and a couple of good outdoor shops – I'd recommend West Coast Leisure at the south end of the main street.

Overnight Options
Camp at the head of Cona Glen, either down by the burn or high up on the ridge.

Escape Routes
You can get out of Cona Glen by simply following the track eastwards to Conaglen House. Once over the watershed to Glenfinnan the easiest route out is by carrying on to the A830, which runs between Fort William and Glenfinnan.

DAY 1
As you cross **Loch Linnhe** on the **ferry** you'll notice that the hill opposite is topped by a TV mast. This is the hill you must first climb to begin the traverse to **Stob Coire a' Chearcaill**, your first destination. I usually leave the pier and turn right for 200m to a stream, then bash up through the trees by the stream and on to the open hillside. This is fine, but hard going,

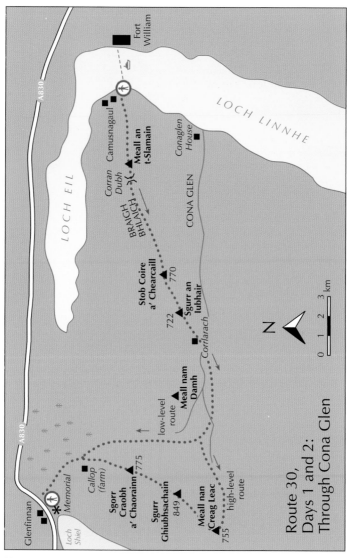

Route 30,
Days 1 and 2:
Through Cona Glen

and you might like to consider going left from the pier, along the road for a short way until clear of the house at Trislaig, then climbing the hill from there. If you're really worried about it, I can also recommend a slightly longer, but easier approach up beautiful Glen Sron a' Chreagain.

Whichever route you take, you'll find yourself on the slopes of Meall an t-Slamain, and you should walk to its top at 467m.

> Look back across Loch Linnhe for superb views of the mass of Ben Nevis, Britain's highest mountain. You are looking at the western slopes from here, which are not quite as impressive as the huge cliffs on the north face, but the mountain is spectacular from any angle. From here you also get a good view of the peaks in the Mamores range that lies to the south of Ben Nevis.

From Meall an t-Slamain head down to the bealach at **Corran Dubh**, then pick up the long, easy angled ridge of **Braigh Bhlaich**, which gets gradually narrower as you approach the summit ridge of Stob Coire a' Chearcaill at 770m, and a great viewpoint.

Head westwards down a broad ridge, then where it begins to get steeper after 1km go southwestwards into a col, then up to the summit of **Sgurr an Iubhair** at 722m.

The long west ridge of Sgurr an Iubhair is lovely to walk. It's a bit rough underfoot, but as you walk you get superb views right into the head of Cona Glen and to the peaks arranged around either side.

Follow this ridge to a little lochan, then onwards to Gearr Leachdann, where there is a narrow southwest ridge leading down to the house at **Corrlarach**. Here you pick up the main track up the glen, which comes from **Conaglen House** down on Loch Linnhe. This is another good way of gaining access to the glen – you can follow this track all the way from the house, but it does mean more road walking at the start!

> I saw my first golden eagle in this glen. I was walking through to Glenfinnan with some friends when we heard a long, deep screeching sound coming from a rocky gully

Bistort is common in Cona Glen, and attracts orange-tip butterflies

high on Sgurr an Iubhair. Out of the gully flew a magnificent golden eagle, and we watched it for half an hour.
Later that day, as we crossed over the pass to drop down
to Glenfinnan, another eagle flew up from a rock just
around a bend, and we had a great view of it as it sailed,
without a single flap of its huge wings, back up and over
the pass.

Turn west on the track from Corrlarach and follow it up
into the glen. The valley here is lovely – there are some magnificent trees growing by the side of the river, and the views
on either side of the mountains are spectacular.

The path passes below a rocky bluff, which makes a great
place for a break, then continues up the glen. Where the path
begins to climb away from the river you can start thinking
about where you're going to camp overnight. I usually camp
discreetly down by the river here.

DAY 2
There are two route options today, depending on how difficult you want things to get! I'll describe the easier route first.

Low Route to Glenfinnan
Regain the track above the river and follow it uphill as it curves
to the north, then northeast, and soon find yourself on a high
bealach between the peaks of Sgorr Craobh a' Chaorainn to
the northwest and Meall nam Damh to the east.

Go over this bealach and follow the track, which is boggy
in places, though not difficult to follow. The path leads you
down to a forest, and you stay on the outside of this, on the
west side. The path continues to the farmstead of **Callop**, and
just beyond this you come to a major track. Turn right over a
bridge and you find yourself on the A830 between Fort William
and Glenfinnan. Turn left on the road and walk into Glenfinnan,
taking care of the traffic.

High Route to Glenfinnan
From your camp you begin the day by heading westwards
along the course of the main Cona River. The going is slightly
easier on the north side, and as it becomes a stream you gain

height and soon find yourself on the bealach between Druim Tarsuinn and Meall nan Creag Leac. Turn right and climb **Meall nan Creag Leac**, a fine little peak at 755m.

Turning to the northeast, now pick up a good ridge route that leads to the summit of **Sgurr Ghiubhsachain** at 849m. The summit here is quite complicated – you need to head southeast for 600m, then turn to the east down to a bealach with a little lochan. From here there is a really good ridge that takes you to the top of **Sgorr Craobh a' Chaorainn** at 775m.

The view to the west is very fine, taking in the peaks of Moidart across Loch Shiel. Mike Tomkies, a well-known wildlife photographer, lived for many years down on the shores of Loch Shiel. Here he studied golden eagles as well as red deer and Scottish wildcats.

The northeast ridge of Sgorr Craobh a' Chaorainn is rocky but not difficult, and leads down to the top edge of a forest where you pick up a path near Callop. This is the path taken by the low route to Glenfinnan. Turn northwards along the outside of the forest and follow the above route to Glenfinnan.

The Glenfinnan memorial stands proud at the head of Loch Shiel. It is at the spot where Bonnie Prince Charlie raised his standard in 1745, and so marked the beginning of the Jacobite uprising of that year. With an army of just 200 Highlanders, the young Prince waited here for Cameron of Loch Shiel to bring his men to join the uprising.

The railway station in Glenfinnan lies 1km further along the road from the memorial, and from there you can catch the train back to Fort William, or put your feet up in one of the hotels in village before heading off the next morning.

The author runs regular navigation and other skills courses for hillwalkers and mountaineers, as well as hillwalking and scrambling holidays. You can get in touch with him via www.wildridgeadventure.com, tel 07720 169191.

Wilderness Scotland also has a good selection of walking trips, often to unusual locations: www.wildernessscotland.com, tel 0131 6256635.

The Scottish Tourist Board has a very useful website: www.visitscotland.com, tel 0845 2255121.
For the northern isles you will also find www.visitshetland.com, tel 08701 999440, and www.visitorkney.com, tel 01856 872856, very useful.

The Mountain Bothy Association website is: www.mountainbothies.org.uk.

The Backpacker's Club is a worthwhile association for anyone interested in backpacking: www.backpackersclub.co.uk.

The Welsh Hewitts Club is a very active hillwalking club. The author is currently the chairman, and you can contact the club through him via his website.

APPENDIX 2:
BIBLIOGRAPHY

The most useful general mountain guidebooks for Scotland are the district guides published by the Scottish Mountaineering Trust.
For wildlife books I find that the Christopher Helm, Poyser and Pica Press publications are invaluable. These are all imprints of A&C Black, and their website gives full details: www.acblack.com/christopherhelm.
For the islands of Scotland the only book worth considering is **The Scottish Islands** by Hamish Haswell Smith, published by Canongate: www.canongate.net.
Books on mountain safety run into the hundreds, but best of all are:
Mountaincraft and Leadership, Eric Langmuir (The Scottish Sports Council and the Mountain Leader Training Board, 1995)
Mountain Skills Training Handbook, Pete Hill and Stuart Johnston (David & Charles, 2004)
Wild Camping, Kevin Walker (Constable, 1989)
Mountain Hazards, Kevin Walker (Constable, 1988)

APPENDIX 3
ROUTE SUMMARY

No	Route Name	Start/Finish	Distance	No. Days	Height	OS Landranger Map	Difficulty
1	Shetland – Esha Ness	Urafirth – North Mainland	52km	2	850m	3	Moderate
2	Shetland – Mainland South	Start – Scalloway Castle Finish – Grutness	68km	2	1570m	4	Strenuous
3	Shetland – Yell	Start – Ulsta Finish – Gutcher	54km	2	690m	1 & 3	Easy
4	Orkney – Western Mainland	Start – Birsay Finish – Stromness	38km	2	380m	6	Easy
5	Lewis – Western Mountains	Mangurstadh	40km	2	1140m	13	Moderate
6	North Harris	Abhainn Suidhe	31km	2	2060m	13	Strenuous
7	South Uist	Howmore	35km	2	1680m	22	Moderate
8	Cape Wrath and Sandwood Bay	Start – Kyle of Durness Finish – Kinlochbervie	47km	2	1530m	9	Moderate
9	Ben Hope	Kinloch Lodge	24km	2	1160m	9 & 10	Easy
10	Inverpolly	Inverkirkaig	36km	2	1200m	15	Easy
11	Assynt from Inchnadamph	Inchnadamph	33km	2	1420m	15	Easy
12	The Munros of the Inverlael Forest	Inverlael	49km	2	2520m	20	Challenging
13	Fisherfield and Letterewe	Start – Poolewe Finish – Corrie Hallie	45km (+13km)	2 (+1)	740m (+970m)	19	Moderate (Strenuous)
14	Applecross Peninsula	Applecross	49km	2	1420m	24	Moderate
15	The Fannichs Traverse	Start – Braemore Junction Finish – Lochluichart	35km	2	1280m	20	Strenuous

No	Route Name	Start/Finish	Distance	No. Days	Height	OS Landranger Map	Difficulty
16	Torridon from Shieldaig	Shieldaig	44km	2	2070m	19	Strenuous
17	Coulin Forest from Torridon	Coulin Forest	39km	2	2470m	25	Challenging
18	Strath Carron Munros from Craig	Craig	48km	2	3070m	25	Challenging
19	The Head of Strathconon	Scardroy	38km	2	1880m	25	Moderate
20	High Level Traverse of Glen Affric	Loch Beinn a' Mheadhoin	59km	3	3400m	25	Challenging
21	Beinn Fhada & A' Ghlas Bheinn	Morvich	35km	2	1750m	33	Strenuous
22	High Level Traverse of Glen Shiel	Kintail village	60km	3	4610m	33	Challenging
23	Shiel Bridge to Glenfinnan	Start – Shiel Bridge Finish – Glenfinnan	71km	5	2310m	33 & 40	Moderate
24	The Mountains of Knoydart	Inverie	42km	2	3510m	33	Challenging
25	Skye – Black Cuillin Lochs and Bealachs	Sligachan Inn	40km	2	1640m	32	
26	Skye – Red Cuillin	Start – Sligachan Inn Finish – Broadford	28km	2	2870m	32	Strenuous
27	Skye – Trotternish Ridge Traverse	Start – Portree Finish – Uig	54km	2	2810m	23	Strenuous
28	Exploring Raasay	East Suisnish	51km	2	930m	24	Easy
29	Discovering Rum	Kinloch	35km	2	1700m	39	Moderate
30	Through the Cona Glen	Start – Camusnagaul Finish – Glenfinnan	38km (50km)	2	1370m (2080m)	40 & 41	Moderate (Strenuous)

Difficulty Grades:
Easy: Low level or short distances each day. Suitable for regular hillwalkers.
Moderate: Numerous hills or longer distances. Suitable for fit hillwalkers.
Strenuous: Multiple peaks traverse, or very long distances. Suitable for experienced Munro-baggers.
Challenging: Long mountain traverses, sometimes over difficult terrain. Suitable for experienced and fit mountain walkers.

Glossary of common names and terms used in this book. Gaelic and Old Norse place names often have a variety of spellings, and only the most common are given here.

Munro   Mountain above 3000 feet (914.4m), originally a list drawn up by Sir Hugh Munro, but now much changed.

Corbett   Mountain between 2500 feet (762m) and 3000 feet (914.4m), with a drop on all sides of at least 500 feet (152.4m), originally drawn up by John Rooke Corbett.

abhainn	river (Gaelic)
allt	burn or stream (Gaelic)
aonach	height (Gaelic)
ban	white (Gaelic)
bealach	col or mountain pass (Gaelic)
beag	small (Gaelic)
beithe	birch (Gaelic)
beinn	hill (Gaelic)
breac	speckled (Gaelic)
binnean	peak (Gaelic)
bodach	old man (Gaelic)
brough	cliff peninsula (Old Norse)
buidhe	yellow (Gaelic)
cailleach	old woman or witch (Gaelic)
carn	hill or stones (Gaelic)
coinneach	mossy place (Gaelic)
ciste	chest or coffin (Gaelic)
clach	stone (Gaelic)
coire	cirque or upland valley (Gaelic)
creag	crag (Gaelic)
dale	valley (Old Norse)
damh	stag (Gaelic)
dearg	red (Gaelic)
dubh	black (Gaelic)
eilean	island (Gaelic)
fionn	white (Gaelic)
fraoch	heather (Gaelic)
fuar	cold (Gaelic)

garbh	rough (Gaelic)
geal	white (Gaelic)
geo	break in the coast (Old Norse)
gleann	glen or valley (Gaelic)
gloup	sea tunnel (Old Norse)
gorm	blue (Gaelic)
hope	sea inlet (Old Norse)
inbhir (inver)	mouth of a river (Gaelic)
lairig	hill pass (Gaelic)
loch	lake (Old Norse)
lochan	small loch or lake (Old Norse)
meall	bare hill or lump (Gaelic)
monadh	hill range (Gaelic)
mor	big (Gaelic)
ness	promontory or headland (Old Norse)
sgor	rocky peak (Gaelic)
strath	valley (Gaelic)
stob	peak (Gaelic)
uaine	green (Gaelic)
uisge	water (Gaelic)
voe	sea loch (Old Norse)
wick	sea loch (Old Norse)

LISTING OF CICERONE GUIDES

Walking the Munros Vol 2 –
    Northern & Cairngorms
Scotland's Far West
Walking in the Cairngorms
Walking in the Ochils, Campsie Fells
    and Lomond Hills
Scotland's Mountain Ridges

IRELAND
The Mountains of Ireland
Irish Coastal Walks
The Irish Coast to Coast

INTERNATIONAL CYCLE GUIDES
The Way of St James – Le Puy to
    Santiago cyclist's guide
The Danube Cycle Way
Cycle Tours in Spain
Cycling the River Loire – The Way
    of St Martin
Cycle Touring in France
Cycling in the French Alps

WALKING AND TREKKING
IN THE ALPS
Grand Tour of Monte Rosa Vol 1
Grand Tour of Monte Rosa Vol 2
Walking in the Alps (all Alpine areas)
100 Hut Walks in the Alps
Chamonix to Zermatt
Tour of Mont Blanc
Alpine Ski Mountaineering
    Vol 1 Western Alps
Alpine Ski Mountaineering
    Vol 2 Eastern Alps
Snowshoeing: Techniques and Routes
    in the Western Alps
Alpine Points of View
Tour of the Matterhorn

FRANCE, BELGIUM AND
LUXEMBOURG
The Tour of the Queyras
Rock Climbs in the Verdon
RLS (Robert Louis Stevenson) Trail
Walks in Volcano Country
French Rock
Walking the French Gorges
Rock Climbs Belgium & Luxembourg
Tour of the Oisans: GR54
Walking in the Tarentaise and
    Beaufortain Alps
The Brittany Coastal Path
Walking in the Haute Savoie, vol. 1
Walking in the Haute Savoie, vol. 2
Tour of the Vanoise
Walking in the Languedoc
GR20 Corsica – The High Level Route
The Ecrins National Park
Walking the French Alps: GR5
Walking in the Cevennes
Vanoise Ski Touring
Walking in Provence
Walking on Corsica
Mont Blanc Walks
Walking in the Cathar region
    of south west France
Walking in the Dordogne
Trekking in the Vosges and Jura
The Cathar Way

PYRENEES AND FRANCE / SPAIN
Rock Climbs in the Pyrenees
Walks & Climbs in the Pyrenees
The GR10 Trail: Through the
    French Pyrenees
The Way of St James –
    Le Puy to the Pyrenees
The Way of St James –
    Pyrenees-Santiago-Finisterre
Through the Spanish Pyrenees GR11
The Pyrenees – World's Mountain
    Range Guide
The Pyrenean Haute Route
The Mountains of Andorra

SPAIN AND PORTUGAL
Picos de Europa – Walks & Climbs
The Mountains of Central Spain
Walking in Mallorca
Costa Blanca Walks Vol 1
Costa Blanca Walks Vol 2
Walking in Madeira
Via de la Plata (Seville To Santiago)
Walking in the Cordillera Cantabrica
Walking in the Canary Islands 1 West
Walking in the Canary Islands 2 East
Walking in the Sierra Nevada
Walking in the Algarve

SWITZERLAND
The Jura: Walking the High Route &
    Ski Traverses
Walking in Ticino, Switzerland
Central Switzerland –
    A Walker's Guide
The Bernese Alps
Walking in the Valais
Alpine Pass Route
Walks in the Engadine, Switzerland
Tour of the Jungfrau Region

GERMANY AND AUSTRIA
Klettersteig Scrambles in
    Northern Limestone Alps
King Ludwig Way
Walking in the Salzkammergut
Walking in the Black Forest
Walking in the Harz Mountains
Germany's Romantic Road
Mountain Walking in Austria
Walking the River Rhine Trail
Trekking in the Stubai Alps
Trekking in the Zillertal Alps

SCANDINAVIA
Walking In Norway
The Pilgrim Road to Nidaros
    (St Olav's Way)

EASTERN EUROPE
Trekking in the Caucausus
The High Tatras
The Mountains of Romania
Walking in Hungary

CROATIA AND SLOVENIA
Walks in the Julian Alps
Walking in Croatia

ITALY
Italian Rock
Walking in the Central Italian Alps

Central Apennines of Italy
Walking in Italy's Gran Paradiso
Long Distance Walks in Italy's Gran
    Paradiso
Walking in Sicily
Shorter Walks in the Dolomites
Treks in the Dolomites
Via Ferratas of the Italian
    Dolomites Vol 1
Via Ferratas of the Italian
    Dolomites Vol 2
Walking in the Dolomites
Walking in Tuscany
Trekking in the Apennines
Through the Italian Alps: the GTA

OTHER MEDITERRANEAN
COUNTRIES
The Mountains of Greece
Climbs & Treks in the Ala Dag
    (Turkey)
The Mountains of Turkey
Treks & Climbs Wadi Rum, Jordan
Jordan – Walks, Treks, Caves etc.
Crete – The White Mountains
Walking in Western Crete
Walking in Malta

AFRICA
Climbing in the Moroccan Anti-Atlas
Trekking in the Atlas Mountains
Kilimanjaro

NORTH AMERICA
The Grand Canyon &
    American South West
Walking in British Columbia
The John Muir Trail

SOUTH AMERICA
Aconcagua

HIMALAYAS – NEPAL, INDIA
Langtang, Gosainkund &
    Helambu: A Trekkers' Guide
Garhwal & Kumaon –
    A Trekkers' Guide
Kangchenjunga – A Trekkers' Guide
Manaslu – A Trekkers' Guide
Everest – A Trekkers' Guide
Annapurna – A Trekker's Guide
Bhutan – A Trekker's Guide

AUSTRALIA AND NEW ZEALAND
Classic Tramps in New Zealand

TECHNIQUES AND EDUCATION
The Adventure Alternative
Rope Techniques
Snow & Ice Techniques
Mountain Weather
Beyond Adventure
The Hillwalker's Manual
The Book of the Bivvy
Outdoor Photography
The Hillwalker's Guide to
    Mountaineering
Map and Compass

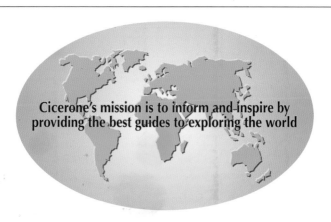

Cicerone's mission is to inform and inspire by providing the best guides to exploring the world

Since its foundation over 30 years ago, Cicerone has specialised in publishing guidebooks and has built a reputation for quality and reliability. It now publishes nearly 300 guides to the major destinations for outdoor enthusiasts, including Europe, UK and the rest of the world.

Written by leading and committed specialists, Cicerone guides are recognised as the most authoritative. They are full of information, maps and illustrations so that the user can plan and complete a successful and safe trip or expedition – be it a long face climb, a walk over Lakeland fells, an alpine traverse, a Himalayan trek or a ramble in the countryside.

With a thorough introduction to assist planning, clear diagrams, maps and colour photographs to illustrate the terrain and route, and accurate and detailed text, Cicerone guides are designed for ease of use and access to the information.

If the facts on the ground change, or there is any aspect of a guide that you think we can improve, we are always delighted to hear from you.

Cicerone Press
2 Police Square Milnthorpe Cumbria LA7 7PY
Tel:01539 562 069   Fax:01539 563 417
e-mail:info@cicerone.co.uk   web:www.cicerone.co.uk

CICERONE